CONTENTS

FROM
DANIEL
TO
DOOMSDAY

FROM
DANIEL
TO
DOOMSDAY

The Countdown Has Begun

JOHN HAGEE

THOMAS NELSON
Since 1798

NASHVILLE   DALLAS   MEXICO CITY   RIO DE JANEIRO

Published in Nashville, Tennessee, by Thomas Nelson. Thomas Nelson is a registered trademark of Thomas Nelson, Inc.

Thomas Nelson, Inc., titles may be purchased in bulk for educational, business, fund-raising, or sales promotional use. For information, please e-mail SpecialMarkets@ThomasNelson.com.

Unless otherwise noted, all Scripture quotations are from THE NEW KING JAMES VERSION. © 1979, 1980, 1982, Thomas Nelson, Inc.

Scripture quotations noted NIV are from the HOLY BIBLE: NEW INTERNATIONAL VERSION®. © 1973, 1978, 1984 by International Bible Society. Used by permission of Zondervan Publishing House. All rights reserved.

Scripture quotations marked NLT are from the *Holy Bible*, New Living Translation, © 1996. Used by permission of Tyndale House Publishers, Inc., Wheaton, Illinois 60189. All rights reserved.

Library of Congress Cataloging-in-Publication Data

Hagee, John C.
   From Daniel to doomsday / John Hagee.
     p. cm.
   ISBN 978-0-7852-6966-3 (hc)
   ISBN 978-0-7852-6818-5 (pb)
   ISBN 0-7852-6868-5 (fl)
   1. End of the world—Biblical teaching. 2. Bible—Prophecies—End of the world.   I. Title.
   BS649.E63H33 1999
   236'.9—dc21

                                      99-31179
                                        CIP

Printed in the United States of America

13 14 QG 18 17 16 15

Lovingly dedicated to
The Salt Covenant Partners
of
John Hagee Ministries,
who make it possible for me
to preach the gospel
around the world and across the nation.

INTRODUCTION

"And lo, I am with you always, even to the end of the age."

—JESUS CHRIST, MATTHEW 28:20B

From the earliest beginnings of recorded time, man has intuitively known that the world will end. The Hopi Indians prophesied that ashes would fall from the sky at the world's death. Nostradamus predicted a coming doomsday. The belief that the world would be destroyed by flood or fire has been found among natives in the Pacific islands, the ancient Persians, and past Nordic cultures. The common proverb "Everything has an end" assures us that whatever has a beginning must logically have a conclusion.

Modern man is not immune from speculation about the end of the world. Movies like *Independence Day*, *Outbreak*, and *Deep Impact* entertain us with roller-coaster thrills even as they force us to think. If you knew sudden and complete destruction would fall upon the earth in twenty-four hours, how would you spend your last day?

The characters in *Independence Day* fought fire with fire—they blasted the threatening aliens out of the sky. The lethal virus in *Outbreak* was countered with a vaccine, and the people threatened by the asteroid in *Deep Impact* succeeded in shattering the huge stone with a nuclear device. Some folks died, sure—but the world was saved.

What else would you expect from Hollywood? Lots of drama, piles of dead bodies, but ultimate victory in the end. In the movies, mankind always wins.

My friend, the end of the world *is* coming, but there's not a thing anyone can do to stop it. The world as we know it will end, neither with a bang nor a whimper, but in stages clearly set forth in God's Word. In 1 Thessalonians 5:3, the apostle Paul used the analogy of a woman giving birth to describe the beginning of the end: "For when they say, 'Peace and safety!' then sudden destruction comes upon them, as labor pains upon a pregnant woman. And they shall not escape."

I've never given birth to a child, but my wife has, and from her experience I know that certain signs signal an impending birth. First, even before labor pains begin, there is a feeling of increased pressure as the baby drops lower into the birth canal, preparing to be born. The mother grows increasingly uncomfortable as the baby grows larger, and she feels pressure on her internal organs as the time of birth draws near. Next, she may experience twinges and sharp contractions—still before labor officially begins. Finally, after days of false starts and unsettling sensations, labor commences. The bag of waters surrounding the child breaks, and the woman's labor pains intensify, growing sharper and more insistent until the child passes through the birth canal and leaves his place of darkness for a world of light.

The analogy of childbirth is a good one, for our world and everyone in it will soon undergo a similar experience. Paul, writing in the eighth chapter of Romans, explains that the earth itself waits for doomsday and the new world to come: "Because the creation itself also will be delivered from the bondage of corruption into the glorious liberty of the children of God. For we know that the whole creation groans and labors with birth pangs together until now" (Rom. 8:21–22).

Two features of birth pangs are universally true: first, when the birth pangs begin, there is no stopping them. Second, the birth pangs come more violently and frequently as time passes until the child—in this case, the new era—is born. As the dispensation of grace races toward its conclusion on planet earth, the birth pangs have begun!

Notice the pattern:

- In 1917, the earth experienced World War I.
- In 1929, the stock market crashed.
- In 1941, the attack on Pearl Harbor drew America into World War II.
- In 1950, The United States entered the Korean Conflict.
- In 1960–72, we fought in Vietnam.
- In 1963, our president was assassinated.
- From 1917 until today, the contractions or wars, rumors of wars, earthquakes, pestilence, and signs in the heavens have not stopped. The new age is about to be born, and the most severe contractions are just before us.

Mark it down, my friends: Doomsday is approaching, but it won't be ushered in by the advent of space aliens or a catastrophic asteroid. It will come like a woman giving birth, and each devastating birth pang will signal this planet's coming doom.

As I write this, we have just entered 1999. As the world anticipates the year 2000, doomsday scenarios are as abundant as dandelions in a pasture. Practically every newspaper or magazine I pick up is quoting some expert on something that could kill us or destroy our way of life by the dawn of the new millennium.

The same thing happened in 1899. One 1890s prognosticator predicted that New York City would be abandoned as unfit for human habitation by the 1930s. He *correctly* projected that the city's population would grow from four to seven million, but then he stated that the amount of horses necessary to provide transportation for so many people would result in a public health hazard—manure piled up to the third floor of every window in Manhattan![1]

A recent *Newsweek* editorial addressed the same subject:

Long before Bill Gates, Rockefeller made the word monopoly a household term with the bullying tactics of Standard Oil. A series of financial and industrial mergers in the last years of the century . . . only fueled the public's fears about the power of big business. The depletion of the Western frontier had Americans concerned about environmental preservation, while the telegraph and automobile were seen as exciting—but ominous—new technologies. Meanwhile, tuberculosis, the 19th-century equivalent of AIDS, continued to baffle physicians and ravage entire towns.[2]

The article went on to say that doomsayers were in full battle dress, predicting disaster on midnight of December 31, 1899. The New York and Chicago newspapers featured full-page ads announcing the Second Coming of Jesus Christ. A story in the *New York Times* quoted scientists' predictions that the sun would eventually go out, leaving the solar system in darkness and the earth an uninhabited ball of ice.

Sound familiar? We're hearing the same types of stories today. While surfing the Internet, I found a story by David Nicholson-Lord, of London's *Independent on Sunday* newspaper. Nicholson-Lord asked an oddsmaker, William Hill, to formulate odds for various end-of-the-world scenarios. The bookie's report is fascinating:

> *Odds that the world will end by natural causes like a "big bang"*: 50 million to 1.
>
> *Odds that the human race will be wiped out due to over-population*: 25 million to 1.
>
> *Odds that the human race will be wiped out by pollution*: 1 million to 1.
>
> *Odds that the world will be conquered by aliens*: 500,000 to 1.
>
> *Odds that life as we know it will be destroyed by changes in climate*: 250,000 to 1.
>
> *Odds that the human race will be wiped out by drought*: 100,000 to 1.
>
> *Odds that the human race will be starved out by famine*: 75,000 to 1.
>
> *Odds that life as we know it will be snuffed out by anarchy*: 50,000 to 1.

Odds that the world will be wiped out by an asteroid:
   10,000 to 1.
Odds that the human race will be wiped out by disease:
   5,000 to 1.
Odds that the human race will be annihilated by war: 500
   to 1.[3]

As I look over William Hill's list of possible doomsday scenarios, I am struck by the realization that many of the situations on this list *will* come to pass. The earth will shudder through several calamities before it is reborn. The Word of God describes famines, disease, war, climate changes, earthquakes, drought, and fire from heaven. A series of events unlike anything the world has ever seen will precede the ultimate doomsday—the day when each individual must stand before the terrifying Great White Throne in heaven and give an accounting for his life. The awful importance of that moment, my friend, makes other doomsday catastrophes seem like insignificant blank spots on the paper of life!

Faced with the threatening possibility that mankind's bent toward evil just might result in total nuclear annihilation, *The Bulletin of the Atomic Scientists* created the Doomsday Clock in an effort to remind the world how close we could come to destruction. In 1947, when the clock first appeared, the hands were set at seven minutes to midnight, with midnight being the moment of ultimate doom. As mankind has alternated between hostility and peace in the succeeding years, the hands of the Doomsday Clock have moved back and forth, constantly reminding us that nuclear destruction is only a few moments away.

God has a similar clock, my friend, and its hands *never*

move backward. Even as the eternal God created man, He devised a plan that allows man free choice, accounts for man's natural disposition for sin, and provides a means for a loving, compassionate God to draw wayward man back into fellowship with Him. This plan began in the Garden of Eden and will end with the creation of a new heaven and a new earth. The crimson threads of God's redemptive plan are woven into Holy Scripture from Genesis to Revelation, and at times they come together to create prophetic images of astounding clarity and beauty.

Nowhere is God's prophetic plan more fully illustrated than in the book of Daniel. Here we see, with startling accuracy, how God plans to let each individual choose his eternal destiny. Peering at the pages of Daniel's writing, we can also understand how future events will reveal themselves.

In designing this book, I've taken a cue from the makers of the Doomsday Clock. The hands on the clock pictured at the beginning of each chapter do not represent an actual moment, of course, but a predetermined event that will come to pass. There is no turning back with God.

Doomsday—the stroke of midnight—is coming.

CHAPTER 1

11:50 P.M.
DANIEL PAINTS THE
PANORAMA OF PROPHECY

This morning I shook out my newspaper, skimmed the lead stories, then turned the page. There, in a prominent position on page two, a headline caught my eye: "Year 2000 Cultists Arrive Home, Hide." The article that followed was an excellent example of what can happen when people misuse prophecy.

You may recall the story: members of a millennial cult based in Denver had flown to Israel because their leader, Kim Miller, told his followers that the way to salvation lies in dying in the city of Jerusalem on the eve of the year 2000. Rightfully fearful that the cult, "Concerned Christians," might actually provoke the violence necessary to achieve their aims, a special Israeli task force detained the group in Jerusalem, then sent them home. The newspaper report described the group's leader, Kim Miller, as a former Procter & Gamble executive with no formal religious training.[1]

1

Miller has told his followers that he will die in Jerusalem in December 1999 and be resurrected three days later.[2]

If you attend a Bible-preaching church, you may find it difficult to understand how professing Christians could sell all their earthly belongings and follow a cult leader like Kim Miller to Israel. The reason, however, is simple: People fall for false doctrine when they don't know the truth. Our nation's mainline denominations and far too many churches dismiss prophecy as irrelevant or something that cannot be humanly understood. Without a complete understanding of what will come to pass in the future, however, believers can fall into deep deception.

Imagine for a moment that you have set your darling two-year-old daughter on the kitchen table. "Come on, honey, jump!" you tell her as you hold out your arms, and she jumps because she *knows* you'll be there to catch her. She trusts your ability to keep her safe, and she knows what you'll do when she takes that literal leap of faith. The same thing is true for us. We need to know what God has planned for the end of our lives, for the end of our planet, for the end of the age. Knowing gives us confidence, strength, and peace, and we come to understand God's plans through the study of biblical prophecy.

Too many people, however, have turned away from the study of prophecy to place their confidence in false doctrine and false teachers. As I write this, Israeli police are preparing for the possibility that misled Christians will try to commit suicide atop the Temple Mount as the millennium approaches. The government has actually allotted $12 million to upgrade security at the site in case extremists attack the Al Aqsa and Dome of the Rock mosques. Israeli mental hospitals are preparing for an influx of patients with *Jerusalem Syndrome*, an actual clinical condition in which religious pilgrims "exhibit strange behavior while sometimes proclaiming that they are ancient religious figures sent on a mission."[3]

You don't have to be carried away on the winds of false doctrine. God wants us to understand His Word, and a large portion of that Word is prophecy. God's plan has existed from the foundations of the earth. Just as God Himself does not change, His plans for the earth will not change, either.

Can you trust the Bible? Absolutely! Bible prophecy proves the divine inspiration of the Word of God. The Bible is different from all other religious books. The books that form the foundation for other major religions and cults interpret the present or deal with the past, but the Bible, when written, was 25 percent prophecy. From Genesis to Revelation, countless prophecies were given, and most have been *exactly* fulfilled. This confirms the inspiration, validity, and authority of the Bible.

The apostle Peter wrote that Bible prophecy would be of benefit to the church "until the day dawns and the morning star rises in your hearts" (2 Peter 1:19). The "morning star" is none other than Jesus Christ (Rev. 22:16). Peter boldly declared that Bible prophecy will benefit the church until the end of the age. As we enter a new millennium and contemplate the future, we will discover that prophecy produces peace in the heart of every believer.

Jesus said, "Let not your heart be troubled; you believe in God, believe also in Me" (John 14:1). The Savior comforted His disciples' hearts—and our own—with a prophetic promise: "In My Father's house are many mansions; if it were not so, I would have told you. I go to prepare a place for you. And if I go and prepare a place for you, I will come again and receive you to Myself; that where I am, there you may be also" (John 14:2–3).

As we watch the newscasts and read shocking headlines about people committing mass suicide, watching for alien spaceships, and trembling at the thought of an economic collapse, we are comforted by the prophetic Scripture that confirms every event is transpiring by divine design. From every book in the Bible, prophetic Scripture shouts, "Lift up your heads and rejoice; God is in charge!"

DANIEL'S VISION OF DOOMSDAY

Probably no prophet's writing is as significant as Daniel's. His book portrays several visions in which the future of the world is revealed, and the revelations that have been fulfilled have proved 100 percent accurate.

In his writings, the ancient historian Josephus told a story about Daniel and Alexander the Great. Nearly 270 years after Daniel wrote his visions and their interpretations, Alexander the Great and his army marched on Jerusalem. As he neared the Holy City, Jaddua, the high priest at the time, went out to meet the Greek emperor and showed him a copy of the book of Daniel and the passage where Alexander was described. Alexander was so impressed by this that instead of destroying Jerusalem, he entered the city in peace and worshiped at the temple.[4]

Our Lord Jesus mentioned Daniel (Matt. 24:15, Mark 13:14), and He quoted from the book of Daniel in his Olivet Discourse. The book of Revelation makes sense when studied along with Daniel, and Paul's "man of sin," or the

Antichrist, becomes a flesh-and-blood being when viewed in the light of Daniel's insight.

God gave the prophet Daniel a glimpse into the future, and one of those prophetic visions shook Daniel so profoundly that he fainted and took to his bed for several days! He saw what was coming, he accepted it as the work of a sovereign and just God, yet still he was astonished and shaken by the sight of future events.

Let's backtrack for a few moments. Daniel's story began in the third year of the reign of Jehoiakim, king of Judah, when "Nebuchadnezzar king of Babylon came to Jerusalem and besieged it" (Dan. 1:1). In 605 B.C., because of Jehoiakim's extreme ungodliness, God allowed Nebuchadnezzar to overthrow the kingdom of Judah, which was centered in Jerusalem.

Nebuchadnezzar was an emotional sort of man, but he was no fool. Rather than simply drag his prisoners of war into slavery, he decided to sift through the lot of captives and loot. He took the choice golden vessels from the temple and put them in the house of his own god. He instructed the master of his eunuchs to evaluate the captives and pull out "young men in whom there was no blemish, but good-looking, gifted in all wisdom, possessing knowledge and quick to understand, who had ability to serve in the king's palace" (Dan. 1:4). Among the young men chosen for royal service were Daniel, Hananiah, Mishael, and Azariah, the latter three better known as Shadrach, Meshach, and Abed-Nego.

Daniel and the captured Israelites had a legitimate right to think the unthinkable—perhaps they thought their own doomsday had come. When God called Abraham to be the founder of a new nation, He gave him a title deed to the

Promised Land (Gen. 15:9–21). In addition, when God raised David to be the king over Israel, He promised David that his seed would sit upon the throne of Israel forever. God had made unbreakable covenants with the nation of Israel, but now it appeared He had deserted his special people. Where was He when they needed Him?

Daniel looked around him and saw foreign faces, heard foreign voices, saw hordes of people worshiping pagan gods. The holy and sacred vessels from David's temple were being used to hold oil and incense for false gods of man's own creation. How could God have allowed this to happen?

Daniel and his people were strangers in a strange land, captives living without the right of self-determination under a pagan king. Had God forgotten his promises—or had He broken the unbreakable covenant? I'm certain Daniel and his friends were wondering if they would ever see Jerusalem again and what they had done to deserve such exile.

The prophecies of the Old Testament make God's reasons for the exile very clear. The prophet Hosea portrayed Israel as an adulterous wife who went whoring after idols. As a picture of God's amazing grace and the redemption of Israel, Hosea literally went to the slave market and redeemed his adulterous wife.

The prophet Ezekiel painted Israel's past sins and deserved doom in a series of visions of the abominations in the temple, the slaying of the wicked, and the departing glory of God. Israel had been a fruitless vine and an adulterous wife, said the prophet, and Babylon would swoop down like an eagle and pluck them up. But Israel's judgment would be followed by restoration.

God wants us to understand what He does and why He

acts as He does. The Israelites of Daniel's day had been warned, just as contemporary men and women are warned. God's nature and character are unchanging; there is no shadow of turning in Him.

Paul wrote, "Yet indeed I also count all things loss for the excellence of the knowledge of Christ Jesus my Lord, for whom I have suffered the loss of all things, and count them as rubbish, that I may gain Christ . . . that I may know Him" (Phil. 3:8, 10). There is a vast difference between knowing *about* God and knowing God. America knows about God, but she has no comprehension of His character. The God of the Bible is a God of majesty, wisdom, truth, love, and grace. He is jealous over His children. He is a God of judgment and wrath, and He never changes. He is just as ready to judge sin today as He was in Daniel's day.

God always judges sin. Israel had sinned repeatedly, without confession, so God sent them into captivity in Babylon.

The man or nation that breaks God's law without repentance will discover God's severity. You don't break God's laws—God's laws break you. You either fall on the cornerstone, Jesus Christ, and are broken, or the cornerstone will fall on you, grinding you to powder.

God cannot change! He is "from everlasting" (Ps. 93:2), the "everlasting King" (Jer. 10:10), "the incorruptible God" (Rom. 1:23), and "alone has immortality" (1 Tim. 6:16). Speaking of God, King David wrote, "But You are the same, And Your years will have no end" (Ps. 102:27).

When my children were young, they often asked me, "Daddy, who made God?" God did not need to be made, for He is eternal; He has always been. He has always existed; He will always exist. He does not grow older. He does not gain or lose power. He cannot evolve or devolve; He does not improve or deteriorate, for He was perfect from the beginning.

Many situations can alter the character of a man— strain, shock, a lobotomy, or attending public school for more than thirty minutes! But nothing can alter the character of God. "The counsel of the LORD stands forever, / The plans of His heart to all generations" (Ps. 33:11).

What God does in time, He planned from eternity. And what He planned in eternity, He carries out in time.

God sent Israel into captivity because His character does not change. *God always judges sin.* This is a message America needs to hear. If God crushed Israel because they became a pagan society, God will crush America for the same reason.

God judged Sodom and Gomorrah because of their inhabitants' homosexual lifestyles.

God judged Noah's generation because "every intent of the thoughts of [man's] heart was only evil continually" (Gen. 6:5).

God judged Israel and sent them into Babylonian captivity because of their godless lifestyle. God will judge America for our slaughter of unborn children in America's abortion mills and for the official endorsement from the White House to the church house of homosexuality as an alternative lifestyle.

America is no longer "one nation under God." We have ridiculed the truth of the Word of God and called it *pluralism*. We have worshiped other gods and called it *multiculturalism*. We have rewarded laziness and called it *welfare*. We have neglected to discipline our children and called it *the building of self-esteem*. We have polluted the air with profanity and pornography and called it *freedom of expression*. We have institutionalized perjury and deception in government and called it *politically correct*.

According to polls in 1998, 67 percent of Americans condoned the immoral lifestyle of our president because "the economy is good." When money matters more than morality, God will crush our economy as a potter crushes an earthen vessel with a rod of iron. If America will not serve the Lord in prosperity, then God will send poverty.

Put it down in your book as a fact for the future—an economic earthquake is coming to America with a severity this nation has never known.

REMEMBER NOAH'S GENERATION

As I write these words, the U.S. stock market is at an all-time high. The majority of Americans consider economic prosperity as a sign of God's approval. Wrong! Examine the biblical record of nations whose economies were at their peak when God's judgment came and shook everything that could be shaken.

The judgment of God came to Noah's generation at the pinnacle of good times. The Bible records, "in the days of Noah . . . They ate, they drank, they married wives, they were given in marriage" (Luke 17:26–27).

Their prosperity continued to break all records until the day Noah entered the ark, God closed the door, and the fountains of the deep were opened up as Almighty God destroyed all living flesh on the face of the earth.

REMEMBER LOT'S GENERATION

Sodom and Gomorrah's economy was as hot as America's ever has been. Ezekiel recorded, "This was the iniquity of your sister Sodom . . . pride, fullness of food, and abundance of idleness . . . and they were haughty" (Ezek. 16:49–50).

When Lot warned his sons-in-law that the judgment of God was coming, they thought he was joking.

When Americans are told that judgment is coming to this nation for the same reasons it came to Sodom and Gomorrah, they mock the messenger as a "right-wing, Bible-believing radical, a homophobic misfit who needs sensitivity training to become politically correct."

REMEMBER BABYLON

John the Revelator graphically describes mystery Babylon of Revelation 18, whose economy was crushed by the hand of God in one hour. John wrote,

> Babylon the great is fallen, is fallen . . . and the merchants of the earth have become rich through the abundance of her luxury . . . The kings of the earth who committed fornication and lived luxuriously with her will weep and lament for her, when they see the smoke of her burning . . . saying, "Alas, alas, that great city Babylon, that mighty city! For in one hour your judgment has come." (Rev. 18:2–3, 9–10)

John does not reveal the identity of mystery Babylon other than to say, "And in her was found the blood of prophets and saints, and of all who were slain on the earth" (Rev. 18:24).

This evidence would point to Rome, as it was the city that made great sport of feeding Christians to the lions in the Roman Coliseum. It was Rome where the apostle Paul was decapitated. It was Rome where Nero wrapped Christians in oily rags and hung them on lampposts, setting them ablaze to light his gardens. It was Rome that orchestrated the Crusades where Jews were slaughtered going to and returning from Jerusalem by the tens of thousands. It was Rome that orchestrated the Inquisitions throughout the known world where "heretics" were burned at the stake or pulled in half on torture racks because they were not Roman Catholic.

The biblical point is absolutely clear: *A thriving economy does not signify God's approval.*

Take a panoramic look at the economies of the world right now. Just a few months ago the world's bankers were tripping over themselves to invest in Asia. Now the Asian economy has fallen like a house of cards, and violent mobs roam the streets in public demonstration of frustration and rage.

- The economy of Indonesia has collapsed.

- Japan's economy is staggering beneath the awesome burden of national scandal.

- Russia's ruble has fallen. Civil servants have not been paid for six months, and soldiers of the once-proud Russian army are digging for potatoes to stave off starvation.

- Brazil has devalued its currency.

- The wizards of Wall Street now see that the ripple of the economic earthquake that began in Asia is about to hit America's shore. Add to this the fact that Europe has just established the Eurodollar, a currency which will be in head-to-head competition with the U.S. dollar.

Why should such things be important to you? How will the situation in Europe affect you? Before the introduction of the Euro, when any country experienced a currency crisis, the rich and powerful sent their money to America and invested in dollars. Now when a country has a currency crisis, they have the choice of going to the United States or Europe. The anti-American attitude of the world will soon make the Euro the most powerful currency on the face of the earth. That means the dollar will become weaker and more unstable than ever.

America must have a revival of repentance, or we will have an economic holocaust in this country!

Nebuchadnezzar's Disturbing Dream

If ever a man was in the right place at the right time, Daniel was. God took him from Jerusalem and planted him in Babylon, the wonder city of the ancient world. The kingdom of Babylon was the first great world empire. The monarchy rose to its zenith during Daniel's lifetime, and Daniel served Babylon's most influential and powerful king.

The city of Babylon itself was a marvel. Ancient historians have reported that its wall was 60 miles in circumference, 300 feet high, 80 feet thick, and extended 35 feet underground so enemies could not tunnel beneath it. Two hundred fifty towers were built into the wall, along with guard rooms for the king's vigilant soldiers.

Inside the city, the Great Temple of Marduk contained a golden image of Bel and a golden table, which together weighed at least fifty thousand pounds. At the top of the temple were golden images of Bel and Ishtar, two golden lions, a golden table, and an eighteen-foot-high human figure of solid gold. Isaiah wasn't exaggerating when he described Babylon as a golden city (Isa. 14:4).[5]

The monarch and absolute ruler of this gilded city was Nebuchadnezzar. The Bible tells us in Daniel 2 that one night King Nebuchadnezzar—king over the Assyrians, the Syrians, and the Egyptians—was troubled by a dream. In Babylonian society, dreams were considered messages from the gods. When the king awoke, however, he retained nothing of his nightmare except a profound sense of doom. He had forgotten the dream, but he remembered enough of the feeling to know that it was important. The dream left a deep, permanent, and powerful impression on his mind.

How could a mere dream, especially a forgotten one, trouble the most powerful king on the face of the earth? Why couldn't he remember it? The dream—and the cloaking of it—were engineered by God. Through Daniel, a captive Jewish boy, the world would learn that the God of Abraham, Isaac, and Jacob was the one true and living God.

When Nebuchadnezzar could not remember his dream, he sent for his magicians, astrologers, sorcerers, and the Chaldeans. The magicians were masters of fortune-telling; the astrologers predicted events based upon the position of the stars. Sorcerers communicated with the dead with the assistance of evil spirits, and the Chaldeans were philosophers who had mastered every field of science. They were the king's "cabinet" and Babylon's "think tank."

These men were not fools—the mere fact that they had access to the royal court speaks volumes about their skill and diplomacy. For years they had been listening to the king's recitations about his dreams, watching his expressions, judging his moods. Then they would perform their specialty acts and structure their answers in such an ambiguous manner that their words would prove true, no matter which way future events developed.

When this cast of characters assembled before him, Nebuchadnezzar looked out and asked the one question they could not answer: "Tell me the contents of my dream and the meaning."

I wish I'd been there to see their startled faces! With one statement Nebuchadnezzar turned the tables on these sycophantic masters of the occult and guaranteed he'd receive a true answer. For if a man had the power to correctly interpret the dream, he certainly ought to have power enough to know what the dream was.

The princes of the occult who stood before Nebuchadnezzar claimed they could communicate directly with the gods, but they were completely powerless when Nebuchadnezzar tossed his question at them. A couple of them protested that the king's question was unfair, but the king's reply was simple: "My decision is firm: if you do not make known the dream to me, and its interpretation, you shall be cut in pieces, and your houses shall be made an ash heap" (Dan. 2:5).

Faced with the ax and the flame, the eager frauds did the only thing they could do—they begged! They tried to buy time; they finagled and bargained and pleaded. But Nebuchadnezzar's patience was at an end. He said,

> I know for certain that you would gain time, because you see that my decision is firm: if you do not make known the dream to me, there is only one decree for you! For you have agreed to speak lying and corrupt words before me till the time has changed. Therefore tell me the dream, and I shall know that you can give me its interpretation. (Dan. 2:8–9)

For once, the Chaldeans answered with the truth:

> There is not a man on earth who can tell the king's matter; therefore no king, lord, or ruler has ever asked such things of any magician, astrologer, or Chaldean. It is a difficult thing that the king requires, and there is no other who can tell it to the king except the gods, whose dwelling is not with flesh. (Dan. 2:10–11)

Emotional Nebuchadnezzar was ready to clean house. He straightway sentenced the entire lot of wise men to death, including Daniel and his companions, who knew nothing of the events transpiring in the royal throne room. When Arioch, the king's captain, came to arrest Daniel, the Jewish captive protested. If given time, he said, he could tell the king his forgotten dream and give the accurate interpretation. By then young Daniel—he was probably between seventeen and twenty years old at the time—was known to the king and respected enough that the king granted him one night's stay. In complete faith, Daniel "went in and asked the king to give him time, that he might tell the king the interpretation" (Dan. 2:16).

THE PRAYER MEETING

After hearing of Nebuchadnezzar's edict, Daniel went out and told Hananiah, Mishael, and Azariah that he was holding a prayer meeting at his house. They might not be living in Jerusalem, the Holy City, but God was still listening to their prayers and available to meet their needs.

As they gathered to pray, every man was aware that his life depended upon the results of this prayer meeting. If God did not send an answer and deliver them, they would die the next morning. The Bible tells us that Daniel and his friends sought "mercies from the God of heaven concerning this secret, so that Daniel and his companions might not perish with the rest of the wise men of Babylon. Then the secret was revealed to Daniel in a night vision" (Dan. 2:18–19).

What a secret it was! Locked within Nebuchadnezzar's dream was the most important prophetic revelation God had yet given to mankind! This dream described events of the future with such graphic and dramatic detail that it could be called the portrait of prophecy.

We are not told how long the prayer meeting lasted, but we know they didn't stop praying until they heard from heaven. Because they had to have an answer for the king the next morning, it is logical to assume they prayed into the night and Daniel fell asleep while an angel, perhaps Gabriel, revealed the meaning of the king's dream.

The next morning, Daniel awoke. With a spirit of gratitude, he blessed the Lord for this supernatural revelation.

Blessed be the name of God forever and ever,
For wisdom and might are His.
And He changes the times and the seasons;
He removes kings and raises up kings;
He gives wisdom to the wise
And knowledge to those who have understanding.
He reveals deep and secret things;
He knows what is in the darkness,
And light dwells with Him.
I thank You and praise You,
O God of my fathers;
You have given me wisdom and might,
And have now made known to me what we asked of
    You,
For You have made known to us the king's demand.

(Dan. 2:20–23)

After profoundly expressing his thanksgiving, Daniel went to Arioch, the king's man, and immediately requested that the death sentence be lifted.

Daniel exhibited unexpected mercy. As the princes of the occult were being led out to be executed, Daniel interceded for their lives. Imagine that! Daniel was the greatest of the prophets, a righteous man submitted in every way to the God of Abraham, Isaac, and Jacob; yet, he interceded to spare the lives of the most spiritually corrupt people in a very corrupt kingdom. What an example of love, grace, and mercy! If Christians would show that same love, grace, and mercy even to other Christians, America would experience a mighty revival of repentance, restoration, and renewal.

THE SCENE CHANGES

As a result of Nebuchadnezzar's dream, God's prophetic "A-Team," Daniel and his three friends were thrust instantly into the national spotlight. This wasn't the first time a Jewish captive had risen to national prominence from nowhere—remember Pharaoh and Joseph? Joseph was literally lifted from prison, cleaned up, and sent to explain Pharaoh's dream. Now another Jewish captive, Daniel, stood waiting in the wings with God's supernatural power of revelation. Daniel 2:25–47 records the story:

It was still early morning; perhaps the evening torches still smoldered on the walls of the king's throne room as Arioch ushered Daniel into the royal chamber. Servants scurried out of the way as Arioch shouldered his way past, but the captain's eyes were filled with hope as he lifted his gaze to meet the king's thunderous expression.

"I have found a man," he said, his voice echoing in the cavernlike stillness of the vast chamber. "I have found a man of the captives of Judah, who will make known to the king the interpretation." Notice that Arioch didn't mention the dream itself—though he had every hope in Daniel, he didn't have faith enough to remind the king that he was seeking the interpretation *and* the dream. Perhaps Arioch was thinking that a night's sleep had softened the king's heart. Perhaps the impulsive ruler had reconsidered his decision to execute every wise man. If this young Hebrew could satisfy the royal curiosity with some sort of innocent babble about the future and the gods . . .

The king, however, had not forgotten. Nebuchadnezzar transferred his gaze from his captain to the young man standing in the shadows. He knew Daniel and remembered granting the Hebrew a few hours to explain the dream. The handsome youth's face stirred a vague memory, then another recollection surfaced. This captive was one of four Hebrews who had caused a bit of a stir when they were first assimilated into palace life. They had wanted only vegetables and water, and to everyone's surprise, that kosher diet made them healthier in appearance than the others who had eaten meat killed in a sacrificial rite to honor the king's gods. This one, the apparent leader, has been given the honored name of Belteshazzar.

"Belteshazzar," the king said, his steely gaze meeting his captive's. "Are you able to make known to me the dream which I have seen, and its interpretation?"

A silence, thick as wool, wrapped itself around the occupants of the throne room as Daniel stepped forward. He did not begin with the ceremonial greetings and wishes for life and health and prosperity; instead he met the king's gaze with determination. "The secret which the king has demanded," Daniel began, his voice ringing with authority, "the wise men, the astrologers, the magicians, and the soothsayers cannot declare to the king." He paused, and Arioch caught his breath, wondering if he would be called upon to execute this youthful wise man on the spot. So far Daniel the Hebrew had displayed nothing but a gift for stating the obvious.

Daniel took another step forward, and his voice softened with something akin to compassion as he held the king's gaze. "But there is a God in heaven who reveals secrets," he continued, "and He has made known to King Nebuchadnezzar what will be in the latter days. Your dream, and the visions of your head upon your bed, were these . . ."

Forgetting all he had ever been taught about royal protocol, Arioch gaped, open-mouthed, as the Hebrew began to paint a verbal picture of kingdoms and rulers and the world to come. Daniel spoke of Nebuchadnezzar, the Babylonian empire, and of a coming kingdom that would never end. He foretold glorious power, terrible destruction, and coming doom.

When he finished, King Nebuchadnezzar, most powerful of the powerful, stumbled from his throne and fell on his face, prostrate before the Hebrew captive. "Bring incense," he called, his voice hoarse. "We will present an offering to Belteshazzar."

Daniel reached out, daring to touch the king's shoulder, and urged Nebuchadnezzar to a standing position, silently refusing his worship. The king's eyes flashed with understanding, then he lifted his hands and closed his eyes, overcome with the realization that today he had honestly heard from God.

"Truly your God is the God of gods, the Lord of kings, and a revealer of secrets," he said, his rough whisper echoing in the vast room. And all who heard it marveled at the power of Daniel's God . . .

NEBUCHADNEZZAR'S DREAM EXPLAINED

One of the most remarkable things about Nebuchadnezzar's dream is that Daniel described future events when he interpreted it. We are living in the dream's time line—we can see the fulfilled events of the first part of the dream, and we can look toward the future for the conclusion.

Let's examine the dream as Daniel described it:

You, O king, were watching; and behold, a great image! This great image, whose splendor was excellent, stood before you; and its form was awesome. This image's head was of fine gold, its chest and arms of silver, its belly and thighs of bronze, its legs of iron, its feet partly of iron and partly of clay. You watched while a stone was cut out without hands, which struck the image on its feet of iron and clay, and broke them in pieces. Then the iron, the clay, the bronze, the silver, and the gold were crushed together, and became like chaff from the summer threshing floors; the wind carried them away so that no trace of them was found. And the stone that struck the image became a great mountain and filled the whole earth.

This is the dream. Now we will tell the interpretation of it before the king. You, O king, are a king of kings. For the God of heaven has given you a kingdom, power, strength, and glory; and wherever the children of men dwell, or the beasts of the field and the birds of the heaven, He has given them into your hand, and has made you ruler over them all—you are this head of gold.

But after you shall arise another kingdom inferior to yours; then another, a third kingdom of bronze, which shall rule over all the earth. And the fourth kingdom shall be as strong as iron, inasmuch as iron breaks in pieces and shatters all things; and like iron that crushes, that kingdom will break in pieces and crush all the others. Whereas you saw the feet and toes, partly of potter's clay and partly of iron, the kingdom shall be divided; yet the strength of the iron shall be in it, just as you saw the iron mixed with ceramic clay. And as the toes of the feet were partly of iron and partly of clay, so the kingdom shall be partly strong and partly fragile. As you saw iron mixed with ceramic clay, they will mingle with the seed of men; but they will not adhere to one another, just as iron does not mix with clay.

And in the days of these kings the God of heaven will set up a kingdom which shall never be destroyed; and the kingdom shall not be left to other people; it shall break in pieces and consume all these kingdoms, and it shall stand forever. Inasmuch as you saw that the stone was cut out of the mountain without hands, and that it broke in pieces the iron, the bronze, the clay, the silver, and the gold—the great God has made known to the king what will come to pass after this. The dream is certain, and its interpretation is sure. (Dan. 2:31–45)

History has proven Daniel's interpretation to be absolutely and totally accurate. As he prophesied, the empire that replaced Nebuchadnezzar's head of gold was the Medo-Persian, the breastplate of silver. The Medo-Persians were displaced by Alexander the Great of Greece, the loins of brass. Alexander's empire fell to the Romans, the strong and mighty domain that eventually divided into eastern and western empires.

Notice that as Daniel's eye traveled down the image, the strength of the metals progressed from soft (gold) to very hard (iron). This corresponds to the military strength of nations that would develop in centuries to come. Mankind has progressed from relatively weak weapons such as spears and cudgels to smart bombs, scud missiles, and thermonuclear devices.

It is important to note that the strength of the iron kingdom seemed to dilute over time. The lower the eye descended, the weaker the material became, until the feet were composed of iron and clay, two materials that simply would not blend with each other. The "partly strong and partly broken" kingdom of Rome did weaken as it aged, until it finally divided into ten toes, or ten kingdoms.

What are the two substances that will not mix? Scholar William Kelly suggests that the final form of power from the old Roman Empire will be a federation composed of autocracies and democracies, represented by iron and clay. In his view, iron represents nations ruled by a monarch; clay represents nations that adhere to a democratic or representative form of government.[6]

These ten toes, or empires, will be some sort of European federation arising from the old iron, or Roman, empire. These ten nations—some ruled by monarchs, some by democratic governments—will be the "ten toes" crushed by the stone cut without hands, Israel's Messiah, the Lord Jesus Christ. Nebuchadnezzar's image, representing the glorious and powerful kingdoms of the world, will be ground to powder and totally obliterated by this stone, who will conquer all dominions and rule a kingdom that will stand forever.

Nebuchadnezzar was thrilled with the interpretation of his dream and gave glory to the God of Israel.

But Daniel wasn't done with dreaming . . . nor was God finished painting a portrait of prophecy.

The Dream of Four Beasts

Many years later, during the first year of Belshazzar's rule over Babylon, Daniel slept, then awoke and wrote down the aspects of another disturbing dream:

> I saw in my vision by night, and behold, the four winds of heaven were stirring up the Great Sea. And four great beasts came up from the sea, each different from the other. The first was like a lion, and had eagle's wings. I watched till its wings were plucked off; and it was lifted up from the earth and made to stand on two feet like a man, and a man's heart was given to it. (Dan. 7:2–4)

In this dream we will see the same parade of nations described in Nebuchadnezzar's vision, but with a different and disturbing twist. Daniel saw four beasts rise up from the sea. The first beast was like a lion with the wings of an eagle: the exact representation of the Babylonian national symbol, a winged lion. Daniel had already seen the fulfillment of the first part of this vision. Nebuchadnezzar, who had risen to staggering heights of accomplishment, took pride in his success, but God struck him to the ground in a supernatural display of real power. Nebuchadnezzar lost his mind and actually ate grass like an ox for seven years, after which God restored his sanity. He returned to his kingdom with "the heart of a man" and a new appreciation for the power of God (Dan. 4).

But Babylon was doomed to failure. On the night of October 13, 556 B.C., Cyrus the Great of Persia defeated Babylon's army on the Tigris River just south of modern-day Baghdad. He entered the city and had Belshazzar executed.

(Interestingly enough, Daniel also foretold the city's fall to the Persians—the story is told in the fifth chapter of Daniel.)

And suddenly another beast, a second, like a bear. It was raised up on one side, and had three ribs in its mouth between its teeth. And they said thus to it: "Arise, devour much flesh!" (Dan. 7:5)

The second beast, a lopsided bear (because the Medes were more prominent than the Persians), represents the Medo-Persian Empire. The three ribs in the bear's mouth graphically illustrate the three prominent conquests of the empire: Lydia in 546 B.C., Babylon in 539 B.C., and Egypt in 525 B.C. A succession of kings ruled this empire, including King Ahasuerus (Xerxes) of the book of Esther. The Persian king Artaxerxes was king during Nehemiah's royal service.

After this I looked, and there was another, like a leopard, which had on its back four wings of a bird. The beast also had four heads, and dominion was given to it. (Dan. 7:6)

The third beast, the leopard with four wings and four heads, represents Greece under Alexander the Great. The leopard is a swift animal, symbolizing the blinding speed with which Alexander's military juggernaut attacked its enemies. Greece's Golden Age produced some of the most notable personalities of the ancient world, including Hippocrates, the father of modern medicine, and Socrates, Plato, and Aristotle, all renowned philosophers.

Through the telescope of history, the significance of the four heads becomes clear. In 323 B.C., at age thirty-two,

Alexander died in Babylon. At his death, his four leading generals divided his kingdom: Ptolemy I took Israel and Egypt; Seleucus I reigned over Syria and Mesopotamia; Lysimachus chose to rule Thrace and Asia Minor; and Cassander took charge of Macedonia and Greece.

> After this I saw in the night visions, and behold, a fourth beast, dreadful and terrible, exceedingly strong. It had huge iron teeth; it was devouring, breaking in pieces, and trampling the residue with its feet. It was different from all the beasts that were before it, and it had ten horns. (Dan. 7:7)

The frightening fourth beast, more terrifying than its predecessors, represents the Roman Empire and the final form of Gentile power on the earth. Rome controlled central Italy by 338 B.C., and the Empire gradually expanded. Pompey, the famous Roman general, conquered the Holy Land in 63 B.C. Rome ruled Palestine with an iron fist during the time of Christ and afterward. In A.D. 70, the Roman general Vespasian ordered his son, Titus, to destroy Jerusalem. The temple was demolished, just as Jesus had predicted it would be.

In A.D. 284, Diocletian separated the Eastern Empire from the West and appointed Maximian to rule the eastern realm. A succession of rulers struggled for control over the years, and in A.D. 476, the last Roman emperor, Romulus Augustus, was dethroned. Notice, however, that the Roman Empire was never conquered—it simply fell apart from struggles rising from within. It fell into separate kingdoms, but the spirit of Rome—Europe—is alive and well today.

The most important thing to notice about this last horrifying beast is not its strength, its ferocity, nor the fact that it has destroyed all the other beasts before it. Notice that it has ten horns.

The ten horns of Daniel's dream correspond to the ten toes in Nebuchadnezzar's dream. The horns represented ten kings or leaders who would lead nations that would rise from the fourth great world kingdom—the Roman Empire.

"I was considering the horns, and there was another horn, a little one, coming up among them, before whom three of the first horns were plucked out by the roots. And there, in this horn, were eyes like the eyes of a man, and a mouth speaking pompous words" (Dan. 7:8).

From among the ten kingdoms will arise one individual who will control the entire federation of nations. Who is this "little horn" and what is his purpose?

Before we consider the answer to those questions, let's look at the end of Daniel's dream.

I watched till thrones were put in place,
And the Ancient of Days was seated;
His garment was white as snow,
And the hair of His head was like pure wool.
His throne was a fiery flame,
Its wheels a burning fire;
A fiery stream issued
And came forth from before Him.
A thousand thousands ministered to Him;
Ten thousand times ten thousand stood before Him.
The court was seated,
And the books were opened.

I watched then because of the sound of the pompous words which the horn was speaking; I watched till the beast was slain, and its body destroyed and given to the burning flame.

As for the rest of the beasts, they had their dominion taken away, yet their lives were prolonged for a season and a time.

I was watching in the night visions,
And behold, One like the Son of Man,
Coming with the clouds of heaven!
He came to the Ancient of Days,
And they brought Him near before Him.
Then to Him was given dominion and glory and a
    kingdom,
That all peoples, nations, and languages should serve
    Him.
His dominion is an everlasting dominion,
Which shall not pass away,
And His kingdom the one
Which shall not be destroyed. (Dan. 7:9–14)

Though Daniel's dream ended with the good news of the permanent reign of Christ, still he was troubled. Four great empires would arise in the time line allotted to the world's kingdoms, and from a final confederation would come a pompous destroyer. The victory would ultimately be God's, but not before the world had suffered greatly.

We will read more from Daniel in the chapters ahead, and we will see how his dreams, visions, and prophesies fit into the entire canon of Scripture. But before we move on, let's consider one other fact about Bible prophecy.

Remember Peter's comment that prophecy would be useful until the morning star, Jesus, rises in our hearts? The apostle went on to add, "knowing this first, that no prophecy of Scripture is of any private interpretation, for prophecy never came by the will of man, but holy men of God spoke as they were moved by the Holy Spirit" (2 Peter 1:20–21).

Prophecy is not of private interpretation—that is, the prophets didn't create it from their own imaginations, but their words were inspired by the Holy Spirit. Since all biblical prophecy comes from the same source, shouldn't one prophecy reinforce another? We must study the entire panorama of prophecy. We cannot be like those unstudied leaders who take one or two verses and create a cult around them.

In the pages ahead, we will see how other biblical writers reinforce Daniel, and how Daniel reveals the future as well as the past. Most importantly, we will see that doomsday, following the sharp, intense pangs of a dying world, cannot be avoided.

CHAPTER 2

11:51 P.M.
MESSIAH THE PRINCE
ENTERS JERUSALEM

The next event on our prophetic doomsday clock was forecast in 575–538 B.C. and partially fulfilled when Jesus Christ, the Jewish Messiah, entered Jerusalem for His final Passover feast. This event is tied to others, however, which we will encounter in the final moments of our doomsday countdown.

In order to fully understand the significance of what happened in A.D. 32, we must look again to the book of Daniel. In a story recounted in the ninth chapter, the prophet was now between eighty-five and ninety years old, stooped and white-haired. He had seen the powerful and glorious Babylonian kingdom fall to the Medes and the Persians; yet in the royal palace he was still respected for his wisdom, his godliness, and his strong convictions.

In the first year of Darius's reign, Daniel was in his private chamber, reading the following words of the prophet Jeremiah:

"And this whole land shall be a desolation and an astonishment, and these nations shall serve the king of Babylon seventy years. Then it will come to pass, when seventy years are completed, that I will punish the king of Babylon and that nation, the land of the Chaldeans, for their iniquity," says the Lord; "and I will make it a perpetual desolation." (Jer. 25:11–12)

Jeremiah had prophesied that God would send the children of Israel into Babylonian exile for seventy years, and those seventy years were nearly complete. Struck by that realization, Daniel began to fervently pray that this time he and his people would walk with God:

Then I set my face toward the Lord God to make request by prayer and supplications, with fasting, sackcloth, and ashes. And I prayed to the Lord my God, and made confession, and said, "O Lord, great and awesome God, who keeps His covenant and mercy with those who love Him, and with those who keep His commandments, we have sinned and committed iniquity, we have done wickedly and rebelled, even by departing from Your precepts and Your judgments." (Dan. 9:3–5)

Daniel closed his eyes and continued to pray, including himself in the confession of Israel's sin. Though Scripture does not record a single sin Daniel ever committed, still he identified himself as a sinner and begged for mercy, forgiveness, and compassion. He extolled God's righteousness and compared it to his own sinfulness. Caught up in a wave of emotion, Daniel prayed, "O Lord, hear! O Lord, forgive! O Lord, listen and act! Do not delay for Your own sake, my God, for Your city and Your people are called by Your name" (Dan. 9:19).

Overcome with emotion, Daniel fell silent and slowly opened his eyes. His breath caught in his throat when he realized he was not alone. Though the door had not creaked and the rushes on the floor had not stirred, a man had come into the room. He stood now before Daniel.

The astounded prophet lifted his gaze, and with a shock of realization he remembered the man's face. This was the angel Gabriel, whom Daniel had seen before . . . in a vision.

With a wry smile, Gabriel acknowledged the prophet's surprise. "I was sent to you from the throne of God the moment you began to pray," he explained. "Because you are greatly beloved, I have come to tell you something important and give you the skill to understand the vision" (Dan. 9:22-23, paraphrased).

Imagine! Daniel was greatly beloved, but, my friend, so are you and I! In Ephesians 1:6, Paul told us that every believer in Christ has been "accepted in the Beloved." We are all beloved by God, just like Daniel! Our prayers are heard, just as Daniel's prayer was heard; the angels are charged to aid us, just as Gabriel was charged to rush to Daniel's side.

Stunned into silence, Daniel gave Gabriel his full attention. Then Gabriel began to explain another vision God wanted Daniel to understand and record.

> Seventy weeks are determined
> For your people and for your holy city,
> To finish the transgression,
> To make an end of sins,
> To make reconciliation for iniquity,

To bring in everlasting righteousness,
To seal up vision and prophecy,
And to anoint the Most Holy.

Know therefore and understand,
That from the going forth of the command
To restore and build Jerusalem
Until Messiah the Prince,
There shall be seven weeks and sixty-two weeks;
The street shall be built again, and the wall,
Even in troublesome times.

And after the sixty-two weeks
Messiah shall be cut off, but not for Himself;
And the people of the prince who is to come
Shall destroy the city and the sanctuary.
The end of it shall be with a flood,
And till the end of the war desolations are determined.
Then he shall confirm a covenant with many for one
    week;
But in the middle of the week
He shall bring an end to sacrifice and offering.
And on the wing of abominations shall be one who makes
    desolate,
Even until the consummation, which is determined,
Is poured out on the desolate. (Dan. 9:24–27)

What do the seventy weeks mean? The interpretation
never fails to send a holy thrill through my soul.

Just as the minutes on our prophetic doomsday clock
do not stand for actual minutes, the phrase "seventy

weeks" does not mean seventy weeks of seven days each. The Hebrew word for *seven* is *shabua*, meaning "a unit of measure."[1] In use, it is similar to our word *dozen*, which we could use to signify a dozen of anything—a dozen people, a dozen eggs, a dozen doughnuts.

In the context of this verse, however, since Daniel had been reading about the seventy years of exile in Jeremiah, the "seventy weeks" or "seventy sets of seven" is generally understood to mean seven times seventy years, or 490 years. In his explanation, the angel subdivided the seventy weeks into a period of seven weeks, another period of sixty-two weeks, and one final week. Each "week" represents seven years on man's calendar.

Why 490 years? According to 2 Chronicles 36:21, the Babylonian exile lasted for seventy years to atone for the 490 years during which Israel lived in the Promised Land and failed to observe the Sabbath year. In Leviticus 25:3–5, God told His people,

> Six years you shall sow your field, and six years you shall prune your vineyard, and gather its fruit; but in the seventh year there shall be a sabbath of solemn rest for the land, a sabbath to the LORD. You shall neither sow your field nor prune your vineyard. What grows of its own accord of your harvest you shall not reap, nor gather the grapes of your untended vine, for it is a year of rest for the land.

The Jews did not honor the law of sabbath rest for the land. For 490 years they violated this commandment— among others—so God sent them to toil in Babylon and the land enjoyed its seventy years of rest. Notice a really interesting fact: Except for the gap between the sixty-ninth and seventieth years, the 490 years leading up to Israel's exile will be equaled by 490 years leading up to its final triumph![2]

THE TIME LINE OF THINGS TO COME

The decree to rebuild Jerusalem—issued during the time of Nehemiah—was given in 445 B.C. For forty-nine years (Daniel's first period of seven weeks), Nehemiah and his men labored to rebuild the wall, and the work was completed in 396 B.C., even in "troublesome times." Nehemiah and his fellow laborers battled discouragement, fear, internal and external strife, ridicule, lying prophets, pure laziness, and Satanic opposition as they struggled to rebuild the wall that would protect and defend Jerusalem.

Daniel prophesied that after the following sixty-two week period (a total of sixty-nine "weeks"), the Messiah would be "cut off." The brilliant scholar Sir Robert Anderson has calculated the beginning and ending of this group of "sevens":

What then was the length of the period intervening between the issuing of the decree to rebuild Jerusalem and the public advent of "Messiah the Prince"—between the 14th March B.C. 445 and the 6th April A.D. 32? *The interval contained exactly and to the very day 173,880 days, or seven times sixty-nine prophetic years of 360 days, the first sixty-nine weeks of Gabriel's prophecy.*[3]

On this day Jesus rode into Jerusalem, publicly and officially offering Himself as Israel's Messiah.[4] That very night, the chief priests, the scribes, and the leaders of the people began to plot his death. Within days, Israel's Messiah was "cut off," just as Daniel predicted.

As an ominous footnote, Daniel added that the people of the prince who is to come (the Antichrist of Revelation) would destroy the city and the sanctuary—just as the Romans destroyed Jerusalem and the temple in A.D. 70.

During His triumphal entry into Jerusalem, Jesus looked over His beloved city and wept, saying:

> If you had known, even you, especially in this your day, the things that make for your peace! But now they are hidden from your eyes. For days will come upon you when your enemies will build an embankment around you, surround you and close you in on every side, and level you, and your children within you, to the ground; and they will not leave in you one stone upon another, because you did not know the time of your visitation. (Luke 19:42–44)

This prophecy was exactly fulfilled to the jot and tittle when the Romans under Titus (A.D. 70) and Hadrian (A.D. 135) surrounded the city in a massive siege and crucified any Jew who tried to escape Jerusalem. There were as many as five hundred Jews being crucified at one time outside the walls of the city.

But one week remains on Daniel's time line. In the last of Daniel's seventy weeks, the Antichrist will arise from a revived Roman Empire, he will confirm a covenant with Israel for one week (seven days equals seven years), but in the middle of the week (after three and one-half years), he will bring an end to sacrifice and offering in the rebuilt temple. "And one who causes desolation will place abominations on a wing of the temple until the end that is decreed is poured out on him" (Dan. 9:27, NIV).

WAS JESUS THE PREDICTED MESSIAH?

Gabriel told Daniel about two princes—"Messiah the Prince," who would appear after sixty-nine weeks, and "the prince who is to come." We'll discuss this latter prince in a later chapter, but first let's make certain Jesus Christ was the "Messiah Prince" of Daniel's prophecy.

When Diocletian abdicated as emperor of Rome, a war of succession between Maxentius and Constantine became inevitable. Maxentius held possession of Rome, but Constantine invaded from Gaul in A.D. 312. In preparation for battle on the Tiber River, Maxentius consulted the Sibylline books for prophetic insight. The relevant oracle declared, "On that day the enemy of Rome will perish." Confident that Constantine's doom was at hand, Maxentius stalked into battle and perished there, unintentionally identifying himself as the "enemy of Rome." The prophecy was going to be fulfilled one way or the other; its intentional vagueness guaranteed it.

Are the Old Testament prophecies about the Messiah equally general? Could any number of Jewish males claim to fulfill them after rising to prominence as spiritual leaders? While that may be true about many messianic prophecies taken in isolation, there are more than three hundred separate predictions about the Messiah in the pages of the Old Testament. Taken together, they form an imposing barrier to accidental fulfillment or fulfillment after the fact.

Think of each of the three hundred messianic prophecies as a filter that strains out everyone who does not meet its requirements, and you will realize how unlikely it is that anyone but the actual Messiah could pass through their rigorous standards. If you try to calculate the odds of someone accidentally satisfying three hundred separate, personal descriptions, you end up with something like one out of a number with 125 zeroes after it—an incomprehensibly unlikely eventuality.

The Old Testament foretold that the Messiah would descend from Eve (Gen. 3:15), Judah (Gen. 49:10), and David (2 Sam. 7:14). He would be born of a virgin (Isa. 7:14) in Bethlehem (Mic. 5:2). He would enter Jerusalem riding a donkey (Zech. 9:9). He would be betrayed by a friend (Ps. 41:9). He would die with sinners but be buried with the rich (Isa. 53:9, 12). None of His bones would be broken (Ps. 34:20) during a violent death in which His hands and feet were pierced (Ps. 22:16) so that He cried out to God (Ps. 22:1). While He died, onlookers would divide His clothes (Ps. 22:18). He would come to save Gentiles as well as Jews (Isa. 49:6). He would rise from the dead (Ps. 16:10).

Yes, Jesus was the predicted Messiah. But prophecies do so much more than merely identify Him. They tell us that as God's Son, He shared the divine nature (Ps. 2:7) and as the Son of man, He shared human nature (Gen. 3:15). As God's suffering Servant, He fulfilled Israel's destiny by keeping the righteous standards of the Law of Moses (Isa. 49:1–3). He established God's new covenant with humanity (Jer. 31:31–34; Matt. 26:28). He is the destiny and focal point of history (Col. 1:16). We wait for His return to establish justice and righteousness in the millennial kingdom (Mal. 4:1–3; Rev. 19:11–20:4).

THE PURPOSE OF THE SEVENTY WEEKS

As Gabriel explained to Daniel in chapter 9:24, there were six things that must be accomplished during this period of seventy weeks.

1. *"To finish the transgression."* This refers to the transgression, or sin, of Israel and all people. The cross of Jesus Christ provided redemption for sin, but not all have accepted it. In the last week, Zechariah 13:1 tells us: "In that day a fountain shall be opened for the house of David and for the inhabitants of Jerusalem, for sin and for uncleanness." This prophecy has not yet been fulfilled.

2. *"To make an end of sins."* The national sins of Israel will come to an end at the Second Coming of Christ. Just as any other people, they are sinners as individuals and as a nation.

3. *"To make reconciliation for iniquity."* During this period of seventy weeks, God atoned for guilt and provided redemption through the death and resurrection of Christ— for Jew and Gentile alike.

4. *"To bring in everlasting righteousness."* This, of course, refers to the return of Christ at the end of 490 years to establish His kingdom.

5. *"To seal up vision and prophecy"* means that all prophetic visions will be confirmed—this and every other prophecy in Scripture. All true prophets and their prophecies will be vindicated at last.

6. *"To anoint the Most Holy"* could refer to the anointing of the Holy of Holies in the millennial temple[5] or to the anointing of the Lord's Messiah as King of heaven and earth.

Why a Gap in the Progression?

Why is there a gap between the sixty-nine weeks and this final week? God has called a "time out," as it were, in His prophetic countdown. At Calvary God stepped in and stopped the clock.

There are many other so-called "gaps" in prophetic Scripture. For instance, in Zechariah 9:9–10 we read:

Rejoice greatly, O daughter of Zion!
Shout, O daughter of Jerusalem!
Behold, your King is coming to you;
He is just and having salvation,
Lowly and riding on a donkey,
A colt, the foal of a donkey.
I will cut off the chariot from Ephraim
And the horse from Jerusalem;
The battle bow shall be cut off.
He shall speak peace to the nations;
His dominion shall be "from sea to sea,
And from the River to the ends of the earth."

Verse nine of this chapter obviously refers to Christ's triumphal entry into Jerusalem. The tenth verse, however, directly applies to Christ's Second Coming and the establishment of the millennial kingdom. Between these two verses, uttered in one prophetic breath, lies a span of at least two thousand years.

We see the same thing in Isaiah 9:6–7a. These two verses read so often at Christmastime actually pertain to two widely separated events in history. In verse six we read, "For unto us a Child is born, / Unto us a Son is given," an obvious reference to Christ's birth; but then, separated only by a semicolon, we read of His millennial kingdom: "And the government will be upon His shoulder. / And His name will be called / Wonderful, Counselor, Mighty God, / Everlasting Father, Prince of Peace. / Of the increase of His government and peace / There will be no end, / Upon the throne of David and over His kingdom."

We find another illustration of this gap in the schedule of Israel's divinely instituted feasts. Before the advent of calendars and clocks, the people of Israel lived by the unchanging calendar of the seasons. The first four festivals—the Feast of Passover, the Feast of Unleavened Bread, the Feast of Firstfruits, and the Feast of Pentecost—are pictures of Christ's death, burial, resurrection, and the advent of the Holy Spirit. The three fall festivals—the Feast of Trumpets, the Feast of Atonement, and the Feast of Tabernacles—depict future events. There is a wide separation—a time gap—between the spring feasts, which serve as a type of Christ's first appearing and the fall feasts, which speak of Israel's regathering and blessing.

The two sets of holidays also coincide with the two annual seasons of rain. Spring brings the former rain; the latter rain comes in the fall. The prophet Hosea knew the seasons and rain cycles were a clear picture of things to come. Inspired by the Holy Spirit, he wrote of the Messiah, saying, "He will come to us like the rain, / Like the latter and former rain to the earth" (Hos. 6:3).

Hosea meant that Jesus Christ, the Messiah, would come twice—once in the former rain, and again in the latter. The four feasts of the former rain—Passover, Unleavened Bread,

Firstfruits, and Pentecost—are Acts I through IV in God's preparation for the divine drama of the Second Coming. The prophetic fulfillment to those feasts lies behind us.

The Jews of Jesus' time rejected Him as Messiah, even attributing His words to Beelzebub (Matt. 12:24). Concerning Israel's unbelief, Jesus quoted Isaiah 6:9–10:

> Keep on hearing, but do not understand;
> Keep on seeing, but do not perceive.
> Make the heart of this people dull,
> And their ears heavy,
> And shut their eyes;
> Lest they see with their eyes,
> And hear with their ears,
> And understand with their heart,
> And return and be healed.

Another time he wept over Jerusalem, saying:

> O Jerusalem, Jerusalem, the one who kills the prophets and stones those who are sent to her! How often I wanted to gather your children together, as a hen gathers her chicks under her wings, but you were not willing! See! Your house is left to you desolate; for I say to you, you shall see Me no more till you say, "Blessed is He who comes in the name of the LORD!" (Matt. 23:37–39)

In this passage, Jesus said Israel would not see Him again until His Second Coming, when He will appear at the end of Daniel's seventieth week. Because He has not yet appeared, and Israel is not yet willing to say, "Blessed is He who comes in the name of the Lord," we know a considerable amount of time has passed between the last two weeks of Daniel's prophecy.

The gap of time between the sixty-ninth and the seventieth week—what is known as the Church Age—really benefits you and me! The apostle Paul told us that because of Israel's rejection of the Messiah, God offered His kingdom to the Gentiles in order to make Israel jealous: "I say then, have they stumbled that they should fall? Certainly not! But through their fall, to provoke them to jealousy, salvation has come to the Gentiles" (Rom. 11:11).

As Daniel listened to Gabriel's explanation of the seventy weeks, I am certain he was wondering how his visions of the statue with the head of gold and the four beasts fit into this seventy-week progression. After all, in both the statue vision and the vision of the beasts, Gentile kingdoms dominated the earth for extended periods of time. Daniel may have even thought that since Israel's seventy years of Babylonian captivity were nearly complete, the exiles would soon return to Jerusalem and welcome the Messiah. So when was this "time of the Gentiles" to occur?

The vision of seventy weeks answers this question. The permanent kingdom of Israel's Messiah would not come immediately, for the seventy sevens must be fulfilled. Israel's seventy weeks runs concurrently with the "time of the Gentiles," and both will end at the same exact moment.

The seventieth "week" will begin when the Church Age ends, at another distinct moment on our prophetic doomsday clock.

CHAPTER 3

11:52 P.M.
AND KNOWLEDGE
SHALL INCREASE

*"But you, Daniel, shut up the words, and seal the
book until the time of the end; many shall run to
and fro, and knowledge shall increase."*
(Dan. 12:4)

The Bible scholar Harold Willmington told us that some-time around 1680, the great scientist Sir Isaac Newton read the above passage and remarked, "Personally, I cannot help but believe that these words refer to the end of the times. Men will travel from country to country in an unprecedented manner. There may be some inventions which will enable people to travel much more quickly than they do now."

Newton went on to speculate that this speed might actually exceed fifty miles per hour! Eight years later, the French atheist, Voltaire, read Newton's words and retorted, "See what a fool Christianity makes of an otherwise brilliant man! Here a scientist like Newton actually writes that men may travel at the rate of thirty or forty miles per hour. Has he forgotten that if man would travel at this rate he would be suffocated? His heart would stand still!"

"One wonders," Willmington added, "what Voltaire would have said had he known that some two centuries after he wrote this, an American astronaut, Edward H. White . . . would climb out of a space craft a hundred miles in the sky and casually walk across the continental United States in less than fifteen minutes, strolling along at 17,500 miles per hour? . . . Or that during the moon landings, man exceeded a speed some twelve times faster than a .22-caliber rifle bullet travels?"[1]

The literal translation of Daniel 12:4 indicates that during the end times, an explosion of knowledge will occur. We are living in that generation.

From the Garden of Eden until the beginning of the twentieth century, men walked or rode horses just as King David and Julius Caesar did. In the span of a few years, however, mankind invented the automobile, the jet plane, and the space shuttle. Today you can fly from New York to Paris in three hours.

There's an interesting little ditty floating around the Internet, and since I can't credit the author, I'll just paraphrase some of the information about the Class of 2002—young people who are in high school today. These students were born in 1980, so they have few meaningful recollections of the Reagan era. They were elementary students during the Gulf War. There has been only one Pope in their lifetime. They do not remember the Cold War, and they have known only one Germany. The explosion of the space shuttle Challenger is at best a fuzzy memory to them, and the Vietnam War is ancient history.

Their lifetime has always included AIDS. They have never had a polio shot and most likely have never even seen anyone with the disease. Bottle caps, for them, have always been the "screw off" plastic variety. Atari and PONG predate them, as do vinyl record albums. They have probably never played an eight-track tape. Compact disc players were introduced when they were infants.

They have grown up with answering machines, color television, cable, and VCRs. They wouldn't know what to do if they had to change television channels with a round television dial.[2]

One lady told me a story that illustrates this point. Though for years she and her husband had lived in a small house without a dishwasher, their daughter was only five when they moved into a newer, modern house. One day, however, the dishwasher broke, and the woman had to wash dishes in the sink . . . by hand. Her daughter, then ten, came into the kitchen, wide-eyed, and asked what Mom was doing. Mom shrugged and said she was washing dishes, to which the daughter replied, "How'd you ever learn to do *that*?"

Twentieth-century technology has increased, not a little at a time, but exponentially. While not necessarily advancing knowledge in the average man or woman, technology has made fathomless depths of data available to us at the click of a button. You can receive faxes in your car, take a message on your sky pager, and explore encyclopedias of vast knowledge that are small enough to fit in the palm of your hand. You can sit in the quiet of your own home and drown yourself in information from the Internet. We used to be in awe of how many volumes of information could fit on a computer's CD ROM disk, but now a DVD can hold up to four times as much as a typical CD!

In the last two generations, we have put men on the moon and redefined life and death. Medical science has the ability to keep a corpse breathing for months on life support. Tiny babies weighing less than one pound can survive outside the womb, and unborn babies can undergo surgery before birth. We can repair DNA before a child is conceived; we can clone sheep, mice, and cattle. We have the technology to clone humans, and before too long, I'm sure someone will.

All this knowledge ought to be a good thing, but still we're on the road to doomsday. Our knowledge has not produced utopia; instead, it has created a generation of people who know more about rock stars than history. Our "enlightened" society seeks freedom and self-expression, but it is actually enslaved by drugs, perversion, and occult practices.

We favor death for the innocent and mercy—even praise!—for the guilty. We tout the benefits of secular humanism, the worship of man's intellect, yet our enlightened, religion-free government finds itself impotent in the face of growing crime. Why? Because knowledge without God can only produce intellectual barbarians, smarter sinners. Hitler's Nazis threw Jewish children alive into the ovens. Many of them were educated men; some had Ph.D.'s, but their education was accomplished without the acknowledgment or the knowledge of God.

"We have grasped the mystery of the atom," General Omar Bradley told a Boston audience in November 1948, "and rejected the Sermon on the Mount . . . With the monstrous weapons man already has, humanity is in danger of being trapped in this world by moral adolescents. Our knowledge of science has already outstripped our capacity to control it. We have too many men of science, too few men of God."[3]

We have built a society upon pillars of technology, a capitalistic economy, and human government. Just like Israel of old, we have forgotten or ignored God's precepts and warnings in order to go our own way. But as the clock nears doomsday, my friend, the birth pangs of the coming new creation are sending shock waves throughout civilization. The pillars of our society are teetering, and they will fall.

TECHNOLOGY: BLESSING OR BURDEN?

"There is no reason for any individual to have a computer in their home."
—KEN OLSON, CONVENTION OF THE WORLD
FUTURE SOCIETY, 1977[4]

I'll be one of the first to admit that computers have made life easier. The simple act of typing a manuscript used to be a major trial—one little mistake, and the page went into the trash can. Then came correcting typewriters, followed by word processors, then computers with word processing programs. Now, instead of actually typing out a book four or five times, writers input the information once, then spend hours cutting, pasting, and correcting before the manuscript is even printed out.

The Internet, while it does collect a shameful amount of trash, is also an ocean of facts and news. Used wisely, it can be a godsend when researching a topic.

Computers are used in virtually every aspect of life today. There are computer chips in your car, your microwave, and your VCR. If you call the phone company or your doctor's office for help, you'll probably be kept on the line until the receptionist can punch your customer number into her computer and pull up your records. Technology has brought us to the place where the phrase "the computer is down" is the most feared expression in modern times. Without computers, we're stuck. Without beepers, we're incommunicado. Without technology, we might as well take the day off and curl up with a good book, but we can't afford to relax for long. Our society hums efficiently only as long as our computers are operating.

VIRTUAL TERRORISM IS REAL

The increase of knowledge in our generation has resulted in a building wave of cyber-terrorism. James Bond is familiar with the scenario—legions of mercenary hackers in league with black-clad terrorist organizations whose wide-eyed leaders want nothing less than to rule the world. You may think such situations belong purely to the world of novelists and screenwriters, but that virus that slipped into your computer wasn't designed by someone with your best interests at heart. Cyber-terrorism is not only possible, but it could spell disaster for millions.

"According to experts in terrorism and information warfare specialists, we are on the verge, if not already in the midst, of the 'cyber-terrorism' age," wrote Arieh O'Sullivan of the *Jerusalem Post*. "Add to this the threat of unaccounted-for nuclear bombs—some that can fit into a suitcase—and biological weapons, and you've got 'super terrorism.'"[5]

In March 1998, a host of computer experts met in Israel to discuss threats of the technological age. Conference organizer Yonah Alexander believes that the globalization of cultures, economies, and securities opens us up to a "new world disorder." Technology has connected the world, but this connection carries a great risk, leaving us vulnerable to attack.

"We are moving toward a new age of Internet 'click' terrorism," said Alexander. "This is the new face of terrorism in the future."[6]

The Internet not only enables groups from around the world to communicate, but Web pages are used for propaganda and psychological warfare. In some ways, Alexander said, the Internet has replaced military training camps. If you want to know how to build a bomb, you can easily find a "recipe" online.

What else could cyber-terrorists do? A movie released a few years ago, *The Net*, showed how easily a person's identity could be erased through computer hacking. Using hacked information, anyone with evil intentions could demolish a person's credit rating, insert a police record, or alter medical records. The organizations whose records had been altered might not even realize they had been invaded by terrorist hackers, and if they did, they wouldn't know how to set things right again.

Marvin Leibstone, an information warfare analyst and former army colonel, believes cyber-terrorism isn't yet a worrisome reality, but the potential for trouble is certainly present. Terrorist groups could negotiate online, break into computers, and demonstrate scenarios they intend to carry out. They could also hold referendums online and show that their groups have political clout, forcing governments to alter their policies.[7]

Kevin Stevens makes his living helping companies protect their computer systems. He knows the potential for trouble, and he noted that only 5 percent of America's $7.5 trillion economy actually exists in hard currency. The rest is "electronic" money—and that's a frightening statistic. How would you react if you woke up tomorrow morning and found that your bank accounts had been wiped clean?

According to *Jane's Defence Weekly*, an online news bulletin, the Pentagon computers suffered over 250,000 break-ins last year. One particularly heavy-duty attack came during one of our crises with Iraq.[8]

"In the 1960s, 1970s, and 1980s terrorism was manifested by the physical actions of attacks, hostage-taking, hijackings, and bombings," said Yonah Alexander. "The 1990s and the next decade will be seen as the decade of super terrorism. The impending doomsday scenario is not a question of *if*. It's a question of *when*."[9]

THE DAY THE DOLLAR DIES

Money is an exciting topic—if you don't think so, just try taking twenty dollars away from the next person you meet on the street. Jesus tried to teach us about dealing with

money—16 out of 38 parables deal with the topic of possessions. There are 500 verses in the New Testament dealing
with prayer, less than 500 dealing with faith, and over 2,000
about how to handle our possessions.

Wall Street is headed for doomsday, don't you doubt it.
Despite the optimistic predictions flowing from our nation's
capital, America is teetering on the edge of economic collapse. The economy is one pillar upon which we have built
our "Great Society," and as the end draws near, that pillar is
going to crack and crumble.

Perhaps you remember President Clinton's celebration of
the so-called budget "surplus" in 1998. After the announce-
ment of this "leftover money," debate raged in Congress and
the national media about how we should spend this supposed windfall. No one, however, talked about the solid
truth underlying all the political hyperbole. The truth, simply put, is this: *There is no extra money*. Despite
Washington's claims that the current administration is wip-
ing away thirty years of red ink, the national debt continues
to grow. As of September 29, 1998, the national debt—the
total amount of outstanding Treasury bonds, bills, and notes
our government owes—stood at $5,523,785,546,399.80.
That's five *trillion* dollars. In fiscal year 1998 alone, the debt
increased by $110,639,535,002.46. In case you're tired of
counting digits, that's over one hundred ten *billion* dollars.[10]

How many is a trillion? If you went into business the day
Jesus Christ was born, stayed open 365 days a year, and lost
a million dollars every day, you'd have to work through
today and for another 700 years before you'd lose a trillion
dollars.

One million dollars can be contained in a stack of one-thousand-dollar bills four feet high. You'd have to stack one-thousand-dollar bills sixty-seven *miles* high before you'd have a trillion.

"The growing national debt is an unwelcome guest at today's surplus party," said Concord Coalition National Policy Director Robert L. Bixby. "But politicians who energetically boast about surpluses today will have a difficult time explaining to their constituents in a few years why they need to raise the debt limit."[11]

DEBT DISASTER

The growing national debt will ultimately murder the American dollar. Proverbs 21:20 tells us, "There is desirable treasure, / And oil in the dwelling of the wise, / But a foolish man squanders it." America has not only devoured all she has, but also all her children will have! By God's accounting system, our nation's spending policy is formulated by fools. We are spending all we have, and all we can borrow from Europe and Japan.

The other day a man told me that Congress raised taxes so they could pay off the national debt. That's a myth! Last year the national media featured shots of Clinton and various members of Congress celebrating the budget surplus. Lots of people made a lot of fuss about extra money, but all that hoopla was nothing but wool being drawn over the eyes of the American people!

Let me explain: In 1998, America experienced a year of economic stability. Unemployment was at a peacetime low. Inflation was negligible. President Clinton announced a $39 billion budget surplus, while the Congressional Budget

Office estimated that it might run as high as $63 billion. People celebrated, Democrats clapped themselves on the back, and Republicans began pushing for tax cuts.

It was all Cinderella talk, and the illusion will vanish at the stroke of midnight.

The explanation lies in history. In 1968, to pay for the war in Vietnam, President Lyndon Johnson decided—for the first time—to include Social Security in the national budget. Social Security, by necessity, takes in more money than it pays out, so the Social Security surplus helped LBJ balance his books.

Today, the Social Security surplus is at least $100 billion a year, and it alone accounts for the federal budget surplus. If you separated Social Security out of the national budget, as in pre-LBJ days, the budget wouldn't show a surplus at all. It would show a *deficit* of over $37 billion.

A deficit budget can be a good thing, for it curtails government spending. But when you start talking about a surplus, politicians begin dreaming up new ways to spend money we don't really have. While the politicos in Washington are arguing over the perception of deficit versus surplus, none of them are talking about the national debt.

The national debt is currently about 67.4 percent of our U.S. Gross Domestic Product, or GDP. Eric Black, a staff writer for the Minneapolis *Star Tribune*, explained why this is important:

Imagine a family that is borrowing money every year, never paying off any of the debt, and therefore paying more interest every year. It's not healthy. But in assessing the magnitude of the problem, you'd certainly want to know whether the family's income was rising fast enough to enable them to pay their growing interest costs without invading the grocery or mortgage money. Expressing the debt as a percentage of GDP indicates which is growing faster . . . Between 1981 and 1996, the GDP grew by 250 percent, a healthy pace. During the same period, however, the national debt grew 500 percent—twice as fast as the economy.[12]

Black went on to explain that the percentage of national debt to GDP did decline slightly in 1997, but it could easily begin to grow again. "One way to think about the phenomenal growth of the national debt is to consider it as the price we pay for putting off a visit to the dentist," said Lawrence Malkin, an economic columnist. Putting off the visit never eases the pain, but only makes it worse.[13]

Over and over in America's history, national debt was created during wartime and paid during peacetime, but after World War II the government decided not to pay off the debt. The debt to GDP ratio in 1945 was more than 100 percent.[14]

Our nation is simply digging itself deeper and deeper into a ditch. If we are to survive, we must send a shocking message to our elected officials: Stop spending this nation into poverty! Stop sending our children and grandchildren into debtors' prison.

What Is a Dollar Worth? Less and Less

The dollar will die because it has no basis. What is money? Have you ever stopped to consider the worth of a single dollar?

The world's first system of exchange was the barter system. If I wanted something from you, I would offer some tobacco, a cow, or a couple of chickens in exchange. Precious metals became the next system of monetary exchange. Then banks were created, and paper receipts represented the value of gold stored in a bank's vault. The American mint printed dollars to represent the gold stored in Fort Knox, but when America was taken off the gold standard in 1933, the dollar in your pocket lost value.

Under the gold standard, the supply of dollars is determined by the supply of gold. Gold must have a fixed dollar value, x dollars per ounce. If the supply of gold increases, then the money supply can grow by x dollars. Under this system, inflation cannot take hold, for the government cannot manipulate the money supply at will. The supply of gold—and money—is limited by the amount of gold mined. Without a gold standard, governments print money at their own discretion, and the free flow of dollars ultimately cheapens the value of goods. When an item is plentiful, its value falls.

America abandoned the gold standard in the midst of the Great Depression, and the world went off the international gold standard in 1971. These days, exchange rates fluctuate freely, and the United States Federal Reserve, headed by Alan Greenspan, controls the American economy.

We Are "Entitling" Our Way to Disaster

The American dollar will die because of entitlements. Did you know that before 1930 it was considered unconstitutional for the government to tax one citizen and give his money to another citizen? For one hundred years the Supreme Court had voted against such programs. But Franklin Delano Roosevelt packed the Supreme Court with liberal judges who voted in favor of entitlements, and the floodgates flew open. The American people discovered that the United States government was willing to provide handouts.

Over two hundred years ago, Professor Alexander Tyler wrote about a powerful Greek society which had fallen two thousand years earlier:

> A democracy cannot exist as a permanent form of government. It can only exist until the voters discover they can vote themselves money from the [public] treasury. From that moment on, the majority will vote for the candidate promising the most benefits from the public treasury, with the result that a democracy always collapses over loose fiscal policy and is always followed by a dictatorship.[15]

In 1964, in his State of the Union address, LBJ announced an "unconditional war on poverty," proclaiming, "One thousand invested in salvaging an unemployable youth today can return $40,000 or more in his lifetime." Fueled by Johnson's belief in the Great Society, Congress enacted an unprecedented amount of legislation instituting poverty reduction programs.

Today, more than thirty years later, we have spent over $5.4 trillion, but America's poverty rate has not budged. In fact, the poverty rate in 1966 was 14.7 percent. By 1993, after spending billions of dollars, the poverty rate had actually increased to 15.1 percent.

How does this translate into everyday reality? In 1993

alone, American taxpayers spent over $324 billion on eighty different welfare programs—that's over $3,300 from each tax-paying household!

With the $5.4 trillion we've spent in fighting the war on poverty, we could have purchased every factory, all the manufacturing equipment, and every office building in the United States. Even after these purchases, we would have enough money left over to buy every airline, railroad, trucking firm, commercial maritime fleet, telephone company, television and radio company, power company, hotel, and every retail and wholesale store in the nation![16]

Welfare has become one of the government's largest categories of spending. By 1994, after adjusting for inflation, welfare spending was six and a half times greater than at the beginning of Johnson's war on poverty![17] "In welfare," said William Lauber,

> You get what you pay for. Ever since President Johnson and Congress enacted the Great Society programs, our government has paid for nonwork and out-of-wedlock births. And, consequently, it has achieved huge increases in both . . . By offering benefits to people without regard to character or behavior, the entitlement system has helped destroy the character and resolve of the poor.[18]

What is the biblical solution to poverty? "Six days shall you labor" (Ex. 20:9). America is the land of equal opportunity: everyone can work and pay taxes. The Bible says, "If anyone will not work, neither shall he eat" (2 Thess. 3:10). Nothing in your life will work until you do!

The Word of God makes provision for the man or

woman who cannot work because of health or age. In Israel, the farmers were forbidden to cut the grain in the corners of the field so widows and orphans might come and glean grain for their needs. The limbs of fruit trees could be flayed only once, so the remaining fruit could be harvested by the poor. It is the responsibility of the church and individuals to provide for those who legitimately cannot work.

THE RUMBLINGS HAVE ALREADY BEGUN

The Federal Reserve has no elected officials, it has never been audited, and it alone sets the rate of interest, which determines what your dollar is worth. Thomas Jefferson once said, "A private central bank issuing public currency is a far greater menace to the liberties of the American people than a standing foreign army."[19]

Economist Patrick Gaughan, director of the New Jersey Economic Research Center, says that Federal Reserve Chairman Alan Greenspan is the most powerful man in America: "He affects all American lives whether they know it or not."[20] Greenspan and his cohorts at the Federal Reserve control interest rates, which directly influence the American economy. Some have even speculated that the Federal Reserve controls American politics—no one denies that the Federal Reserve Chairman and the president of the country must treat each other with wary respect. "The worst thing you could do is create a recession during an election year," says Sung Won Sohn, chief economist at Norwest Bank, a large Minneapolis holding company. "That would create a political backlash that could curb the independence of the Federal Reserve."[21]

James Stack, editor of *InvesTech Research*, says that federal interest rate cuts are the only thing that will keep the stock market from running into a ditch in 1999. "The Federal Reserve chose to reinflate the Wall Street bubble in the fall [of 1998] and flood the financial markets with liquidity [by lowering interest rates]. But it's like a junkie hooked on drugs. When the infusion stops, or in this case, the Fed has to reverse directions, the withdrawal will be horrendous."[22]

The United States is standing in a line of dominoes that have already begun to topple. In the summer of 1997, Thailand devalued its currency, the *baht*, and few Americans even noticed. But devaluation is serious business. (What would happen if our government suddenly announced that the dollar was worth, say, only fifty cents?) As other Asian countries followed suit, foreign investors panicked and pulled out of Asian investments.

Japan was the next country to be affected, because 40 percent of its trade is with other Asian countries.[23] The loss of exports pushed its already weak economy into a terrible recession. Japanese banks were left with more than $500 billion in bad debts, and though the Japanese government tried to bail out its banking system, the economy is still in sad shape. Japanese pension funds have enormous losses while a sizeable percentage of Japan's work force will be retiring in the next twenty years. Japanese government bonds have *negative* interest rates, but most people are more willing to accept losses in government bonds than to risk putting their wealth into Japanese banks.

The investor exodus hit Latin America and Russia next. To stop investors from converting local currencies into dollars or a more stable currency, countries raised interest rates.

But high rates mean slow economic growth; the dominoes had rattled almost half the world economy.

Korean banks that had invested heavily in the Russian market had to sell their positions in order to pay their own creditors. The Russian ruble began to fall while interest rates began to increase, hitting heights of 70 to 90 percent in July 1998. Finally, in mid-August, the Russian government literally ran out of dollars and announced it would no longer convert the unstable ruble into dollars. The stock market went into free fall; the financial system collapsed. Currently, real family income in Russia is less than three hundred dollars per year, lower than in Haiti.[24]

Next in line for hits were the huge hedge funds, investment banks, and commercial banks that invest in foreign markets.[25] Few people paid attention last fall when newspapers and magazines reported that the Federal Reserve Board had put together a multibillion dollar rescue of a struggling hedge fund. If you asked the average person on the street what a hedge fund was, few could tell you, and even fewer would care. But this is something you need to understand, for issues like this may greatly influence your life in the coming months.

Newsweek magazine began its story about the hedge fund rescue by telling a joke: "If you owe a bank a million dollars and can't pay, the bank owns you. But if you owe a *billion* dollars, you own the bank, because it doesn't dare foreclose and take a huge loss."[26]

That's the best explanation I've heard of what happened in October 1998. Long-Term Capital Markets, located in Greenwich, Connecticut, owed so much money to important institutions that the Federal Reserve and Wall Street didn't dare let it collapse. Why not? Because if Long-Term Capital failed, businesses to whom they owed money would go bankrupt, forcing still other businesses to go out of business. Talk about a domino effect!

The most incredible irony is that those who poured money into the fund to save it will also pay the Long-Term Capital executives a management fee for the right to pull their fat from the fire.

A hedge fund generally makes very short-term investments—usually ranging from five minutes to two weeks—and speculates on short-term price changes in security markets. It generally borrows very large amounts of money for these speculations; Long-Term Capital, for instance, did not want to handle any investment less than ten million dollars. Long-Term Capital's ratio between borrowed money and investors' money was one hundred to one—in other words, they borrowed one hundred dollars for every dollar the partners or equity holders invested. When they lost, they lost big, and they lost in October 1998.

Newsweek explained the firm's failure this way:

> The firm's computer wizards expected markets to move one way, but markets kept doing things—like having 27-year U.S. Treasury bonds decline in value relative to 30-year-Treasuries—that the computer insisted would never happen. The firm's chief executive, John Meriwether . . . has told people he considers this summer's market a "10-sigma" event. Translated from the Greek, this means a chance of less than one in a billion billion billion.[27]

When will financial wizards and their computers learn that God controls the affairs of men?

Let me make one thing clear: Your tax dollars did not go to save the skins of a few fat cats. Not yet, at least. Though the Federal Reserve did play a role in assembling the fourteen players who agreed to bail out the Long-Term Capital hedge fund, no tax money was involved. But people in the know are already grumbling about the appearance of unfairness. Why will the government's big boys step in to bail out some players and not others, and how did the Federal Reserve come to have so much power?

Last fall, *Standard & Poor's* chief international economist Nariman Behravesh spoke in San Antonio and reported that the chances of a full-blown world recession, including the United States, have increased to 35 percent from 25 percent last summer. At that same meeting, Norwest Bank's chief economist Sung Won Sohn forecast a 50 percent chance for a world recession in 1999. Citing the fact that 40 percent of the world economy is shrinking, Sohn calculated a 25 percent chance the United States will be hit hard enough to fall into recession next year. "The world economy is out of our control," Sohn declared. "Greenspan cannot fix the problem."[28]

The simple facts are these: If the world is gripped by a recession, the United States will be affected sooner or later. Since 1997, prices of raw materials such as oil, wheat, copper, and coffee have dropped 10 to 40 percent on world markets. Robert Samuelson said, "At home, consumer buying can stay strong only if Americans continue to spend almost all their current income—a shaky assumption of most forecasts."[29]

I don't know when this horrendous crash will begin, but I'm certain it is coming. For every article I read about our prosperous economic outlook, I read another that foretells economic doom. More alarming than the economic reports, however, are the spiritual indicators that tell me God is ready to send America a message via an economic crash.

WHY WOULD GOD ALLOW
AN ECONOMIC CRASH?

God will allow an economic crash to affect America and the world because America's number one false god is the god of money. Don't believe me? Consider these facts:

- *We sacrifice our health to the god of mammon (money).* We ruin our health to get wealth . . . then spend all our wealth to regain our health! This is madness. America's hospitals and doctor's offices are filled with patients suffering from stress-related illnesses. Why so much stress? Because we're spending all we have and borrowing more to keep up with the Joneses. It's time for most Americans to consider plastic surgery—cut up those credit cards and get out of debt!

- *We sacrifice our marriages and our children in the mad pursuit of more money.* How much time did you spend talking to your children yesterday? How much time did you spend at work? How much time watching TV? The average father in America talks to his children forty-eight seconds per day. Make sure you value your priceless human relationships above your career.

- *America's new cathedrals of worship are banks.* The next time you enter one, look at the lavish furniture and notice how the typical customer goes in to talk to a loan officer. Nine times out of ten, he or she will enter with a solicitous and almost reverent manner. If we honored God like that, revival would sweep America. Banks aren't the source of our wealth— God is!

- *In Deuteronomy 28:17–18, God announced the curses that will fall upon the nation who does not obey Him:* "Cursed shall be your basket and your kneading bowl. Cursed shall be the fruit of your body and the produce of your land, the increase of your cattle and the offspring of your flocks." The basket (for gathering produce), the kneading bowl (for making bread), the produce of the land, the increase of cattle and the offspring of flocks all have to do with a nation's economy. Men may think they control the economies of nations, but they do not. God does!

- *God will allow an economic crash because such a scenario fits into His prophetic plan.* The coming Antichrist's economy will be a cashless society in which every financial transaction is electronically monitored. John, author of the book of Revelation, described the situation: "He causes all, both small and great, rich and poor, free and slave, to receive a mark on their right hand or on their foreheads, and that no one may buy or sell except one who has the mark or the name of the beast, or the number of his name"

(Rev. 13:16–17). I'm going to save the complete discussion of this future economic system for a later chapter, but know this: In the resulting confusion of a worldwide economic crash, the Antichrist will rise to power, just as Hitler rose to power because of Germany's economic crisis.

God Almighty will topple America's false god, mammon. He says to us, "I am the Lord your God, and there is none other beside me. I am your shield, your buckler, your high tower, your provider. Remember, America, the power to gain wealth does not come from Alan Greenspan, the President, Congress, the Federal Reserve, or Wall Street. God rules in the affairs of men!"

THE DEADLY EDGE OF KNOWLEDGE

A true mystery: In September 1984, in a small town in northwest Oregon, 4 people came down with fever and violent nausea. A week later, the number of sick had risen to 30. After two weeks, nearly 200 people had been bitten by the same mysterious "bug." Health officials identified it as salmonella, and by the time the disease abated, 751 people were seriously ill, including babies—nearly a tenth of the town.

The origin of the disease was a mystery until an informant from the Rajneeshis cult came forward and confessed. Cult members, who lived on the edge of town, had a secret underground lab where they cultivated salmonella in liquid. They had taken vials of it into local restaurants and poured the liquid over salad bars, in salad dressing, in coffee creamers. Their purpose? To make people too sick to vote against cult interests in a local election.[30]

In the recent movie *The Siege*, Hollywood filmmakers depicted the deployment of American soldiers in New York City, a response to terrorist bombings on our own shores. The movie, which came under intense media fire for portraying Arabs in a negative light, was fictional.

In reality, however, New York City is fighting terrorists of a far more menacing variety than those portrayed in *The Siege*. Without drawing a lot of attention, New York City officials have been buying germ detectors and making arrangements with regional hospitals for emergency care. They're not thinking of explosive bombs or even nuclear warheads, but of something far more insidious—germ warfare.

Although the city has not been directly threatened by a biological or chemical attack, it has undertaken an extensive training program to teach four thousand police officers and firefighters how to handle a biochemical emergency. Incidents like the World Trade Center bombing and the Tokyo nerve gas attack have hammered home one point: any city is vulnerable to chemical attack. And large cities, where there are more people per square foot, are more vulnerable than most.

At any moment, our cities may be struck by silent, deadly weapons that cannot be smelled or tasted.

HISTORY OF CHEMICAL WARFARE

Chemical warfare is nothing new, though the means of production has certainly grown more sophisticated in the last ten years. The ancient Spartans burned sulfur with pitch, creating the gas sulfur dioxide. Byzantine soldiers used a compound that, when burned, created toxic fumes.[31]

Early Greek and Roman literature tells us that ancient warriors engaged in a crude sort of biological warfare by contaminating the enemy's wells. One documented case tells how the English spread smallpox among an Indian tribe by deliberately distributing disease-contaminated blankets among the tribe.[32]

Modern chemical warfare began during World War I. In 1914 the French employed tear gas grenades against the Germans, who retaliated with tear-gas artillery shells. The first lethal agent employed was chlorine, launched by the Germans against the French and British at Ypres in Belgium in 1915. At least 5,000 men died in that attack. Later in that same war, the Germans developed phosgene and mustard gas. By the end of World War I, chemical weapons had caused 1.3 million casualties, including 90,000 deaths.[33]

The Geneva protocol, adopted by the League of Nations after World War I, banned the first use of chemical and biological weapons, but did not restrict preparations for such warfare or protection against it. The Italians were the first to violate the Geneva protocol—in 1936–37, they used mustard gas against the Ethiopians.

And scientists kept experimenting. Tabun, the first nerve gas, appeared in Germany in 1936; Sarin followed in 1939. Though the Germans manufactured nerve agents throughout World War II, they were not used in warfare.

During the 1950s the United States experimented with the development of nerve gases. One of these, called VX, was produced in Utah, but production halted when an accident at the plant at Dugway poisoned six thousand sheep. Herbicides began to attract military interest during the Vietnam War, and the best-known, Agent Orange, was intended mainly for defoliation and the destruction of crops.

In 1983, the United Nations learned that Iraq was using chemical weapons in its war with Iran. Weapons inspectors authenticated these reports and discovered that Iraq had used mustard gas and the nerve agent Tabun against the Iranians. In 1987–88 Saddam Hussein used poison gas against the Kurds, an ethnic group within his own country.

Perhaps even more terrifying than chemical weapons are biological weapons; they are certainly more stealthy, for a person can be exposed to a biological weapon and not become ill until days afterward. They leave no fingerprints, they give a terrorist time to get away, and they also provide more "bang for the buck." One single aircraft spraying a deadly organism over a city the size of New York could kill one out of two people—that's one hundred times the impact of a chemical weapon.[34]

After World War I, with an eye toward developing biological weapons, several countries began experimenting with anthrax, tularemia, plague, and yellow fever. Disarmament negotiations in Geneva during the 1960s, however, included biological weapons, and an agreement ratified in April 1975 forbade the production, storage, and use of biological and toxin weapons. Though the United States, the Soviet Union, Great Britain, and France ratified the agreement, violations were suspected almost immediately. An anthrax epidemic in the Sverdlovsk region of the Soviet Union was widely assumed to be the result of an accident in a factory for biological weapons, but the Soviets claimed it resulted from illegal distribution of infected meat.[35]

The United States *did* stop manufacturing biological weapons. The Russians didn't.

In a July 1998 report for *Primetime Live*, Diane Sawyer and the ABC News team visited Sverdlovsk and discovered the truth. In 1979, someone forgot to turn on the military compound's filtration system one night, and a small amount of anthrax powder went up in a gust of wind and floated out into the atmosphere. According to Sawyer,

> It blew over a neighborhood just south of the military plant in a plume that stretched ten miles. American scientists say the number of dead [was] 62. But the director of a military hospital there told us she documented 259 victims, but the KGB confiscated all her records. The infected were treated with everything available—penicillin, cephalosporin, chloramphenicol, anti-anthrax globulin, and corticosteroids. Nothing worked!

> For more than a decade the Russians refused to admit that their military had released the anthrax. But these two local pathologists who suspected the truth risked their lives by hiding samples of infected brain tissue, hoping some day they could send it to the U.S. for confirmation . . . In January, American experts reported that those tissue samples not only contained anthrax, but four different strains of it, raising the question [of

whether] the Russians [were] creating germs that can resist vaccines.[36]

In 1989, the CIA learned that a vast complex of buildings in the heart of Russian Siberia was the center of what is called "black biology." The program is called Vector, and it contains a bank of 10,000 viruses, including 140 strains of smallpox and three kinds of Ebola.

Diane Sawyer interviewed Russian biological warfare expert Ken Alibek, who has been called the most important defector ever. He confirms that as late as 1992, just before he left Russia, Russian authorities had directly targeted American cities in the event of war for a biological first strike. He specifically told Diane Sawyer that plague, smallpox, and anthrax were to be used against the United States because they were contagious, had a high mortality rate, and could cause serious panic.[37]

Smallpox is a dread disease that causes fever, pain, and numerous pustules. It is so contagious that it wiped out entire tribes of Native Americans when the Europeans brought it to North America in colonial days. *Wait*, you may be thinking, *smallpox has been eradicated. I remember having the vaccination when I was a kid; in fact I still have the small scar on my arm.* Well, my friend, the world hasn't eradicated smallpox. It is not a scourge in civilized countries, but samples of it still live in research labs . . . and our government stopped giving the vaccinations in 1971. Those vaccinations lasted only ten years, so today *no one is immune.* Of people who haven't been vaccinated, 25 to 30 percent of those infected with smallpox will die.

Dr. Donald Henderson has reported the story of a man

who returned to Germany after a visit to Pakistan. He became ill and was admitted to a hospital. Even though he was isolated and had contact with only two nurses, he passed a smallpox infection to nineteen others as the virus passed through the air, even to a room two floors above him.[38]

Richard Preston, author of *The Hot Zone*, a nonfiction work on the Ebola virus, says there are seven million doses of smallpox vaccine on hand in the United States. If a major outbreak occurred in this country, that vaccine would become "more valuable than diamonds."[39]

To be useful for biological warfare, a microorganism must be easy to grow in cultures for large-scale production, able to withstand the stress caused by dispersion, able to survive in air for several hours or in water or food for several days, and it should cause severe disease for a long time. Agents that qualify include influenza, yellow fever, dengue fever, Venezuelan equine encephalitis, anthrax, tularemia, plague, dysentery, Q fever, and coccidioidomycosis.[40]

As technology has increased, so has the potential for the creation of truly fearsome biological weapons. Using microbiological techniques, scientists could feasibly adapt certain viruses and bacteria so that they are even more dangerous and more suitable for use in biological weapons. The Ebola virus, for example, could be modified so that it is airborne. Certain fatal strains of influenza could be adapted for ease of distribution in a crop duster, sprayed from a boat cruising through a crowded harbor, or placed inside a fragile light bulb left to roll around on the floor inside a city bus.

A Russian military scientist recently published a report in the British journal *Vaccine* announcing the creation of a vaccine-proof anthrax. The Americans asked to see it, and the Russians refused. If that's not frightening enough, Alibek told Diane Sawyer that Russian scientific publications have reported a genetic marriage between smallpox and a brain virus called VEE. He believes they have engineered yet another deadly genetic merger—smallpox and Ebola.[41] The mortality rate of such an altered virus would be 90 to 100 percent, and there are no treatments.

The possibilities are endless, and so are the occasions for fear. Dr. Michael Osterholm, Chair of the Public Health Committee of the American Society for Microbiology's Public and Scientific Affairs Board, addressed the congressional subcommittee on Labor, Health, and Human Services in June 1998:

Infectious diseases may be introduced into an unsuspecting U.S. population not only from natural human, animal, or plant sources but also deliberately as part of a 'bio-terrorism' scheme—that is, as part of a release of pathogens intended to harm humans directly or to damage the animals or plants on which we depend. Although casualties may be limited if unsophisticated groups deploy biological weapons, the threat of mass deaths from a biological weapons attack is of grave concern . . .

Unlike nuclear or conventional bombs or even chemical weapons, a biological weapon is unlikely to cause instant harm. Thus, because symptoms take time to develop, an act of bio-terrorism may go undetected for days or even weeks after it occurs. For example, if a biological agent were secretly released in a busy metropolitan travel center such as Washington's Ronald Reagan National Airport, cases affecting travelers might not begin to appear until 2 to 14 days later and, by then, among individuals in scattered locations throughout the United States and other parts of the world. If the disease were even moderately contagious, secondary cases would occur among contacts of ill persons and would also be randomly distributed. Delay in detecting these cases by hours could mean the difference between an order of magnitude in the increased number of serious illnesses and deaths. In particular, for agents such as anthrax, plague, and even smallpox, a delay of hours in responding to these potential disease problems will result in many more cases and deaths.[42]

Dr. Osterholm went on to point out that infected individuals would not be met by trained "first response" teams, but would seek medical attention in emergency rooms, doctors' offices, and clinics in scattered locations. The man with the slight cough sitting next to you at church, the woman who shook your hand as you entered the door—anyone who had come in contact with a biological agent could pass a fatal disease to you without knowing it.

Have I scared you? The folks in Washington are scared, too. Concerned about the broad availability of biological agents to terrorists and national enemies, the government has awarded $4.5 million to Texas researchers to develop a protective vaccine. The three-year grant went to the University of Texas Southwestern Medical Center at Dallas, and one of the program's aims is to develop a wide-spectrum vaccine against any biological pathogen and make production so simple it could be manufactured in a theater of war within one day of detection.[43]

The job won't be easy. Not only are scientists dealing with unknown and sometimes unpredictable reactions of the human body, but there are at least six dozen bacteria, toxins, viruses, fungi, and plant and animal pathogens that could be used as biological warfare agents. Saddam Hussein's Iraq has acknowledged a biological weapons program that includes anthrax, botulinum, and aflatoxin, some of the deadliest agents known to man. Botulinum toxin is the most toxic substance known—one ounce is enough theoretically to kill 420 *million* adults.[44]

The Aum Shinrikyo religious cult in Japan, which killed 12 and injured 5,000 people by releasing nerve gas in a Tokyo subway, was also involved in efforts to make Ebola, anthrax, and botulinum toxins.[62] The 10,000-member cult had its own lab and microbiologists funded by $300 million in assets. As the leader of that cult called for Armageddon, one of his top assistants tried unsuccessfully to spray deadly bacteria from the top of a Tokyo building.[45]

What if another group succeeds?

Michael Osterholm told the story of a Minnesota woman who walked into a local sheriff's office carrying a small, red Folger's coffee can. Inside was a strange powder and a small bottle of green gel. The powder was Ricin, a deadly biotoxin made from castor beans. The gel was a liquid that makes Ricin seep into the skin. The woman's husband and three others were arrested and charged with planning to kill IRS agents, U.S. marshals, and the local sheriff.

They had made the Ricin from a twelve-dollar kit they had ordered from a catalog.[46]

Other dissident groups have pretended to be registered research labs and written to a bio-research supply house where they obtained deadly germs. A supply house in Rockville, Maryland, sold the salmonella culture to the Rajneeshi in Oregon. It also sold Iraq its first strain of lethal anthrax.[47]

THE HOMETOWN SCENARIO

While most of us think a biological weapons attack would be directed at Washington, D.C. or New York City, experts say an even more likely scenario is the "hometown event." Dr. Stephen Joseph, former New York City commissioner of health, said that a hometown scenario "might in the end prove even more significant than a larger-scale attack on a major city" because most state and local jurisdictions are not aware, trained, or equipped to cope with such an incident.[48]

Most people suffering with the early symptoms of anthrax or plague would be treated by local physicians and sent home; only after many people became extremely ill would officials even begin to suspect something like a biological weapons attack. "Very few American physicians," said Dr. Joseph, "whether office- or hospital-based, have even a basic familiarity with plague, anthrax or smallpox, let alone more exotic potential agents."[49]

Dr. Michael Osterholm has told Diane Sawyer, "It is not a matter of *if* [a biological attack] will occur. It's a matter of *when* it occurs and *where* it occurs, and how much panic and how much death are we willing to accept at the time it occurs.[50]

Sawyer went on to reveal that the FBI is training a hazardous materials or "hazmat" unit—a cutting-edge biological SWAT team of scientists, marksmen, and hostage negotiators.

The Marines have a unit called "C-birth" for treating the casualties of a biological attack. This unit, created by a secret presidential directive, PDD 39, directs government agencies to begin preparing for a new and horrifying reality.[51]

When President Clinton addressed the U.S. Naval Academy in 1998, he said that antidotes, antibiotics, and new treatments should be stored in emergency warehouses around the country. But according to the National Security Council, there are not enough supplies to treat casualties for more than one major America city.[52]

Though President Clinton has appointed a "germ warfare czar" to coordinate federal preparations for response to a biological attack, Dr. Michael Osterholm says no money has been appropriated for stockpiling antibiotics and vaccines or to train emergency room personnel. Experts say the threat of the new millennium will not be nuclear but biological, and we are not prepared.[53]

ANTHRAX: THE GERM OF CHOICE

What is anthrax? The disease is normally associated with plant-eating animals like sheep, goats, cattle, and, occasionally, swine. It is called by the bacteria *Bacillus anthracis* and has been recognized as an illness for centuries. It still naturally occurs in Africa and Asia, where animals are not routinely vaccinated. Inhalation of anthrax, when the disease is contracted from breathing anthrax spores, is always fatal.

In August 1998, Kenneth Bacon, a Defense Department spokesman, announced that the Defense Department would immediately begin to vaccinate the entire armed forces, reserves and active, for anthrax. The first forces to be vaccinated were those stationed in the high-threat areas of Southwest Asia and Korea. Vaccination itself is not a simple matter—it requires six doses given over a period of eighteen months, with an annual booster.[54] The vaccine is safe, licensed by the FDA, and has been used by livestock workers and veterinarians since the early 1970s.

At a briefing on the anthrax inoculation program, Dr. Susan Bailey, assistant secretary of Defense for Health Affairs, stated that our country knows of as many as ten nations that either have or are suspected to have capability in biological/chemical warfare.[55] Iraq has admitted to producing and weaponizing anthrax.

There is no doubt that anthrax is the bioterrorist's germ of choice. The grayish brown powder of anthrax spores is stable, destroyed neither by sunlight or temperature. A lot of animals carry anthrax, and spores can survive in horse hair for one hundred years. Unlike a virus, which needs live cells to serve as its host, you can order anthrax from a medical research company or obtain it from an infected animal. After a couple of days in a liquid growth medium, one milliliter of anthrax culture can produce one billion spores—enough to kill 1,250 human beings.[56]

If you were on a bus, casually sitting under an air conditioner that someone had dusted with anthrax spores, you'd hop out at your stop under a death sentence—and you wouldn't even know it. At this point, a massive dose of antibiotics combined with anthrax vaccination *might* save your life, but you have no symptoms, and you don't know what you've been exposed to.

After about three days, you'd think you were coming down with a cold. You'd develop a slight cough. Your chest would feel tight when you breathed. Then, at what is known as the anthrax eclipse, you'd begin to feel better. *No sweat,* you'd think as you got ready for work. *I've kicked whatever bug I had.*

Then, on day four, you would suddenly develop lethal anthrax pneumonia, and your lungs would fill with sputum. You might go to the doctor, and as you struggled to catch your breath and describe how you're feeling, you would suddenly stop breathing and die in midsentence.

Anthrax isn't a pretty picture, and some people in Wichita, Kansas, learned just how ill-prepared they were to deal with it. In August 1998 a state office building was evacuated when an envelope containing a powdery substance was found in a stairwell. Twenty to twenty-five people may have been exposed to the powder found in the envelope and on control panels in three elevators. Thankfully, the powder wasn't anthrax, but if it had been, Wichita would still be in mourning today.

OUR CITIES ARE VULNERABLE

Our country is extremely vulnerable to terrorist attack with chemical and biological weapons.

In 1996 Congress mandated a five-year, $150-million program to prepare our 120 largest cities for antiterrorist training. Under a 1997 program, $42.6 million dollars were set aside for training a multiservice "Chem-Bio Quick Response Force" of up to five hundred people. Members of the force are now traveling around the country training local officials to prepare for terrorists armed with weapons of mass destruction.[57]

In October 1997, officials began to assess the largest 120 American cities for training programs to deal with biological or chemical attacks. Denver was the program's pilot city, and other cities either in training or scheduled for the training program are New York; Los Angeles; Chicago; Washington, D.C.; Kansas City, Kansas; San Diego; Philadelphia; Detroit; Phoenix; San Antonio; San Jose, California; Baltimore; Indianapolis; San Francisco; Jacksonville, Florida; Columbus, Ohio; Milwaukee; Memphis; Boston; Seattle; Atlanta; Honolulu; Miami; and Anchorage, Alaska.

Major General George Friel, who runs the U.S. Army Chemical and Biological Defense Command, says, "It's no longer a question of 'if.' It is now a question of *when*. The World Trade Center [bombing] woke up America, and the Tokyo subway bombing is a reality to the world."[58]

During a training exercise in Boston, emergency forces found that most people involved in the mock attack would have died while victims ran from the scene, contaminating city streets and a nearby hospital. In Washington, D.C., emergency personnel responded to a drill using the scenario of a nerve gas attack at an RFK Stadium rock concert. They discovered that downdrafts from emergency helicopters would have spread the gas. In San Jose, fire and police units responding to a mock gas attack on City Council offices waited outside for three hours while personnel struggled to don the unfamiliar protective gear. In Boston, rescuers waited 90 minutes until personnel with airtight suits could check the scene.[59]

Training personnel to cope with a biological or chemical attack will take time and skill. Realistically, if tomorrow a terrorist organization or a lone gunman were to spray anthrax over your city street, it's highly likely that hundreds would be contaminated and fall sick before anyone even knew exactly what had happened.[60]

OUR COUNTRY IS VULNERABLE

Yes, our cities are vulnerable to terrorist attack, and the United States is unprepared. We've already seen how Russia has continued research and the production of biological weapons, and Russia is a strong ally of Saddam Hussein. President Clinton has allowed Saddam Hussein to continue his work with biological and chemical weapons for far too long. The Iraqi arsenal will be used, and one day soon—against Israel or her allies, including the United States.

Recently a high-ranking member of our government sat in my office with an ashen face and told me the following shocking story: As a candidate for reelection, he was on the campaign trail, giving a speech to doctors and hospital administrators in South Texas. After he spoke, a general in the U.S. Army stood and addressed the group, saying, "We believe without doubt that Saddam Hussein will attack America with germ warfare—probably anthrax. For our purposes of discussion tonight, we want to assume that the anthrax attack has happened and that 250,000 people in San Antonio are dead or dying. Brackenridge Park [a local park] will become the city morgue and mass treatment center. Where do we go from here?"

The politician leaned forward in his chair, looked at me, and said, "I've started looking for vaccine for my family, and the only vaccine available is for military use. America has no idea what's about to happen . . . and it will happen!"

In February 1998, Saddam Hussein's government announced it would no longer allow full and unfettered searches by the United Nations Special Commission weapons inspectors who were supposed to be sure Iraq complied with its promise to destroy its weapons of mass destruction. Knowing that Saddam still possessed a vast arsenal of chemical and biological weapons—at least 6300 chemical bombs and 630 *tons* of chemical agents—national security adviser Samuel Berger declared Saddam's reckless pursuit of weapons to be "one of the most dangerous security threats our people will face over the next generation."[61]

Clinton himself saw the danger in allowing Saddam to continue unchecked and threatened to launch a serious reprisal by U.S. warplanes. Saddam backed down, and weapons inspections resumed.

"But," wrote columnist Michael Kelly,

> Saddam knew that with this president and this administration, everything really depends on what the meaning of "is" is, or whatever. So he bided his time a bit, and then did precisely what he had been warned not to ever, no never, dare attempt. On August 3, the Iraqi government declared that it would not allow inspections at any new sites. And the Clinton administration, mindful of its unambiguous commitment to meet defiance with force, and mindful also of the great danger posed by following what the president had called "some ambiguous third route" did nothing whatsoever.[62]

Actually, the administration did do something—it urged Secretary of State Madeleine Albright to call Richard Butler, the head of the UN inspectors, and asked him to call off a no-notice inspection scheduled for August 6. He rescheduled the inspection for August 9, then, after another call from Washington, ordered his inspectors home.

Immediately thereafter, Scott Ritter, a top American on the United Nations weapons inspection team in Iraq, blew the whistle and resigned. His reason was the weak stance the Clinton administration has taken toward Iraq. "The illusion of arms control is more dangerous than no arms control at all," Ritter wrote in his letter of resignation.[63]

Michael Kelly continued his comments:

> And so on October 31, 1998, a day that would live in the infamy of this administration if the calendar wasn't already so crowded, Iraq announced that the UN inspectors were banned from doing any work at all. This, of course, surprised the White House. If Saddam doesn't back down again, the president will order up a spot of bombing, or 23 spots, or 37, or whatever the number is that the focus groups tell him the American people would regard as a fitting show of might. But it won't matter. The damage is abundantly done; there is nothing this administration will do to really stop Saddam from rebuilding his arsenal, and he knows it. Someday, I guarantee you, he'll use that arsenal.[64]

Mark it down, my friends—this world is a seething cauldron of unrest and violence. It is only a matter of time before doomsday erupts on our planet.

GOD WILL TOPPLE AN UNJUST GOVERNMENT

"The use of fetuses as organ and tissue donors is a ticking time bomb of bioethics."
—ARTHUR CAPLAN, *TIME*, JANUARY 12, 1987

Twentieth-century technology has brought mixed blessings—the doctors who save tiny babies in the womb can also perform what are euphemistically called "partial-birth abortions." Medical professionals and politicians who champion the rights of women trample on the rights of unborn babies without seeing any irony in their views. In America today it is illegal to touch the egg of an endangered bald eagle, but in most states a thirteen-year-old girl can have an abortion without notifying her parents. We want to save the whales, save the manatees, and we've got animal-rights activists who routinely go around splashing red paint on women wearing furs, but it is "politically incorrect" to speak out in defense of a generation of babies who died before even taking a breath. Forty *million* babies have died in America since the *Roe v. Wade* decision in 1973.

In a recent column, George Will told the story of two boys from Chino Hills, California. While they were out riding their bicycles, the school-age youngsters found boxes at the bottom of an embankment. They went home and told their parents they had found boxes of "babies."

"Do not be impatient with their language," wrote Will. "They have not read the Supreme Court opinions. So when they stumbled on the boxes stuffed with 54 fetuses, which looked a lot like babies, they jumped to conclusions. Besides, young boys are apt to believe their eyes rather than the Supreme Court."[65]

Local authorities got involved, of course, and talked about the problems of "solid waste disposal." Someone put the trucker who had dumped the boxes in jail for seventy-one days—the charge was improper disposal of medical waste.

A few decent people in Chino Hills, however, asked the

coroner to give them the fetuses for proper burial. These folks were members of Cradles of Love, a group of church-going Americans who are opposed to abortion. Shortly after the Cradles of Love people made their request, the coroner's phone started ringing with calls from the American Civil Liberties Union.

"[That organization]," wrote Will,

> professed itself scandalized by this threat to . . . what? The ACLU frequently works itself into lathers of anxiety about threats to the separation of church and state. However, it is difficult to identify any person whose civil liberties were going to be menaced if the fetuses were 'released to the church groups for the express purpose of holding religious services.' The ACLU said it opposed 'facilitation' of services by a public official.[66]

For once the ACLU failed to intimidate goodness. In November 1998 the babies were buried in a plot donated by a cemetery in Riverside. Each baby was given a name, and each name was engraved on a brass plate fixed to each of the fifty-four little white coffins made, at no charge, by a volunteer. Fifty-four doves were released at the conclusion of the services.

And, Will wrote, "the ACLU trembled for the Constitution."[67]

My friend, every time I pick up a newspaper, I grow more and more convinced that God's doomsday clock is ticking out the final seconds on the last hour. On one page I read of children killing other children on school playgrounds; on another page I read about parents stuffing their young children into hot ovens. The headlines are filled with stories about our president committing vulgar acts and flagrant infidelity in the Oval Office itself, while our country applauds and his approval ratings rise to new heights! America has become a nation where a Vietnam veteran can walk the streets homeless while a draft dodger sleeps in the White House.

Our national conscience is dead. American society, founded upon the principles of faith and freedom, has left its moral underpinnings and chased after the wind. We are like King Solomon, who said,

> Whatever my eyes desired I did not keep from them.
> I did not withhold my heart from any pleasure,
> For my heart rejoiced in all my labor;
> And this was my reward from all my labor.
> Then I looked on all the works that my hands had done
> And on the labor in which I had toiled;
> And indeed all was vanity and grasping for the wind.
>
> (Eccl. 2:10–11)

America is a soulless mockery of what she once was. Our society, like ancient Rome's, is headed for destruction.

As I write this, 11:52 is exactly where we are on God's prophetic doomsday clock. There is no turning back.

CHAPTER 4

11:53 P.M.

DELIVERANCE FROM DOOMSDAY—THE RAPTURE

How the End of the World Will Be Reported
USA Today:
MILLIONS ARE MYSTERIOUSLY MISSING!
The Wall Street Journal:
DOW JONES PLUMMETS AS WORLD ENDS
New York Times:
AMERICA'S CHURCHES PACKED WITH THOSE
LEFT BEHIND!

The world has zero knowledge of the biblical concept of the Rapture, and many mainline churches belittle this prophetic truth. While most people have heard of "judgment day," far too many think it is a myth, some story created just to keep people in line. Most people have heard of Armageddon, though many think it is merely a synonym for world war, while others would immediately relate it to the

1998 Bruce Willis movie in which the world was threatened by an asteroid. But few Americans have heard of the Rapture, and even fewer fully understand it. It is the next event on God's prophetic doomsday clock.

According to the Millennial Prophecy Report, there are 1,100 groups in the world who believe the end is imminent.[1] Thousands of people today are at least wondering about the end of the earth. As we've already seen, some people are expecting the world to die by famine, pollution, or during an alien invasion. Others are expecting nuclear war, biological terrorism, and cyber-devastation. But Bible believers are expecting none of the above. We are anticipating at any moment the appearance of the Son of God in the clouds of heaven with power and great glory. Jesus Christ will come for His church at the Rapture, and those who have placed their faith in Him will be instantly snatched into heaven.

Daniel, the prophet who saw the future, didn't mention the Rapture. He saw the "times of the Gentiles" and the future of Israel, but he never mentioned anything about a snatching away of believers. So how do we know the Rapture will occur?

THE RAPTURE IS A MYSTERY

In 1 Corinthians 15:51-52, Paul wrote, "Behold, I tell you a mystery: We shall not all sleep, but we shall all be changed— in a moment, in the twinkling of an eye, at the last trumpet. For the trumpet will sound, and the dead will be raised incorruptible, and we shall be changed."

Paul found it necessary to explain this "mystery" to the church at Corinth because age and illness were beginning to claim church members—and they had expected Jesus to come back for them before any of them passed away. So Paul shared with them a "mystery," a term used in Scripture to denote something God had not previously chosen to share with men. They wanted to know if those who had died would have a part in the eternal kingdom to come.

Paul gave them a succinct explanation of the Rapture: At the sound of the trumpet, the dead in Christ will rise instantly, in "the twinkling of an eye" with supernatural, immortal bodies. Those who remain alive will be caught up to meet the Lord, too, and also given glorified bodies of absolute perfection. This mass gathering of believers is commonly called the Rapture.

If you were to ask ordinary church members in America what they thought of the Rapture, far too many would look at you with puzzled expressions on their faces. Some have never heard the word mentioned from their pulpits and haven't the faintest notion what it means. Though most evangelical churches have preached the doctrine of the Rapture for years, they are now falling under attack for teaching that a literal gathering of the church will occur. The thundering liberal herd is bellowing, "There will never be a Rapture! We're going through the Tribulation, so prepare yourself!"

Their position reminds me of a story of a small, Midwestern town. A man came running down Main Street screaming, "The dam broke! Run for your life!"

Two ladies coming out of the grocery store heard him. "The dam broke?" They ran after him, squealing in panic as they spilled groceries all over the sidewalk.

A trio of men in the barber shop heard the commotion. They saw the panicked man and the frightened ladies, then they fled, too. "The dam broke," they shouted, the barber's aprons flapping on their chests as they sprinted for the edge of town. "Run for your life!"

At the firehouse on main street, the fire chief heard the noise and punched the alarm button. The siren echoed through the town, drawing more people into the frightened flood of refugees. The police chief, the mayor, the city clerk all deserted their posts and jumped into the fleeing mob.

An elderly fellow from the barber shop reached the corner of 14th Street and Main, then retreated into a sheltered spot before a doorway, too breathless to run any farther. "I guess this is where it ends for me," he said, bracing himself for the rush of water. Then, from nowhere, a startling thought crashed into him: *Wait a minute. I've lived here all my life, and we don't have a dam!*

My friend, dominion theologians and liberal preachers are running down Main Street screaming, "We're going through the Tribulation," and those who are more loyal to the message of a man than the Word of God are joining the stampede. Saints of God, stop running like lemmings over a cliff. Look up! Pray up! Pack up! We're going up! Your redemption draws nigh, for the King of kings is coming!

Let's look at 1 Thessalonians 4:13–18:

> But I do not want you to be ignorant, brethren, concerning those who have fallen asleep, lest you sorrow as others who have no hope.

> For if we believe that Jesus died and rose again, even so God will bring with Him those who sleep in Jesus. For this we say to you by the word of the Lord, that we who are

alive *and* remain until the coming of the Lord will by no means precede those who are asleep.

For the Lord Himself will descend from heaven with a shout, with the voice of an archangel, and with the trumpet of God. And the dead in Christ will rise first.

Then we who are alive and remain shall be caught up together with them in the clouds to meet the Lord in the air. And thus we shall always be with the Lord.

Therefore comfort one another with these words.

At the time of the Rapture, both the dead and the living in Christ will be changed in a flash, a microsecond. Bodies that are dead and decaying will be revitalized; bodies still living will become immortal and supernatural. At this moment, the Christian will experience victory over death, hell, the grave, the world, the flesh, and the devil. Hallelujah!

When and How Will Jesus Come for the Believers?

Jesus said, "But of that day and hour no one knows, not even the angels in heaven, nor the Son, but only the Father" (Mark 13:32). Despite the thousands of people who would like to predict the exact year, month, date, or hour of Christ's return, Jesus said no man knows—not even *He* knows. But God the Father knows when He will send Jesus to fetch His bride home. While we do not know the day and hour, we can know by prophetic Scripture that the Rapture is very, very near. Jesus said, "But as the days of Noah were, so also will the coming of the Son of Man be" (Matt. 24:37).

How was it in the "days of Noah"? Noah did not know the date nor the hour of the flood, but he knew it was very, very near. Why? Because God put him and his family on the ark with all the animals, and God Himself closed the door. When Noah heard the door close, he knew the flood was imminent.

Today, with the portrait of tomorrow clearly revealed in prophetic Scripture, the door of the dispensation of grace is closing, and the coming of King Jesus could happen before you finish reading this page!

When you merge the prophetic references with common sense, you can paint the following picture of the Rapture: Without warning, Jesus Christ, the Prince of Glory, will appear in the heavens in a burst of dazzling light. Instantly, the trump of God will sound, announcing the appearance of royalty, for Jesus is the Prince of Glory, the King of kings, and Lord of lords. The voice of the archangel shall summon the dead from their resting places, and all over the earth, graves will explode as their occupants soar into the heavens. Marble mausoleums will topple as the bodies of resurrected saints rise to meet the Lord in the air.

In the next moment, empty cars will careen down the highway, their drivers and occupants absent. Homes of believers will stand empty with supper dishes on the dining table, food bubbling on the stove, and water running in the sink. The occupants of those homes will have been snatched from this vale of tears to a land where there is no crying, no parting, and no death to celebrate the marriage supper of the

Lamb of God and his radiant bride, the Church, without spot or blemish!

The next morning, headlines will scream, "MILLIONS ARE MISSING!" The church of Jesus Christ—which includes every born-again believer—will be completely absent from the earth. A few politically-correct pastors, New Age church members, and secular humanist religious leaders will remain, and they will be hard-pressed to explain why they didn't vanish with the true saints of God. Telephone lines will be jammed with families trying to contact their mysteriously missing loved ones. (I've got news for you— your telephone company doesn't reach that far!)

Over the next few days, TV cameras will cover airline crashes in which Christian pilots vanished without a trace. Families will contact their lawyers to sue hospitals because Christian doctors vanished in the midst of surgery. CNN will run a series of telecasts in which spectacled know-it-alls will gather around a table and try to explain what has happened. Among the "experts" will be a New Age prophet who jabbers about an invasion of space ships who "beamed up" millions of earthlings. A psychologist will say the missing were victims of mass hysteria, while a theologian will say the world is better off without the "right-wing, Bible-believing, politically-incorrect fundamentalist hate-mongers" who believed in some nonsensical allegory called the Rapture.

Over the next few months, churches will be packed with weeping people who will have realized, too late, that God's prophetic doomsday clock has advanced, shearing away another event on the prophetic time line. The world, and everyone in it, is moving inexorably toward the greatest tribulation the world has ever known.

DIFFERENT VIEWS OF THE RAPTURE

There are some theologians who believe in the Rapture, but they are not convinced the Rapture will occur before the time of great Tribulation. There are actually five different views of the Rapture.

1. No Rapture Position
2. Partial Rapture Position
3. Midtribulation Rapture Position
4. Posttribulation Rapture Position
5. Pretribulation Rapture Position

1. NO RAPTURE

This position is espoused by those who support a belief sometimes called "dominion theology" or "kingdom now." This view holds that the Church will become so victorious on the earth that it will usher in the millennial kingdom and there will be no Rapture of anyone at any time.

This view must be rejected in the light of Paul's teaching in 2 Timothy. Paul wrote, "But evil men and impostors will grow worse and worse, deceiving and being deceived" (2 Tim. 3:13). In this chapter, Paul was describing the last days, and his description of men becoming worse—not better—does not fit with kingdom theology. Even science and the Second Law of Thermodynamics teaches us that organized systems become more disorganized over time—the nature of mankind is becoming more corrupt, not less!

This view must also be rejected on the basis of 1 Thessalonians 4:16–17: "For the Lord Himself will descend from heaven with a shout, . . . " Paul wrote, "then we who are alive shall be caught up together . . . in the clouds to meet the Lord in the air." There's no getting around the fact that this verse describes a literal Rapture.

The *no rapture* view must also be rejected because of the teaching of Acts 1:11. The angel told the disciples that Jesus would come in the same manner they saw him leave, and that means an appearance in the clouds.

2. PARTIAL RAPTURE

Those who hold the *partial rapture position* believe that when Jesus comes in the clouds of glory, He will take only those who have had a second work of grace or who are sanctified in their daily lives. According to this view, the body of Christ will be divided into two parts: a sanctified part that will ascend into heaven, and an unsanctified part that will be left to go through the Tribulation in the hope that their sins may be purged through this great time of trial.

This view must be rejected on the basis that the death of Jesus Christ removes all sin. The Bible says, "Their sins and their lawless deeds I will remember no more" (Heb. 10:17). Because our redemption at Calvary was complete, there is not one reason God could not receive anyone who has confessed Christ and accepted His substitutionary death at Calvary.

This view also should be rejected because the bride of Christ is a body, perfect and complete: "For by one Spirit we were all baptized into one body—whether Jews or Greeks, whether slaves or free—and have all been made to drink into one Spirit" (1 Cor. 12:13). To suggest that part of the body must remain on earth while the other part is in heaven is contrary to Scripture.

This view must also be rejected because it implies that salvation comes by *our* works. We do not sanctify ourselves—there's no way we could. We are saved and sanctified only through the sinless blood of Jesus Christ.

3. MIDTRIBULATION RAPTURE

Some Christians believe that the Church will endure the first three and one-half years of the seven-year Tribulation and be raptured before the beginning of the second half of the Tribulation. This position is known as *midtribulation rapture*.

This view must be rejected because the first three and one-half years of Tribulation consist of wars, pestilence, famine, disease, desolation, and death, as the beginning of God's wrath is poured out upon the earth. Because the purpose of the Tribulation is to punish the ungodly, not the Church, the Church cannot go through *either* half of the Tribulation.

4. POSTRIBULATION RAPTURE

This position holds that the Church will go through the entire seven-year Tribulation period. It will endure the judgment and the wrath of God and will be caught up to meet the Lord in the air to return immediately with Him to the earth.

A Scripture often used to justify this position is John 16:33: "In the world you will have tribulation."

In Scripture, the word *tribulation* is used in two different ways. First, it is used to describe any severe trial that comes upon an individual in his walk with Christ. In this sense the believer must expect tribulation. Second, the word is used to describe that specific seven-year period (Daniel's seventieth week) when the wrath of God will be poured out upon men for their rejection of Jesus Christ and the gospel.

The purpose of the Tribulation is to punish those who have rejected the Word of God, and the Bible assures us that there is no "condemnation [judgment] to those who are in Christ Jesus" (Rom. 8:1). So this position must be rejected for this reason as well as several reasons cited earlier. It is not only unscriptural but illogical to think the Church would suffer through the Tribulation.

5. PRETRIBULATION RAPTURE: GOD'S PREMILLENNIAL, PRETRIBULATION PLAN

The *pretribulation rapture position* states that the church will not go through any portion of the Tribulation. I believe this is the correct position for several reasons.

First, the very nature of the Tribulation precludes the church from suffering any of it. The Tribulation is a horrendous time of wrath, judgment, indignation, darkness, destruction, and death—and it leads to doomsday. Paul wrote, "There is therefore now no condemnation [judgment] to those who are in Christ Jesus" (Rom. 8:1).

The Church has been cleansed by the blood of Jesus and needs no other purification. Some ask, "Don't Christians need to be cleansed?" The answer is yes, but they are cleansed through confession of sin and the blood of Jesus Christ, not personal suffering. "If we confess our sins, He is faithful and just to forgive us our sins and to cleanse us from all unrighteousness" (1 John 1:9).

Another reason I believe the pretribulation rapture position to be scripturally correct is Paul's teaching in 2 Thessalonians 2. The believers in Thessalonica were experiencing great persecution. They wanted to know whether the persecutions they were enduring were part of the Tribulation and whether Paul was right when in his first letter he told them Christians would not go through the Tribulation.

Paul told them "not to be soon shaken in mind or troubled, either by spirit or by word or by letter, as if from us, as though the day of Christ [or better, the Day of the Lord] had come" (2 Thess. 2:2).

Paul said they were not in the Tribulation. He wrote, "that Day will not come unless the falling away comes first, and the man of sin is revealed, the son of perdition" (2 Thes. 2: 3).

The "man of sin" is the coming Antichrist, who will come from the federated states of Europe, the final form of Gentile world power. He will be the leader of the "ten toes" Daniel saw in his dream of the statue with the head of gold.

The Antichrist has not appeared yet, "For the mystery of lawlessness is already at work; only He who now restrains [hinders] will do so [keep on hindering] until He is taken out of the way" (2 Thes. 2:7).

Who is restraining Satan from presenting the Antichrist to the world as God? The Church, the salt of the earth, that conquers corruption on contact. When the Lord Jesus appears in the clouds of heaven to remove the Church from the earth, God's restraint will be removed, and Satan can then accomplish his purpose of dominating the world—but not until the Church has been raptured from the earth.

Another reason I believe that the pretribulation position is scripturally correct is Revelation 4:4. John wrote, "Around the throne were twenty-four thrones, and on the thrones I saw twenty-four elders sitting, clothed in white robes; and they had crowns of gold on their heads."

Notice that these elders are seated, robed, and crowned. This is clearly symbolic of the Church. In Ephesians 2:6 we read that God has "made us sit together in the heavenly places in Christ Jesus." In Revelation 19:8 we read, "And to her [the Church] it was granted to be arrayed in fine linen, clean and bright." Also, we read in 2 Timothy 4:8, "Finally, there is laid up for me the crown of righteousness, which the Lord, the righteous Judge, will give to me on that Day, and . . . to all who have loved His appearing."

The critical question is this: When is the Church seen in heaven in its glorified position? It is seen at the very beginning of the Tribulation that John described in Revelation 4–19. It is seen in heaven, seated, robed, and crowned. Thus, the Rapture must precede the Tribulation.

One final reason I believe the pretribulation position to be true is found in 2 Thessalonians 1:7–8, where Paul spoke of giving "you who are troubled rest with us when the Lord Jesus is revealed," and "taking vengeance on those who do not know God, and on those who do not obey the gospel of our Lord Jesus Christ." The wrath of God during the Tribulation is to be poured out on "those who do not know God," not on the Church.

God saved Lot from the destruction of Sodom and Gomorrah because he was a righteous man. Since he was a righteous man (2 Pet. 2:7), the angels said, "Escape for your life! Do not look behind you nor stay anywhere in the plain. Escape to the mountains, lest you be destroyed . . . For I cannot do anything until you arrive there" (Gen. 19:17, 22). The presence of one righteous man held back the wrath of God.

The same thing happened at the time of the Genesis flood. The earth was terribly wicked, entirely corrupt, but "Noah found grace in the eyes of the LORD" (Gen. 6:8). God planned a way for Noah to escape His wrath and waited until Noah and his family were safely aboard the ark. Then God shut the door, and the floodwaters covered the earth and consumed every living thing.

In the same manner, the Church has to be removed before the wrath of God can be poured out upon the earth.

THE EARLY CHURCH BELIEVED IN A PRETRIBULATION RAPTURE

The members of the early Church counted the doctrine of the Rapture as one of their most blessed beliefs. The writers of the Epistles spoke of the appearance of the Lord in terms of hope, joy, and comfort. They longed for His appearing.

The disciples who followed Jesus to the summit of the Mount of Olives saw Him rise majestically into the air until He vanished from their sight. Baffled, they stood squinting and searching the heavens, until an angel appeared and said, "Men of Galilee, why do you stand gazing up into heaven? This same Jesus, who was taken up from you into heaven, will so come in like manner as you saw Him go into heaven" (Acts 1:11).

The disciples probably ran back to tell the others what had happened, and in the telling they reiterated the angel's words: "He's coming back! Just like we saw him go, through the clouds!"

The other day I was watching a religious program on television. Some very respected preachers were on a panel, and the host asked one of them to give his reasons for believing in the Rapture. "Of course you know," the host added, "that the early Church fathers didn't believe in the Rapture."

That's wrong! The disciples saw Jesus ascend into

heaven, and they knew He would return in the same way. They had also heard Jesus Himself say He would return to give His followers an *escape* from the coming tribulation: "Watch therefore, and pray always that you may be counted worthy to escape all these things that will come to pass, and to stand before the Son of Man" (Luke 21:36).

The disciples knew the truth from firsthand experience, and they shared it with the other followers of Christ.

Grant Jeffrey has completely debunked the notion that the early Church didn't believe in a pretribulation Rapture. He discovered an old manuscript from A.D. 373, in which Ephraem the Syrian wrote, "For [at the Rapture] all the saints and Elect of God are gathered, prior to the Tribulation that is to come, and are taken to the Lord lest they see the confusion that is to overwhelm the world because of our sins."[2]

FALSE CHRISTS WILL ARISE

If you don't believe in the Rapture, how will you know when the real Jesus comes to earth? Anyone can stand on the Mount of Olives and say, "I'm Jesus." Anyone can wear a white robe. Anyone can claim to be a descendant of King David. Any cult leader could have his followers crown him king of the "new Israel" on the Temple Mount in Jerusalem.

A false messiah could have scars placed in his hands and feet. He could call fire from heaven and perform miracles. There are warlocks and witch doctors on the earth right now who can call fire from heaven and perform miracles. You can turn on your television and watch "psychic healers" perform surgery with their fingernails. But remember this: A man with supernatural power is not necessarily from God. The devil has supernatural power, too, as do his demons.

God knew that imposters and frauds would come and claim to be Christ, especially in the last days. Look at Matthew 24:23–27, in which Jesus told His disciples about His return and the advent of false christs:

> Then if anyone says to you, "Look, here is the Christ!" or "There!" do not believe it. For false christs and false prophets will rise and show great signs and wonders to deceive, if possible, even the elect. See, I have told you beforehand. Therefore if they say to you, "Look, He is in the desert!" do not go out; or "Look, He is in the inner rooms!" do not believe it. For as the lightning comes from the east and flashes to the west, so also will the coming of the Son of Man be.

USA Today once ran a full-page ad that read, "Christ Is Now on the Earth." The *New York Times* carried a similar ad proclaiming, "Christ Is Now Here." Those ads ran in the early 1980s, and I threw them away after showing them on national television. Christ isn't on the earth in bodily form, for when He comes again, the entire world will know about it!

One of our church members once told me, "Pastor Hagee, a lady told me she was driving in California and that suddenly Jesus appeared in the car with her. What do you think?"

"I don't believe it," I answered. "Because if Jesus were here, I'd be gone. I wouldn't be talking to you right now."

Jesus is not in California, New York, Rome, or Brussels.

He is seated at the right hand of God the Father, where He will stay until Gabriel blows the trumpet to call the dead in Christ from their dusty couches of slumber to mansions on high.

How will you be able to tell the real Jesus from the false pretenders? Jesus knew pretenders would come, so God installed a fail-safe mechanism that is so staggering in supernatural power, so earth-shattering, that not even Satan himself could imitate it, much less duplicate it. That fail-safe method is the Rapture!

SOME GLAD MORNING, I'LL FLY AWAY

The old hymn writers knew about the joy of the Rapture. They wrote about it, sang about it, lifted their voices in confidence and praise. They knew, as I know, that just beyond the clouds the saints of God will gather home! From east and west, north and south we will come, ten thousand times ten thousand. God will wipe away every tear from our eyes, and there will be no more parting, no more suffering, no more pain, no more sorrow, no more death, no more disease.

My mother and father will rise. My grandparents will rise, with resurrected, healthy bodies. My family and I will fly to meet them, our bodies changed and clothed in immortality. My glorified body will sail through the heavens past the Milky Way into the presence of God. I'll know I'm with the real Jesus when I stand in His glorious presence with my brand new disease-proof, never-dying, fatigue-free body that looks better, feels better, and *is* better than Arnold Schwarzenegger's.

Does It Matter If I Believe?

Some of you may be saying, "Well, it doesn't really matter if I believe in the Rapture or not. It's just one of those prophetic things that can be interpreted a hundred different ways."

I beg to differ with you, friend. Though the word *rapture* does not appear in Scripture, the word *trinity* doesn't appear in the Bible either, yet over and over it refers to the "oneness" of God and the "threeness" of God.[3] Likewise, there are very clear references to this "snatching away" of believers. The *term* may not be in the Bible, but the *truth* certainly is. Hebrews 9:28 tells us, "To those who eagerly wait for Him He will appear a second time, apart from sin, for salvation." If you're not eagerly looking for Him, you're not going with Him!

Believers in Christ will escape doomsday! Mark it down, take it to heart, and comfort one another with these words. Doomsday is coming for the earth, for nations, and for individuals, but those who have trusted in Jesus will not be present on earth to witness the dire time of tribulation.

The apostle Peter warned that doubters will arise in the end times.

> Knowing this first: that scoffers will come in the last days, walking according to their own lusts, and saying, "Where is the promise of His coming? For since the fathers fell asleep, all things continue as they were from the beginning of creation." (2 Peter 3:3–4)

The fact that the teaching of the Rapture has fallen on hard times is actually a proof that Jesus will be coming soon!

If you listen closely, you can almost hear the footsteps of the Messiah in the clouds of glory.

Other critics of the Rapture say that the doctrine is nothing but escapism, or an attempt to flee from the real world. Well, right now I'm living in the real world, and if I wanted to escape it, I could think of no better way than working and waiting for the coming of my Lord. I'm thrilled that Jesus Christ is my Lord and Savior, heaven is my home, and that I'm not going to walk in the fires of an eternal hell. If that's escapism, so be it.

Let's face it, everyone wants to escape from the coming doomsday. Environmentalists want to escape a doomsday caused by pollution. The peaceniks want to escape the doomsday of nuclear war. The Bible teaches us to prepare for our escape which will come at the Rapture. "How shall we escape if we neglect so great a salvation?" (Heb. 2:3). How do we prepare? We accept Jesus Christ as our Lord and Savior, and we look for His coming.

Yes, my friend, your belief in the Rapture does make a difference. John Calvin, the great reformer, once wrote, "It ought to be the chief concern of believers to fix their minds fully on His Second Advent."

And Martin Luther, in his Sermon of Consolation, wrote,

If thou be not filled with a desire after the Coming of this day, thou canst never say the Lord's prayer, nor canst thou repeat from thy heart the creed of faith. For with what conscience canst thou say, "I believe in the resurrection of the body and the life everlasting," if thou dost not in thy heart desire the same? If thou didst believe it, thou must, of necessity, desire it from thy heart, and long for that day to come; which, if thou doest not desire, thou art not yet a Christian, nor canst thou boast of thy faith.[4]

THE BRIDEGROOM WAITS FOR HIS BRIDE

In order to understand the meaning behind some of the symbolic language used to describe the Rapture, we must understand the Jewish roots of our faith. The mystery of the Rapture is explained in the nuptial chain of events in a traditional Hebrew wedding.

In the ancient ceremony, the bridegroom or an agent of the bridegroom's father went out in search of a bride. (An example is when Abraham sent his servant to secure a bride for Isaac.) A bride would often agree to the marriage without ever seeing her future groom.

Next, a price would be established for the bride—twenty camels, a dozen silver bracelets, or whatever the groom had to offer. The agreed-upon price was called a *mohar*. The bride and groom were then betrothed and legally bound to each other, though they did not yet live together. A scribe would draw up a *ketubah*, or marriage contract, stating the bride price, the promises of the groom (to honor, support, and live with her), and the rights of the bride.

Finally, the groom would present the bride with gifts. Most grooms today give their brides a ring as evidence of love and commitment, but in ancient times the gift could have been almost anything. If the bride accepted her groom's gift, together they shared a cup of wine, the cup of the covenant, and the betrothal was complete. Before leaving her home, however, the groom would tell his bride, "I go to prepare a place for you. If I go, I will return again to you."

The second stage of a Hebrew wedding is the consummation of the marriage. The groom prepares a place for his bride, then journeys to her father's house to get her. Amid great rejoicing, the groom returns with his bride, calls his friends, and arranges for a festive wedding supper.

Christians are betrothed to Christ through the new covenant written on our hearts and sanctified by the blood of Christ. We love a heavenly groom we have not seen and believe He may come at any moment. The bridegroom then went to his father's house to prepare a *chupah*, or wedding canopy. During the following year or so of betrothal, the bride was consecrated and set apart while she waited for her groom. She enjoyed a *mikvah*, or cleansing bath, to purify her for the coming wedding. She had to make herself ready, and she had to *stay* ready, for she had no idea when her groom would return. Often she kept a light burning in the window and an extra jar of oil on hand, lest the bridegroom come in the night and find her unprepared.

No engraved invitations were sent out for the wedding. If people preparing a calendar wanted to reserve a day for the celebration, they had a problem. When the young bridegroom was asked for the date of his wedding, he could only reply, "No man knows except my father." Why? Because he could not go get his bride until the father approved of his son's preparation.

When the groom's father decided everything was in place and released his son to go fetch his bride, the groom arrived at the bride's house with a shout and the blowing of a trumpet, or *shofar*. Thus announced, the bridegroom presented the marriage contract to the father of his intended bride. He claimed her as his own and took her to his father's house.

His father would be waiting to receive the couple, and then the groom's father would take the hand of the bride and place it in the hand of his son. At that moment, she became his wife. That act was called the *presentation*.

After the presentation, the bridegroom would bring his bride to the bridal chamber he had gone to prepare. There he would introduce her to all the society of his friends who had heard the trumpet and come to celebrate the marriage at the marriage feast. In 2 Corinthians 11:2, Paul wrote to the Church, "For I am jealous for you with godly jealousy. For I have betrothed you to one husband, that I may present you as a chaste virgin to Christ."

What a powerful picture of what God has prepared for us! We are the betrothed bride of Christ, sought by the Holy Spirit and purchased at Calvary with Jesus' precious blood. Paul said, "For you were bought at a price" (1 Cor. 6:20). The Almighty Father looked down from heaven and accepted the price of our redemption. We, the bride, accepted the Groom and the evidence of His love for us. Our betrothal contract is the Word of God, for it contains every promise our loving Groom has made on our behalf.

We exchanged gifts at our betrothal. When we accepted Him, Jesus gave us eternal life! God Himself has given us the Holy Spirit, who has bestowed His own gifts of grace, faith, love, joy, peace, longsuffering, kindness, goodness, faithfulness, gentleness, and self-control. Like the bride in her purifying *mikvah*, we have been baptized with water and by the cleansing power of the Holy Spirit (Luke 3:16; Acts 1:5).

In this interim, as we wait for our Bridegroom, Jesus has returned to His Father's house to prepare everything for our arrival. Before He departed this earth, Jesus said, "In My

Father's house are many mansions; if it were not so, I would have told you. I go to prepare a place for you. And if I go and prepare a place for you, I will come again and receive you to Myself; that where I am, there you may be also" (John 14:2-3).

How do we publicly demonstrate our acceptance of Christ? Just like the bride, each time we take the communion cup and drink the wine, we proclaim our wedding vows to our beloved Lord. We demonstrate that we love only Him, that we are loyal to Him, and that we are waiting for Him. Like the eager bride, we keep our lamps burning and strive to be ready, for we don't know when He might arrive.

Our Bridegroom will soon come for us. Make no mistake; we must wait with our ears attuned to hear the trumpet sound.

We're not going into or through the Tribulation. We're going home, to the city where there will be no death, no parting, no sorrow, no sickness. We're going to the city where the Lamb is the Light, to the city where roses never fade, to the city inhabited by Abraham, Isaac, Jacob, and King Jesus.

We have not seen our Bridegroom, but we love Him. And though we do not see Him, we believe, and rejoice with joy inexpressible and full of glory (1 Peter 1:8).

OUR WEDDING GARMENTS

What happened in an ancient Hebrew wedding after the bridegroom took his bride home? She stood before him and awaited his appraisal. If she was wise, she had prepared a trunk with her wedding clothes, and she adorned herself in beautiful garments she had prepared out of her love for her bridegroom.

In biblical times the marriage feast was a celebration to honor not the bride, as is our custom, but the bridegroom. All the guests who assembled at the marriage supper were expected to compose poems and sing songs to honor him as they appreciated the beauty and grace of his bride.

The Blessed Bridegroom has been presented with a bride, and now He is coming to display the bride to all His friends, not that they might honor the bride, but that they might honor the Bridegroom because of the bride's beauty. Jesus will be honored, not because of what we are, but because of what He has made us. In Ephesians 5:27, Paul referred to this analogy when he wrote that Christ gave Himself for the church so that "He might present her to Himself a glorious church, not having spot or wrinkle or any such thing, but that she should be holy and without blemish."

We're not holy by nature. We're not holy by practice. But the bride is the Father's love gift to the Son to honor the Son for His obedience to the Father's will. When Jesus, the Bridegroom, is presented with His bride, He will say, "She is beautiful, without spot or wrinkle." He will rejoice to lead her to the marriage banquet.

Imagine this, if you will: After bringing the bride to his house, the bridegroom takes her into his chamber, looks her in the eye, and says, "Soon I will take you in to meet all my friends. They will want to praise you and exclaim over your beauty. So look into your trunk and pull out those garments you have prepared for our marriage feast."

What would you do if you looked into your hope chest and found nothing? Or if you found only slipshod, poorly prepared garments? You would be embarrassed beyond words before your loving bridegroom, his father, and the assembled witnesses.

J. Vernon McGee said,

> The wedding gown of the church is the righteous acts of the saints . . . The wedding gown will be used only once, but we will be clothed in the righteousness of Christ throughout eternity . . . Through the ages believers have been performing righteous acts which have been accumulating to adorn the wedding gown. By the way, what are you doing to adorn that wedding gown?[5]

THE JUDGMENT SEAT OF CHRIST

The analogy of wedding garments translates into the reality of Christ's Judgment Seat. Soon after the Rapture, we Christians will stand before the Judgment Seat (the "*bema* seat") of Christ. While Jesus took the full weight of God's judgment of sin for us, we must still stand before God for a final review of our faithfulness. As the nations of the world rise and fall because of their morality, our personal decisions and actions are creating evidence for the coming judgment upon us. We will either receive crowns and commendation or reproof and reprimand. Our garments will either be designed to glorify our Bridegroom, or they will appear as filthy rags.

In ancient Greece, the *bema* seat was never used as a judicial bench where criminals were pardoned or punished. The word refers instead to a raised platform in the sports arena on which the umpire sat. From this platform he rewarded all contestants and winners. As Christians, we run the race set before us. If we play by the rules established in the Word of God, we will be ushered to the *bema* seat to stand, not before heads of state, but before the Son of God.

The qualities under examination will be our character and faithfulness. Paul wrote, "For we must all appear before the judgment seat of Christ, that each one may receive the things done in the body, according to what he has done, whether good or bad" (2 Cor. 5:10).

At this Judgment Seat, we are not judged on whether we are saved, for everyone before the *bema* seat is a believer. Paul said the believer's works are brought into judgment, in order that it may be determined whether they are good or bad. Concerning the word *bad* (*phaulos*), Dwight Pentecost observed that Paul did not use the usual word for bad (*kakos* or *poneras*), either of which would signify that which is ethically or morally evil, but rather a word that means "good for nothing" or "worthless."[6] The Lord does not intend to punish us for sins, but to reward deeds done in the name of the Lord.

This is why Paul wrote, "But I discipline my body and bring it into subjection, lest, when I have preached to others, I myself should become disqualified" (1 Cor. 9:27). Paul wasn't worried about losing his salvation, but that his deeds might be found to be worthless.[7]

There's a false concept about the Judgment Seat of Christ that says God will punish believers for all the sins they commit after they accept Jesus Christ as Savior. This concept purports that when an individual accepts Christ, the blood of Jesus washes away all sin from the time of birth until that moment. However, from that moment on, he must answer to God for every sin.

This teaching must be cast off because Scripture plainly

teaches that God does not blot out some of our sins and leave others for us to face on Judgment Day. In Isaiah 44:22 we read, "I have blotted out, like a thick cloud, your transgressions, / And like a cloud, your sins." The psalmist said, "As far as the east is from the west, / So far has He removed our transgressions from us" (Ps. 103:12). My favorite verse is found in both the Old and New Testaments: "For I will forgive their iniquity, and their sin I will remember no more" (Jer. 31:34, Heb. 8:12).

Another false teaching about the Lord's *bema* seat is that if a believer confesses his sins, he's forgiven the sin he confesses, but if he refuses or forgets a sin, God will judge him at the Judgment Seat. This concept must be rejected for the aforementioned reasons. If God is going to present me with a list of sins at the *bema* seat, Christ's death on the cross was meaningless.

Paul wrote, "There is therefore now no condemnation to those who are in Christ Jesus" (Rom. 8:1). Christ took *all* my judgment at Calvary. If He took all my judgment, there is no sin judgment to face at the *bema* seat of Christ.

When we appear before Christ's Judgment Seat, that which is within us will be revealed to all present. The Bible says, "Man looks at the outward appearance, but the LORD looks at the heart" (1 Sam. 16:7). It's not possible for us to know what motives drive men to serve God. For one it may be an absolutely altruistic expression of servanthood. Another, who works just as diligently, may serve to receive applause and recognition from other men. Your motives will be revealed and exposed before all at the Judgment Seat of Christ.

In 1 Corinthians 3:11–15, Paul wrote,

For no other foundation can anyone lay than that which is laid, which is Jesus Christ. Now if anyone builds on this foundation with gold, silver, precious stones, wood, hay, straw, each one's work will become clear; for the Day will declare it, because it will be revealed by fire; and the fire will test each one's work, of what sort it is. If anyone's work which he has built on it endures, he will receive a reward. If anyone's work is burned, he will suffer loss; but he himself will be saved, yet so as through fire.

On display at the *bema* seat will be five great crowns for loyal and trustworthy servants of Christ.

1. To steadfast believers tested by prison and persecution even to the point of death, God will give a Crown of Life (Rev. 2:10).
2. A never-fading, never-tarnishing Crown of Glory awaits the self-sacrificing pastor-shepherds of the flock (1 Peter 5:2–4).
3. Everyone who ran life's race with patient endurance and perseverance will receive a Crown of Righteousness (2 Tim. 4:8).
4. Evangelists and soul winners can eagerly anticipate receiving the Crown of Rejoicing (1 Thess. 2:19-20).
5. Finally, all who overcome will be handed a wonderful Victor's Crown (1 Cor. 9:25).

Which crown will you wear?

Which of your works will be burned, and which will endure?

Will you take your Bridegroom's arm with the scent of

smoke upon you? Or will you join Him, dressed in white, with a glowing crown upon your head? John warned all believers, "Hold fast what you have, that no one may take your crown" (Rev. 3:11). Run the race to win!

> "Let us be glad and rejoice and give Him glory, for the marriage of the Lamb has come, and His wife has made herself ready." And to her it was granted to be arrayed in fine linen, clean and bright, for the fine linen is the righteous acts of the saints. Then he said to me, "Write: 'Blessed are those who are called to the marriage supper of the Lamb!'" (Rev. 19:7–9)

The marriage of the Lamb to His Church will take place in heaven, after the *bema* seat. The marriage supper, however, is an event that involves Israel and will take place on earth . . . at a later date. We'll discuss this later, for it will occur at another fateful moment on God's prophetic doomsday clock.

Today the Master's Son, Jesus Christ, waits to come for His bride. When He comes to fetch her away, anyone who has trusted Him, Jew or Gentile, will go with Him to the place He has prepared. If you are a believer in Christ, a place under the wedding canopy is reserved for you.

CHAPTER 5

11:54 P.M.
RUSSIA INVADES ISRAEL

*"Mankind's greatest collective fear, the doomsday fear,
currently seems to have fascinated an incredible
variety and number of people. Prophecies of doom are
nothing new. Some of mankind's oldest myths have
to do with the destruction of the world by fire . . .
Today, much of the doomsday thinking centers on
nuclear war."*
—EDWARD TELLER,
THE PURSUIT OF SIMPLICITY, 1980

*Y*ou are a citizen of Iraq. Your life in recent months has
been made difficult by sanctions against your country.
Your wife no longer sings in the house; she spends every
spare moment at the market, trying to barter yesterday's
bread for cough syrup so your little ones can sleep through
the dark night. These are dark days, but you and your countrymen endure them because the president assures you that
the day of victory will make all sacrifices worthwhile.

You come home from your work, sit on the carpet in your living room, and turn on the old television in the corner. The president's face instantly fills the screen, and again he is denouncing the Americans, the Jews, the United Nations. "But the time has come," he says, his eyes brightening as the camera zooms in on his face, "for us to settle the old scores. The dead will be avenged, and Allah will be uplifted! We will march upon the settlement of Israel and rid the land of the invaders. Those who have distorted the faith and exchanged the gift of God for heresy and rebellion will be purged from the land!"

The camera pulls back, and you see that the president stands in a row of men, several in dark green uniforms, others in traditional Arab dress. They are all nodding at the president's words, then, in an instant, the screen flickers and changes to a jubilant group of your countrymen dancing in the streets of Baghdad. "The invasion has begun!" The president's voice underlines the joyous celebration. "Our stalwart allies, the people of Russia, and our brothers in arms have united to cleanse Palestine once and for all! Victory to Allah!"

A tide of goose flesh races up your arms and collides at the back of your neck. In public, of course you will praise the president; you might even go to the nearest government office and volunteer for the marching army. But here, in the privacy of your small home, you cannot help but wonder if this time will end like the last time—with bombs and death and humiliation in the face of Iraq's enemies.

But surely the president has learned an important lesson. He would not attack again without a sure and certain confidence that this time he would be victorious. And surely, with

Russian weapons, commanders, and technology behind him, this time he will be.

You breathe a sigh of relief as you consider the implications. Hitler needed to conquer the world to destroy the Jewish people, but the president and his allies need only to conquer a tiny territory, inhabited by fewer than five million people. What can five million do against 804 million Arabs plus the forces of Russia?

Absolutely nothing.

THE CLOCK EDGES FORWARD

Make no mistake—at some moment in the countdown to doomsday, Russia, together with her Arab allies, will lead a massive attack upon the nation of Israel that probably will involve nuclear weapons. The prophet Ezekiel clearly describes the coming battle, which I believe will take place just before the Antichrist steps forward to take his place on the world stage.

To be perfectly honest, I cannot be dogmatic about this event's occurrence after the Rapture. We know the battle over Israel will occur, and I believe it will result in the Antichrist's stepping in to offer Israel and her enemies a seven-year peace treaty. We also know the church will be taken away in the Rapture *before* the Antichrist is revealed. We cannot, however, unequivocally say whether the church will be snatched up before or after Russia's attack upon Israel.

John Wesley White believes this war might occur very soon after the Rapture—that the Rapture might even trigger it. *Thinking the Unthinkable,* he wrote,

With their multitudes of born-again people suddenly raptured away from the distinguished posts of leadership
which they occupy, would provide an opportune moment
for the [Russians] to make their move . . . What would
hinder the Russians and their Islamic satellites from
launching what Hitler called a "final solution" to the
Jewish problem?[1]

Let's take a look at the biblical basis for this prophecy.

THE VALLEY OF DRY BONES

In the thirty-seventh chapter of Ezekiel, the prophet was
caught up by the Spirit of God and taken to a valley of dry
bones. Some Bible scholars believe Ezekiel was taken bodily
to the ruins of Jerusalem, where those who had died in
defense of the city lay unburied outside the walls. In any
case, Ezekiel looked at a multitude of dry bones, scattered by
wind, rain, and wild animals, and wondered what God had
in mind by bringing him to such a place.

God then asked the prophet a strange question: "Son of
man, can these bones live?"

Nonplussed, Ezekiel lifted his brows. Perhaps it was a
trick question, because those bones had been dead a long
time, but with God anything is possible. The prophet, ever a
diplomat, gave a careful answer: "O Lord GOD, you know."

God then told Ezekiel to prophesy to the valley of dry
bones, and as Ezekiel spoke, the bones began to clatter and
clack. An arm bone rushed to join its mate; a thigh bone
snapped to a leg bone. Broken ribs came together; crushed
skulls curved to their original state. And then, as the prophet

watched, sinews, or ligaments, grew over the bones, then skin appeared to cover them over. In moments, the bones were miraculously changed into human bodies, complete and whole, but they did not move or breathe.

Then God spoke again. "Prophesy to the breath," He told Ezekiel, "prophesy, son of man, and say to the breath, 'Thus says the Lord GOD: "Come from the four winds, O breath, and breathe on these slain, that they may live."' "

So Ezekiel obeyed, and breath came into the bodies, and they opened their eyes and lived. They stood, an exceedingly great army of men.

And God said to Ezekiel,

Son of man, these bones are the whole house of Israel. They indeed say, "Our bones are dry, our hope is lost, and we ourselves are cut off!" Therefore prophesy and say to them, "Thus says the Lord GOD: 'Behold, O My people, I will open your graves and cause you to come up from your graves, and bring you into the land of Israel. Then you shall know that I am the LORD, when I have opened your graves, O My people, and brought you up from your graves. I will put My Spirit in you, and you shall live, and I will place you in your own land. Then you shall know that I, the LORD, have spoken it and performed it,' says the LORD." (Ezek. 37:11–14)

The prophecy is not concerned with Israel as individuals, but with Israel as a nation. The Jewish people were scattered throughout the world like the bones in the valley, but God brought them back together in 1948. J. Vernon McGee noted, "They have a flag, they have a constitution, they have a prime minister, and they have a parliament. They have a police force and an army. They have a nation, and they even have Jerusalem. They have everything except spiritual life."[2]

At this moment, Israel can be compared to the bodies who lacked the breath of life in Ezekiel's vision. They are physically complete, but they are lacking the breath of spiritual life itself. They have not recognized their Messiah, but they will, at an appointed time after the battle described in the next chapter of Ezekiel.

GOG AND MAGOG ARE DRAWN TO ISRAEL

In Ezekiel 38 the prophecy continues: "Now the word of the LORD came to me, saying, 'Son of man, set your face against Gog, of the land of Magog, the prince of Rosh, Meshech, and Tubal, and prophesy against him.'"

The leader is "Gog," and his kingdom is "Magog." Magog is referred to as one of the sons of Japheth in Genesis 10:2 and in 1 Chronicles 1:5.

Who is Gog? He is called the prince of "Rosh, Meshech, and Tubal," provinces of Asia Minor. However, that geographical area is today occupied by Iran, Turkey, and the southern provinces of the CIS, the Commonwealth of Independent States. The CIS, which originally consisted of three former Soviet republics—Belarus, Ukraine, and Russia—grew to include eight other republics two weeks after the commonwealth's establishment in December 1991. The republic of Georgia joined in 1993, bringing the total of former Soviet republics to twelve. The CIS states operate much like the American states—they are responsible to a central organization while governing themselves, but they are far from stable.

The CIS has been characterized by infighting between member states from its inception. Ethnic and regional hostilities that had been restrained by decades of central Soviet authority have reemerged in bloody civil wars. More important, a fundamental disagreement has arisen over the goals and purpose of the CIS. One camp, led by Russia and Kazakhstan, envisions the CIS as a vehicle for closer economic and political integration; another camp, led by Ukraine, visualizes the CIS as a transitional organization preparing individual republics for complete independence.[3]

Moscow is the capital and largest city in Russia, one of the founding members of the CIS. I believe "Rosh" of Ezekiel 38 is a combination of Russian states. Seeking long-lost power and glory, the Russian states, headed by a military leader from Moscow, will learn that strength lies in unity.

The geographic identification of Gog and Magog as Russian states is reinforced by linguistics. Many people believe that "Rosh" is related to the modern word *Russia* and that "Meshech" and "Tubal," respectively, are variations of the spellings of *Moscow* and *Tobolsk*, an area in the Ural section of Russia. The name *Russia* does not appear in Scripture, but this detailed description of the invader of Israel clearly fits that now unstable nation.

A great military movement under the leadership of Gog, the prince or leader of Rosh, is described in Ezekiel 38:4: "I will turn you around, put hooks into your jaws, and lead you out, with all your army, horses, and horsemen, all splendidly clothed, a great company with bucklers and shields, all of them handling swords."

Next God identified the invaders that will join Russia: Persia, Ethiopia, Libya, Gomer, and Togarmah (Ezek. 38: 5–6).

Persia is easily identified as Iran. Ethiopia and Libya refer to the Arab Islamic nations of the Arabian Peninsula. I believe when Ezekiel spoke of Persia, Ethiopia, and Libya he was speaking of the contemporary Arab states that are constantly calling for holy war to exterminate Israel. Gomer and Togarmah most likely refer to the region now occupied by the nation of Turkey. Since Israel is the fourth-greatest military power on the face of the earth, there is no way the Arabs could defeat Israel by themselves. So they will enter into an agreement with Russia, who will be more than willing to share military organization, know-how, and weapons.

In brief summation, it is reasonable to assume that Russia will lead a massive pan-Islamic military force to invade Jerusalem. Russia's motive is to control the oil-rich Persian Gulf, which will bring America and the West to their knees. The fundamentalist Islamics have a burning passion to control Jerusalem. This Russian/pan-Islamic union is an unholy alliance that will lead to holy war.

ISRAEL, THE KEY TO END TIMES

It is not possible to understand Bible prophecy without an understanding of Israel's past, present, and future. Israel will be the epicenter of the earth's shuddering travails in the last days, and all pivotal events will center around the Holy Land and the people of Abraham.

Israel was founded by a sovereign act of God. God said to Abraham: "Get out of your country, / From your family / And from your father's house, / To a land that I will show you" (Gen. 12:1). Upon Abraham's arrival in the Promised Land,

God repeated this promise: "To your descendants I will give this land" (Gen. 12: 7).

There are presently two controversies concerning Israel: the first states that God's promise to Abraham was not a promise of literal land, but a promise of heaven. Those who embrace this position teach that Israel lost favor with God through disobedience and the church is now Israel. The second controversy holds that the promise to Abraham and his descendants is literal, but conditional, based upon Israel's obedience to God.

This common confusion is instantly corrected by the clear teaching found in the Word of God. In Genesis 22:17, God told Abraham, "Blessing I will bless you, and multiplying I will multiply your descendants as the stars of the heaven and as the sand which is on the seashore."

God mentioned two separate and distinct elements: stars and sand. The "stars of the heaven" represent the Church. Stars, as light, rule the darkness, which is the commission of the Church. Jesus said, "You are the light of the world" (Matt. 5:14). Jesus is called the "Bright and Morning Star" (Rev. 22:16). And Daniel 12:3 tells us that "Those who are wise shall shine / Like the brightness of the firmament, / And those who turn many to righteousness / Like the stars forever and ever."

Stars are heavenly, not earthly. They represent the Church, Abraham's *spiritual* seed.

The "sand of the seashore," on the other hand, is earthly and represents an earthly kingdom with a literal Jerusalem as its capital city. Both stars and sand exist at the same time, and neither ever replaces the other. Just so, the nation of Israel and the Church exist at the same time and do not replace each other.

The Bible clearly teaches that God's promise to Abraham was *literal* and *unconditional*. Let's examine the Scripture to verify beyond any doubt that God intended Abraham and the Jewish people to possess a literal land.

In Genesis 13, God told Abraham, "Lift your eyes now and look from the place where you are—northward, southward, eastward, and westward; for all the land which you see I give to you and your descendants forever . . . Arise, walk in the land through its length and its width, for I give it to you" (Gen. 13:14–15, 17).

Genesis 15:18 states, "On the same day the LORD made a covenant with [Abraham], saying: 'To your descendants I have given this land, from the river of Egypt to the great river, the River Euphrates.' " Then God listed the heathen tribes living in that area at that time. This is a very literal land. Heaven is not described, even allegorically, as the area between the river of Egypt (the Nile) and the Euphrates.

God told Abraham, "Know certainly that your descendants will be strangers in a land that is not theirs, and will serve them, and they will afflict them four hundred years. And also the nation whom they serve I will judge; afterward they shall come out with great possessions" (Gen. 15:13–14). Israel's departure from the Promised Land was literal because they physically left and journeyed into a literal Egypt. After four hundred years they became a nation of two to three million people, and they physically left a literal Egypt for a literal Promised Land. The books of Exodus, Leviticus, Numbers, Deuteronomy, and Joshua deal with Israel's return to a literal Promised Land—not heaven.

The title deed to the Promised Land was passed to Isaac from Abraham. In Genesis 26:3, God said to Isaac, "Dwell in this land, and I will be with you and bless you; for to you and your descendants I give all these lands, and I will perform the oath which I swore to Abraham your father."

The title deed to the Promised Land was then passed to Jacob from Isaac. In Genesis 28:13, God told Jacob, "I am the LORD God of Abraham your father and the God of Isaac; the land on which you lie I will give to you and your descendants." You have to be in a very literal land to lie upon it!

Was God's promise to Abraham conditional? Those who believe God's promise depended upon Abraham's obedience simply do not understand the blood covenant.

In the Old Testament, there were three covenants: a shoe covenant, a salt covenant, and a blood covenant. In the blood covenant, the most solemn and binding, the contracting parties would agree on the terms of the covenant. Then they would take an animal or animals, kill them, split the carcasses in half down the backbone and place the divided parts opposite each other on the ground, forming a pathway between the pieces.

The two would then join hands, recite the contents of the covenant, and walk between the divided halves of the slain animals. The blood covenant meant they were bound until death, and if either one broke the terms of the covenant, his blood would be spilled just as the blood of the animals that had been killed. A blood covenant was a permanent and unconditional promise. God gave to Abraham, Isaac, and Jacob and their descendants an unconditional promise of a Promised Land in which they were to live literally and forever by blood covenant.

In Genesis 15, God commanded Abraham to take a heifer, a female goat, a ram, a turtledove, and a pigeon. All were split in half except the birds. Because no man can look upon God and live, God placed Abraham in a deep sleep as He prepared to enter a blood covenant with him.

In his sleep, Abraham saw "a smoking oven and a burning torch that passed between those pieces" of the slain animals (Gen. 15:17). In the Old Testament, the burning lamp signified the presence of the Shekinah glory of God. God was binding himself by blood covenant to Abraham and his descendants forever, saying: "To your descendants I have given this land" (Gen. 15:18). Never did God suggest the covenant was conditional. Exactly the opposite is true; this covenant depends only on the faithfulness of God, and He is ever-faithful.

Psalm 89:30–37 confirms this unconditional promise. God said:

If his [Israel's] sons forsake My law
And do not walk in My judgments,
If they break My statutes
And do not keep My commandments,
Then I will visit their transgression with the rod,
And their iniquity with stripes.
Nevertheless My lovingkindness I will not utterly take
    from him,
Nor allow My faithfulness to fail.
My covenant I will not break,
Nor alter the word that has gone out of My lips.
Once I have sworn by My holiness;
I will not lie to David:
His seed shall endure forever,
And his throne as the sun before Me;

It shall be established forever like the moon,
Even like the faithful witness in the sky.

God clearly said He would not break covenant with Israel, even though Israel disobeyed Him. He also said that the moon is a witness of this covenant. When you walk out at night and see the moon shining in the heavens, you are seeing God's eternal witness speaking to all men in all languages that His covenant with Israel is forever and unconditional.

GOD'S THOUGHTS OF FUTURE ISRAEL

What about the future of Israel? Israel was reborn as a nation in a day on May 15, 1948, when the United Nations recognized the state of Israel. This was a fulfillment of Isaiah 66:8: "Who has heard such a thing? / Who has seen such things? / Shall the earth be made to give birth in one day? / Or shall a nation be born at once? / For as soon as Zion was in labor, / She gave birth to her children."

Through the prophet Ezekiel, God wrote, "I will bring you out from the peoples and gather you out of the countries where you are scattered, with a mighty hand, with an outstretched arm . . . Then you will know that I am the LORD" (Ezek. 20:34, 38).

Regarding the restoration of Israel, the prophet Amos wrote:

I will bring back the captives of My people Israel;
They shall build the waste cities and inhabit them;
They shall plant vineyards and drink wine from them;
They shall also make gardens and eat fruit from them.

I will plant them in their land,
And no longer shall they be pulled up
From the land I have given them,"
Says the LORD your God. (Amos 9:14–15)

The prophets declared that the nation of Israel would be reborn, rebuilt, and restored. The Jewish people would never again be removed. No matter who looks toward Israel with covetousness—Gog, Magog, or any Arab country—she will not be pulled out of her land again. That is God's promise.

WHY WOULD THE ARABS WANT TO ATTACK ISRAEL?

Every other week you can pick up your local paper and read something about the peace process currently occupying the Israeli government. From the look on Yasser Arafat's face during press conferences after the Oslo peace accords, you might believe he has wanted nothing more than peace with Israel throughout his entire life.

Think again, friend. The enmity that exists between Israel and the Arabs goes all the way back to Abraham, Hagar, and Sarah. The Arab tribes are descended from Ishmael, the son of Abraham's impatience, while the Israelites are descended from Isaac, the son of God's promise. You can read the entire story in Genesis chapters 16 and 21.

God honored Ishmael—He promised that Ishmael would be fruitful, the father of twelve rulers and a great nation. But in His sovereignty, God established His covenant with Isaac, the child of promise. The title to the Promised Land of Israel passed from Abraham to Isaac and then to Jacob.

The conflict between Arabs and Jews goes deeper than dis-
putes over the lands of Palestine. It is theological. It is Judaism
versus Islam. Islam's theology insists that Islam triumph over
everything else. The Muslims believe that while Jesus, Moses,
David, and several other Hebrews were prophets,
Muhammad was the greatest prophet. Though Muslims
revere the Bible, including the Torah, the Psalms, and the
Gospels, they hold that the *Al-Quran* (the Koran) is the
absolute true word of God, revealed through the angel
Jibraeel (Gabriel) to Muhammad. Muslims believe that Allah
is God, that he has neither father nor mother, and that he has
no sons.

Understand this: No matter what the Arabs say about
peace, their religion demands that they defeat the Jews.
Islam proclaims a theology of "triumphantism." Put simply, Muslims believe it is the will of God for Islam to rule
the world. Islamic law stipulates that to fulfill
Muhammad's task, every "infidel domain" must be considered a territory of war. According to Moris Farhi, author
of *The Last of Days,* Muslims believe there can be no peace
with the Jews or the Christians or any other non-Islamic
people, and that if peace must be made, only a truce is per-
missible—and that "for a maximum of ten years as an
expedient to hone our swords, whet our blood, and
strengthen our will."[4]

Palestinian leader Yasser Arafat frequently compares the
existing peace accords to the Khudaibiya agreement made by
the prophet Muhammad with the Arabian tribe of Koreish.
The pact, slated to last for ten years, was broken within two
years when Arab forces, having used the time of truce to
grow stronger, defeated the Koreish tribe. Comparing the

peace accords to the Khudaibiya pact is tantamount to stating they are temporary arrangements.[5]

As recently as November 15, 1998, just weeks after the October 1998 Wye River accord, Arafat told a rally, "We chose the peace of the brave out of faith in the prophet, in the Khudaibiya agreement."

In another ancient example, Saladin was a Muslim leader who, after a cease-fire, declared a holy war against the Crusaders and captured Jerusalem. Chairman Arafat told an audience of Egyptian TV viewers that Muhammad was able to sign a treaty he did not intend to keep by not including his title "messenger of Allah" in the agreement.

> Then, Omar bin Khatib and the others referred to this agreement as the "inferior peace agreement." Of course, I do not compare myself to the prophet, but I do say that we must learn from his steps and those of Salah a Din [Saladin]. The peace agreement which we signed is an "inferior peace." . . . We respect agreements the way that the prophet Muhammad and Salah-a-Din respected the agreements they signed.[6]

Are you beginning to see that the Arabs *will not* respect peace? Fundamentalist Muslims must destroy the Jews and rule Israel, or Muhammad is a false prophet and the Koran is not true. Such a thought is inconceivable, so the Muslims must attack Israel in order to be loyal to their prophet. The strategy of Islamic *jihad* (holy war) is as simple as it is satanic: "Kill so many Jews that they will eventually abandon Palestine."[7] The late imam Hasan al-Banna of the Islamic Resistance Movement, HAMAS, summed up their philosophy so well that his statement was included in their covenant: "Israel will exist and will continue to exist until Islam will obliterate it, just as it obliterated others before it."[8]

Jerusalem, the city of God, is caught in a supernatural cross fire. Trading land for peace will not bring rest to that troubled city. Giving Yasser Arafat and the Palestinian Liberation Organization (PLO) part of Jerusalem to establish a Palestinian city or a Palestinian state will not bring permanent peace.

THE QUOTABLE ARAFAT—IN 1998

We've seen many pretensions of peace in the last few years— Arafat shaking Yitzhak Rabin's hand in the White House Rose Garden and signing the Oslo accord of 1993 and the Wye River Memorandum of October 1998. In the Wye River document, Arafat and the Arab Palestinian Authority promised to combat terrorism, confiscate illegal firearms, limit the number of Palestinian police, prevent hostile propaganda, and amend the PLO charter in response to Israel's withdrawing from the West Bank city of Hebron.[9]

Israel has withdrawn from Hebron, but the Palestinian Authority has not yet remedied any of the violations listed in the Note for the Record. Most glaring is their halfhearted effort to amend and publicly repudiate the Palestinian National Charter, a thirty-year-old document that declares, "The liberation of Palestine will destroy the Zionist and imperialist presence."[10]

In 1993, Arafat convened a special meeting of the Palestinian National Council in Gaza. There, by a vote of

504 to 54, the body approved a decision to amend the National Charter by canceling articles that contradict the peace process. But Benjamin Netanyahu's Israeli government has questioned whether anything has truly been altered.

Why should he doubt the Palestinians? Because they are continuing to spread their anti-Semitic propaganda.

Listen to Arafat's own words—and notice the dates he spoke them.

- November 15, 1998, only a few weeks after the Wye River accord, addressing a rally in Ramallah: "Our rifles are ready and we are ready to raise them again if anyone tries to prevent us from praying in holy Jerusalem . . . There are agreements and they better be carried out, because the 'generals of the stones' [intifada rioters] are ready . . . For a hundred years we have faced this enormous global power [Zionism], and our people are still steadfast in Jerusalem. Yes, we will establish a state on May 4, 1999."

- November 14, 1998, addressing a rally in Nablus: "We will declare our independent state on May 4, 1999 with Jerusalem as its capital, yes Jerusalem, the eternal capital of our state, whether they like it or not. Now we are on our land and we are regaining this holy land inch by inch until we set up our state in 1999."

- August 1, 1998, an interview with the Algerian newspaper Sawt al-Ahrar: "The Palestinian Authority has taken steps to actively struggle against the Israeli Judaization scheme . . . The Palestinian Authority is ready to restart the intifada in order to stop the assault on the Arab character of Jerusalem."

- July 29, 1998, a speech to the Organization of the Islamic Conference's Jerusalem Committee: "The Israeli policy of ethnic cleansing has taken on the ugliest of forms in recent months . . . Israel has started the war over Jerusalem . . . but with Arab and Islamic assistance, this shall be our faithful jihad to defend holy Jerusalem from the danger of Judaization and the Zionist plot."

- July 1, 1998, a speech broadcast on official Palestinian television: "The battle for Jerusalem is a battle of life or death, life or death, life or death."

- May 14, 1998, leading Palestinian marchers in a chant: "With our soul and blood we will redeem you, O Palestine!"

- April 16, 1998, message marking the tenth anniversary of the slaying of PLO leader Abu Jihad: "My colleagues in struggle and in arms, my colleagues in struggle and in jihad . . . Intensify the revolution and the blessed intifada. Reinforce the strong stance and strengthen the faith. We must burn the ground under the feet of the invaders."[11] Palestinian television continually blasts Israel, referring to cities in disputed areas as "colonies" and "settlements," or as "cities of occupied Palestine." The State of Israel is called by names that indicate a complete unwillingness to recognize it, such as "the Zionist entity," "the Zionist enemy," "the occupation," and "the Tel Aviv government."[12]

WHY WOULD RUSSIA WANT
TO ATTACK ISRAEL?

Why should Russia decide to invade Israel? There are several likely reasons.

First, instability within the CIS might lead to such an invasion. The Russian economy is dangerously weak, but they do have valuable assets: military weapons, knowledge, and organization. Why not offer these assets to the Arab nations who desperately need them?

Second, although Russia is rich with oil reserves and other natural resources, those resources tend to be located in remote areas that are difficult to access. Therefore, it must establish alliances with the countries that sit upon and control the world's vast oil fields—the Arab nations surrounding the Persian Gulf.

In order to transport that oil—and engage in military defense and shipping—Russia desperately needs a warm-water seaport. You need only to look at a map of Russia to see that her seaports are primarily located in the frozen Arctic Ocean and to the east. Russia needs a western seaport that opens into the Mediterranean Sea. Currently, Russian ships must travel through the Black Sea, then through the narrow Bosporus, then through the Sea of Marmara and the Aegean before reaching the Mediterranean. Israel, however, is located right on the Mediterranean—prime shipping territory.

The signs are already appearing. Listen to the words of Uri Dan and Dennis Eisenberg, writers for the *Jerusalem Post*:

> The thunderous roar of US missiles raining down earlier
> this month on military targets in southern Iraq provoked

hostility among most European and Middle-Eastern Arab countries. In sharp contrast, the action taken by Bill Clinton was warmly welcomed by Britain and Israel. This positive attitude was underlined by Prime Minister Binyamin Netanyahu, who told this column minutes before seeing the American president . . . that he had emphasized to his host the dangers to peace in the Middle East posed by Iran, Iraq, and other countries. In all probability Netanyahu singled out Russia, which has reverted to the policies of the former Soviet Union and is aiming to become a dominant power in the Middle East once again. The Russian bear has already hugged Iran in a honeyed embrace by building a nuclear reactor for the mullahs of Teheran. It is also working hard to take Syria back into its bosom, holding out modern arms for Damascus as bait. But Iraq is clearly the prize maiden being wooed by Moscow.[13]

The writers went on to explain that Russia is offering Iraq, a leading Arab state, an all-out effort to get the UN to lift the oil embargo that prohibits the sale of Iraqi oil to world markets, as well as two billion dollars worth of high-tech equipment for enhancing the flow of oil from Iraq to Russia. "Though the situation isn't as dangerous as it was when the Soviet Union was a superpower," Dan and Eisenberg wrote, "The Israeli government is aware of the problem of an increasingly hostile Russia as the Kremlin woos Mideastern Arab states primarily for their oil. Israel will have to learn to handle the way the Kremlin operates."[14]

In 1996 Moscow signed energy agreements with Iraq worth up to $10 million that are to go into effect once UN sanctions are lifted. And it has reached agreement with Iran

on delivery of defense-related goods (read—weapons!) total-
ing $4 *billion* over the next four to five years.[15]

Why is Russia wooing the Arab nations of the Middle
East? Contemporary observers see one overwhelming reason:

> The real factor driving Russian interest [in the Middle
> East] is a geopolitical or strategic one. Economics enters in
> a big way only when it is a question of selling arms. Here
> the Russian defense industry exerts tremendous pressure
> to enter the Middle East regardless of any strategic conse-
> quences, even by low-balling other competitors and selling
> at what appear to be dumping prices to anyone who will
> buy.[16]

In other words, Russia is so eager to have a presence in the
Middle East that she will practically give weapons away! She
needs economic partners, she needs a strategic port, and, in
the light of her crumbling economy, she does not want to
become a "welfare nation." One writer said, "We err if we
underestimate how deeply Russian elites fear becoming a
Western economic colony."[17]

When the Islamic nations, which despise Israel, join
forces with Russia, they will greatly benefit from the strength
of Russia's armed forces. The Islamic nations have oil and
cold, hard cash. Russia has military might and the organiza-
tional skills necessary to launch a military invasion. Together,
they will make a treaty guaranteeing mutual support.

Russia will say to the Islamic nations, "You want
Jerusalem and the Temple Mount as a holy site. We want the
Persian Gulf oil. Let's join forces to rule the world!" Russia
is already friendly with the Islamic nations—she protested

loudly when the United States began its recent bombing of Saddam Hussein's military installations in Iraq.

The final and most compelling reason for Gog and Magog to invade Israel is the "hook" that God will put in Gog's jaw. Regardless of the human or economic reasons, God will inexorably draw Gog and his forces toward Israel.

The end result? A massive pan-Islamic military force led by Russia's high command will come against Israel "like a cloud, to cover the land" (Ezek. 38:16).

THE GUARDIAN OF ISRAEL NEVER SLEEPS

Like so many things, what man intends for evil, God intends for good. This monumental battle between Israel and the coalition of Islam and Russia is no exception. For while this dreaded army believes they have devised this battle of their own accord to serve their own ends, in fact it is God the Father who has brought them.

Ezekiel 38:4–6 declares:

> I will turn you around, put hooks into your jaws, and lead you out, with all your army, horses, and horsemen, all splendidly clothed, a great company with bucklers and shields, all of them handling swords. Persia, Ethiopia, and Libya are with them, all of them with shield and helmet; Gomer and all its troops; the house of Togarmah from the far north and all its troops—many people are with you.

In Ezekiel 38:16 we see again that the Lord has orchestrated this battle: "It will be in the latter days that I will bring you against My land."

Gog will not see the hand of God, he sees only Israel, "the land of those brought back from the sword and gathered from many people on the mountains of Israel, which had long been desolate; they were brought out of the nations, and now all of them dwell safely" (Ezek. 38:8). As a result of Israel's peace treaties with the Palestinians in which she has traded valuable land for peace, she will appear to be more vulnerable than ever—a "land of unwalled villages . . . a peaceful people, who dwell safely, all of them dwelling without walls, and having neither bars nor gates . . . and against a people gathered from the nations, who have acquired livestock and goods, who dwell in the midst of the land" (Ezek. 38:11–12).

As a result, the coalition will "come from [its] place out of the far north, [it] and many peoples with [it], all of them riding on horses, a great company and a mighty army. [The coalition] will come up against My people Israel like a cloud, to cover the land" (Ezek. 38:15–16).

One note—the Bible says Israel will be a land of "unwalled" villages, a description that certainly does not fit the land today. If you've been to Israel, you know that security is their top priority—soldiers, machine guns, tanks, walls, and concertina wire are everywhere! How will the Israelis relax to the point that the prophet could describe the land as "unwalled"? I can't be dogmatic, but the answer may lie in the current peace process.

When Israel is at peace, when ancient enmities are cloaked and smoldering beneath plastic smiles, the Russians will gather their allies and look toward Jerusalem. But what the invaders do not realize is that God has sworn by His holiness to defend Jerusalem. Since God created and defends Israel, those nations that fight against Israel fight against God Himself.

The invaders find an easy entry into the Promised Land. With gratefulness to Allah (or the Russian military commander), they embark on their plan of plunder and genocide.

The vast majority will never know what hit them. Their defeat will be sudden, horrible, and complete.

GOD'S RESPONSE TO THE THREAT

God said that when Gog sweeps down from the north, "My fury will show in My face" (Ezek. 38:18). King David said, "Behold, He who keeps Israel / Shall neither slumber nor sleep" (Ps. 121:4). After watching the Jews of the Holocaust walk into the gas chambers, after seeing the "apple of His eye" thrown into the ovens and their ashes dumped by the tons into the rivers of Europe, after seeing the "land of milk and honey" run red with Jewish blood in five major wars for peace and freedom, God will stand up and shout to the nations of the world, "Enough!"

God will shatter His silence.

First, He will send a mighty earthquake so devastating it will shake the mountains and the seas, and every wall shall fall to the ground.

> Surely in that day there shall be a great earthquake in the land of Israel, so that the fish of the sea, the birds of the heavens, the beasts of the field, all creeping things that creep on the earth, and all men who are on the face of the earth shall shake at My presence. The mountains shall be thrown down, the steep places shall fall, and every wall shall fall to the ground. (Ezek. 38:19–20)

Second, God will send massive confusion to the multinational fighting force, and "every man's sword will be against his brother" (Ezek. 38:21). This is exactly what God did when He commanded Gideon to blow the trumpets and break the pitchers. The Philistines became divinely confused and turned their swords on each other. Gideon won a great military victory without one casualty. God will do it again in defense of Israel.

Third, God will open fire with His divine artillery. "And I will bring him to judgment with pestilence and bloodshed; I will rain down on him, on his troops, and on the many peoples who are with him, flooding rain, great hailstones, fire, and brimstone" (Ezek. 38:22).

This passage could be interpreted in two ways: First, the "fire and brimstone" may refer to Israel's release of nuclear weapons in a last-ditch attempt to prevent annihilation. "Pestilence" might refer to cheaper, more nefarious implements of war—Russia and Iraq have the world's largest store of chemical and biological weapons. I can easily imagine a scenario in which they fire biological weapons upon Israel, but God miraculously turns the anthrax-laden missiles or causes them to misfire, so that the invaders are destroyed by their evil intention!

The second interpretation is that this event is a repeat of Sodom and Gomorrah. God will blast Israel's enemies into oblivion by raining fire and brimstone from heaven. In either case the results will be equally catastrophic.

AMERICA'S NUCLEAR DOOMSDAY?

Ezekiel 39:6 presents a possible scenario that I find interesting in the light of today's technology. Let's look at the verse: "And

I will send fire on Magog and on those who live in security in the coastlands. Then they shall know that I am the LORD."

When God says He will "send fire," I have to wonder whether He is referring to actual fire and brimstone, like that which fell upon Sodom and Gomorrah, or if this is a reference to nuclear war. Sometimes God acts in miraculous ways; at other times He uses men to accomplish His purposes. I believe the fire that fell on Sodom was real and from heaven; I believe the walls of Jericho fell because the people shouted and God worked, not because the sound of so many trumpets caused an unsteady wall to crumble.

Most important, I believe that God's intervention on Israel's behalf in this battle will be of obvious supernatural origin. Scripture tells us that the world will know God intervened on Israel's behalf. Tiny Israel could not defeat a Russian-Arab coalition without God's help, for though she has nuclear weapons, so does Russia.

However, God could certainly use man's implements to work His will, and this verse about "fire from the sky" falling upon people who "live in security in the coastlands" deserves another look.

Consider this scenario: Israel has said she will never be the first to introduce nuclear weapons into the Middle East,[18] but she may feel forced to use them if a gigantic Russian-led military force descends on her from the north. Stan Goodenough, a writer for the *Jerusalem Post*, pointed out that with every inch of territory Israel gives away in the name of peace, she is being backed into a corner from which she would have no choice but to defend herself with nuclear weapons.

"The smaller Israel becomes," he wrote,

The more its defensive options will be restricted to the non-conventional [weapons]. In simple terms, a 1967-size Israel will find itself almost impossibly limited in terms of the time and space it needs to mobilize for a conventional war. As long as Judea and Samaria and Gaza and the Golan Heights are under Israeli control, attacks by the Arab states can be better anticipated and more easily repulsed by conventional means . . . Confronted by an Arab onslaught without these vital pieces of land, however, Israel would have virtually no choice but to go the non-conventional route, or risk immediate and complete annihilation."[19]

Goodenough also pointed out that it would take only three Hiroshima-type bombs on Tel Aviv to completely decimate the country. Casualty estimates would be upwards of 400,000, and Israel could never survive such a blow.[20]

Suppose Israel decided to launch a nuclear attack upon Russia in a desperate attempt to halt the approaching Russian-Arab army . . .

WILL NUCLEAR BOMBS FALL ON THE UNITED STATES?

There's something you should know about the old U.S.S.R. During the height of the Cold War, Soviet scientists designed and built a "doomsday machine," which they named "Dead Hand." The Russian military maintains it to this day. According to Dr. Bruce Blair of the Brookings Institution, this doomsday machine, with backups and fail-safes aplenty, was designed to detect any attack upon Russia and automatically send a message to a complex of communications rockets. Assuming that Russian commanders had been wiped out by an American first strike, the "Dead Hand" would feed orders into the rockets, which would launch automatically. From space, these communications rockets would relay orders to nuclear-armed warheads, which would fire out of their silos or off their mobile trucks and zoom toward their preassigned targets.[21]

Unfortunately, the preassigned targets assigned in Soviet Cold War days were American cities.

Are we the people "living in security in the coastlands" upon whom the fire will fall?

The nuclear doomsday dreaded by Americans since the beginning of the Cold War could come upon us quite by accident. Though in 1991 the Bush administration took our long-range nuclear bombers off alert, and in 1994 the Clinton administration made the oceans instead of Russia the standby aim points for our intercontinental ballistic missiles on alert, Washington still has more than three thousand strategic warheads on land- and submarine-based missiles that can be launched within minutes.[22] If missiles begin to fly at us, I think it's a pretty safe bet that our people would give the order to launch as well.

We will certainly sustain damage from this war, for God says: "All men who are on the face of the earth shall shake at My presence. The mountains shall be thrown down, the steep places shall fall, and every wall shall fall to the ground" (Ezek. 38:20). Whether this devastation arises from nuclear war, hydrogen bombs, a massive earthquake, a combination of all three, or something else altogether, every living person on the face of the planet will tremble as God wreaks destruction upon Israel's enemies.

During the 1980s, United Press International disseminated a story about the dreams—reportedly occurring on the same night—of three distinguished Jewish rabbis. Each man dreamed that the Gog-Magog war was not far away. The UPI report noted, "The chief rabbi of the Wailing Wall in Jerusalem's old city is sure Israel will confront the Soviet Union in a battle over the holy city. 'And it will be a nuclear war,' they contended, drawing in both superpowers."[23]

GOG AND MAGOG ARE ANNIHILATED

Ezekiel's graphic account of the battle's aftermath makes clear just how thorough and disastrous will be the defeat of this Russian-Muslim coalition. The prophet opened chapter 39 by stating: "Thus says the Lord GOD: 'Behold, I am against you, O Gog.'" As the news cameras of the world survey millions of bloated bodies lying in the hot, Middle-Eastern sun, this comment will go down in history as one of the greatest understatements of all time.

Why is God against Russia? I can think of several reasons, including the fact that Soviet leaders imposed atheism upon millions of people for most of this century. For years during the Cold War we watched atheism emanate from Moscow and infiltrate scores of countries around the world. Tim LaHaye said,

No nation in the history of the world has destroyed more flesh than Russia through the spread of Communism . . . but her greatest sin has not been the destruction of flesh, as serious as that is. Her greatest sin has been the soul damnation caused by her atheistic ideology . . . No nation has done more to destroy faith in God than Communist Russia, thereby earning the enmity of God.[24]

The most crucial reason God is set against Gog, I believe, has to do with the fact that God promised Abraham, "I will bless those who bless you, And I will curse him who curses you" (Gen. 12:3). For years, Russia has cursed and persecuted the Jews.

The Russian word *pogrom*, which pertains to the massacre of a helpless people, passed into the international lexicon after the devastation of Russian Jews in the Ukraine in 1903. The Russian nation has been persecuting Jews since the time of the czars. In the span of time between the two world wars, the entire Jewish population of the Russian Western War Zone— including the old, sick, and children—were forcibly evacuated into the interior of the country on twelve hours' notice.

In August 1924, *Dawn* magazine reported:

Wholesale slaughter and burials alive, rape and torture, became not merely commonplace but the order of the day. There were pogroms that lasted a week; and in several cases the systematic and diabolic torture and outrage and carnage were continued for a month. In many populous Jewish communities there were no Jewish survivors left to bury the dead, and thousands of Jewish wounded and killed were eaten by dogs and pigs; in others the Synagogues were turned into charnel houses by the pitiless butchery of those who sought refuge in them. If we add to the figures quoted above the number of those indirect victims who in consequence of the robbery and destruction that accompanied these massacres were swept away by famine, disease, exposure and all manner of privations—the death total will be very near half a million human beings.[25]

The blood of over 500,000 innocent Jews cries out for justice, and God will deliver it in His battle against Gog and Magog.

THE AFTERMATH OF THE BATTLE

Ezekiel did not tell us how many will die in the battle, but he told us how many will be left alive: only a "sixth part" (Ezek. 39:2 KJV). The casualty rate for this battle will be 84 percent, an unheard-of figure in modern warfare.

The prophet's narrative of the end results continues. Ezekiel says the bloated bodies of the enemies of Israel will be a banquet for buzzards. The beasts of the field will have a feast unlike anything since dogs ate the body of Jezebel.

And as for you, son of man, thus says the Lord GOD,
"Speak to every sort of bird and to every beast of the field:
'Assemble yourselves and come;
Gather together from all sides to My sacrificial meal
Which I am sacrificing for you,
A great sacrificial meal on the mountains of Israel,
That you may eat flesh and drink blood.
You shall eat the flesh of the mighty,
Drink the blood of the princes of the earth,
Of rams and lambs,
Of goats and bulls,
All of them fatlings of Bashan.
You shall eat fat till you are full,

And drink blood till you are drunk,
At My sacrificial meal
Which I am sacrificing for you.
You shall be filled at My table
With horses and riders,
With mighty men
And with all the men of war,' says the Lord GOD." (Ezek. 39:17–20)

Peter C. Craigie said the participation of beasts in the demise of the invaders stresses the finality of the event. Human beings who were to have been the masters and stewards of the earth have, in the pursuit of evil, become victims of the natural order.[26]

The people of Israel will set about burying the dead in a mass grave eerily reminiscent of the huge trenches the Nazis used to bury Jewish dead in the Holocaust:

"It will come to pass in that day that I will give Gog a burial place there in Israel, the valley of those who pass by east of the sea; and it will obstruct travelers, because there they will bury Gog and all his multitude. Therefore they will call it the Valley of Hamon Gog. For seven months the house of Israel will be burying them, in order to cleanse the land. Indeed all the people of the land will be burying, and they will gain renown for it on the day that I am glorified," says the Lord GOD. "They will set apart men regularly employed, with the help of a search party, to pass through the land and bury those bodies remaining on the ground, in order to cleanse it. At the end of seven months they will make a search. The search party will pass through the land;

and when anyone sees a man's bone, he shall set up a marker by it, till the buriers have buried it in the Valley of Hamon Gog. The name of the city will also be Hamonah. Thus they shall cleanse the land." (Ezek. 39:11–16)

Some Bible scholars believe this valley of the dead might be in modern-day Lebanon. It is a country of mountains that run from north to south, with a valley in between two mountain ridges and a logical path for a Russian-led attack on Israel. The prophet Habakkuk mentioned Lebanon in a passage dealing with the last days: "For the violence done to Lebanon will cover you" (Hab. 2:17) and Zechariah 11:1 declares, "Open your doors, O Lebanon, / That fire may devour your cedars."

The dead bodies of the invaders will be strewn in the fields and mountains surrounding Israel, and the seven-month burial detail will involve every Israeli citizen. Every last bone shall be buried. *Hamon-Gog* is a Hebrew word for "the multitude of Gog," which is to become the name of this vast cemetery for the invaders of Israel.

Not only will there be tremendous carnage, but the weapons left by these devastated forces will provide fuel for Israel for seven years—through the years of the Tribulation.

> "Then those who dwell in the cities of Israel will go out and set on fire and burn the weapons, both the shields and bucklers, the bows and arrows, the javelins and spears; and they will make fires with them for seven years. They will not take wood from the field nor cut down any from the forests, because they will make fires with the weapons; and they will plunder those who plundered them, and pillage

those who pillaged them," says the Lord GOD. (Ezek. 39:9–10)

Can you imagine weapons burning for seven years? I was in Israel during the "Peace in Galilee War" led by General Ariel Sharon back in the eighties. I personally saw Israeli eighteen-wheel trucks bringing back the spoils of war in a convoy that stretched farther than my eye could see. The trucks, bumper-to-bumper coming out of Lebanon, were carrying loads of war booty back to Israel. These were supplies that had been stored in Lebanon by the Soviet Union and were said to be enough to keep 500,000 men in combat for six months. As great as those spoils were, it was only a matter of days before the Israeli army collected and stored them. But Ezekiel describe a war so vast it will take seven years to gather and dispose of the weapons of war.

Israel will derive an unexpected benefit from this. The prophet said the war booty from this massive invasion will provide Israel with fuel for seven years, and because of this the forest will be spared. In that verse alone, we find proof that this will occur in the latter days—even contemporary times. Prior to the State of Israel's establishment in 1948, the land was almost entirely deforested, a desert wasteland. But the Israelis have worked hard to make the Promised Land bloom again.

It has been my pleasure over the years to plant a tree each time I go to Israel. We have a "Night to Honor Israel" plot in an Israeli forest that we systematically add to each time we visit. I'm glad to know that the invading armies will leave such a massive amount of fuel that "my" trees will survive the war!

THIS IS NOT ARMAGEDDON

Though the world will reel at the damage sustained in this battle, it is important to realize that this is not Armageddon, the battle that is to come later on God's prophetic doomsday clock. This battle involves only a select group of nations, while Armageddon will involve all the kings of the earth, a true world war. In this battle, Gog's armies are arrayed in the open field (Ezek. 39:5), while at Armageddon they will be in the city of Jerusalem. Christ will appear at the end of Armageddon to establish His millennial kingdom, but at the end of this war, Israel will turn her eyes back to the God of Abraham, Isaac, and Jacob.

ISRAEL ACKNOWLEDGES THE HAND OF GOD

Why does God allow the nations to make war upon Israel? There is only one answer: for His glory. Ezekiel wrote, "I will magnify Myself and sanctify Myself, and I will be known in the eyes of many nations. Then they shall know that I am the LORD . . . So the house of Israel shall know that I am the LORD their God from that day forward" (Ezek. 38:23; 39:22).

Mankind worships a pantheon of so-called gods! Some worship Buddha, others Muhammad, some Satan, some gods of their own making, but who is the Almighty God? When the God of Abraham, Isaac, and Jacob finishes mopping up the enemies of Israel on the mountains (notice that Jerusalem and the cities will be saved), there will be no doubt that Jehovah God is the Almighty God.

"It will be in the latter days that I will bring you against

My land, so that the nations may know Me, when I am hallowed in you, O Gog, before their eyes" (Ezek. 38:16).

Truly the only way we can understand the significance of this incredible defeat is to accept it as an act of God. The defeat of Gog and Magog will accomplish the purpose of glorifying God before Israel and the world. Ezekiel wanted the world to know that God supernaturally will neutralize the enemies of Israel and destroy them that His name might be glorified.

A second reason for this great display of God's power is to testify to His beloved Jewish people that He alone is their God. Through their miraculous deliverance, the hearts of the Jewish people will begin to turn again to the God of Abraham, Isaac, and Jacob:

> So the house of Israel shall know that I am the LORD their God from that day forward. The Gentiles shall know that the house of Israel went into captivity for their iniquity; because they were unfaithful to Me, therefore I hid My face from them. I gave them into the hand of their enemies, and they all fell by the sword. According to their uncleanness and according to their transgressions I have dealt with them, and hidden My face from them.
>
> Therefore thus says the Lord GOD: "Now I will bring back the captives of Jacob, and have mercy on the whole house of Israel; and I will be jealous for My holy name—after they have borne their shame, and all their unfaithfulness in which they were unfaithful to Me, when they dwelt safely in their own land and no one made them afraid.

When I have brought them back from the peoples and gathered them out of their enemies' lands, and I am hallowed in them in the sight of many nations, then they shall know that I am the LORD their God, who sent them into captivity among the nations, but also brought them back to their land, and left none of them captive any longer. And I will not hide My face from them anymore; for I shall have poured out My Spirit on the house of Israel," says the Lord GOD. (Ezek. 39:22–29)

Israel, the spiritually dead body of Ezekiel's vision, will know beyond all doubt that God orchestrated her victory in this attack. This may be the impetus needed for officials to begin construction of another temple on the Temple Mount, quite possibly alongside the existing mosque. I don't know exactly how it will happen, but I do know that Israel will rebuild her temple, and it is logical to assume her spiritual reawakening will be the result of seeing God's mighty hand acting in the nation's defense.

Please note very carefully that, at this point, the Jewish people have yet to accept Jesus as their Messiah. The Bible is very clear that this will happen at the end of the Tribulation, an interval yet to come on God's prophetic clock. But because of this cataclysmic battle on the soil of the Holy Land, the nation of Israel will begin to turn toward the Most High God . . . but some of them will be distracted by a newcomer on the world stage, a charismatic man who comes to Israel with outstretched arms, promising peace and safety.

CHAPTER 6

11:55 P.M.
THE TIME OF
TRIBULATION BEGINS

According to a 1994 survey, 60 percent of Americans
believe Jesus will return; 44 percent believe in the
Battle of Armageddon; 49 percent believe an antichrist
will arise, and 44 percent believe in the Rapture.[1]
—THE DALLAS MORNING NEWS,
OCTOBER 24, 1998

God's prophetic doomsday clock has advanced to 11:55 P.M. The time is the beginning of the seven-year period of tribulation, and this moment represents the first three and one-half years. Many characteristics mark this interval, including war, pestilence, famine, earthquakes, and destruction.

THE PURPOSE OF THE TRIBULATION

The term *great Tribulation* strikes terror into the hearts of men, and justly so. God's portrait of the seven-year

Tribulation reveals a time of unspeakable horror that can only be described as hell on earth.

Why does God allow this time of trouble? There are several purposes, and the first is to bring Israel to the place where she will recognize Jesus Christ as the Messiah. In Matthew 23:37–39, Jesus prophesied that Jerusalem would be desolate until she was ready to say, "Blessed is He who comes in the name of the LORD!" And in Ezekiel 20:33–38, God Himself promised to bring Israel out from the nations where she was scattered, "with a mighty hand, with an outstretched arm, and with fury poured out." God promised to purge the rebels from among the people. Those who transgress against Him will not enter the land of Israel. "Then you will know that I am the LORD" (Ezek. 20:38).

A second purpose of the Tribulation is to judge the Gentile nations for their efforts to exterminate the nation of Israel. "I will bless those who bless you," God told Abraham, "And I will curse him who curses you" (Gen. 12:3). That promise is no less valid today than it was when God spoke it.

A third purpose of the Tribulation is to allow a Christ-rejecting world to personally experience the sorrow and suffering created by Satan's evil empire. Just as salt preserves meat, the world has been preserved by faithful Christians living in it, but after the Rapture all Christians will be gone. The Holy Spirit will no longer be restraining the forces of evil.

A fourth purpose for the Tribulation is for God's wrath to be poured out on all who have rejected the gospel. Physical suffering will be so great that men will want to die, but they cannot. Revelation 6:16–17 tells us that men will say to the mountains, "Fall on us and hide us from the face of Him who sits on the throne and from the wrath of the Lamb! For the great day of His wrath has come, and who is able to stand?"

Scripture also refers to the Tribulation as "the time of Jacob's trouble" (Jer. 30:7), "the indignation" (Isa. 26:20), and a "time of trouble" (Dan. 12:1). The entire seven-year period is known as the "Tribulation," while the last three and one-half years are known as "the great Tribulation" because the intense suffering created by the wrath of God will be unspeakable.

One of the most graphic descriptions of this time is found in Zephaniah 1:12–18:

> And it shall come to pass at that time
> That I will search Jerusalem with lamps,
> And punish the men
> Who are settled in complacency,
> Who say in their heart,
> "The LORD will not do good,
> Nor will He do evil."
> Therefore their goods shall become booty,
> And their houses a desolation;
> They shall build houses, but not inhabit them;
> They shall plant vineyards, but not drink their wine.
>
> The great day of the LORD is near;
> It is near and hastens quickly.
> The noise of the day of the LORD is bitter;
> There the mighty men shall cry out.
> That day is a day of wrath,
> A day of trouble and distress,

A day of devastation and desolation,
A day of darkness and gloominess,
A day of clouds and thick darkness,
A day of trumpet and alarm
Against the fortified cities
And against the high towers.

I will bring distress upon men,
And they shall walk like blind men,
Because they have sinned against the LORD;
Their blood shall be poured out like dust,
And their flesh like refuse.

Neither their silver nor their gold
Shall be able to deliver them
In the day of the LORD's wrath;
But the whole land shall be devoured
By the fire of His jealousy,
For He will make speedy riddance
Of all those who dwell in the land.

In Matthew 24:5–8, Jesus specifically described the first three and one-half years of the Tribulation:

For many will come in My name, saying, "I am the Christ," and will deceive many. And you will hear of wars and rumors of wars. See that you are not troubled; for all these things must come to pass, but the end is not yet. For nation will rise against nation, and kingdom against kingdom. And there will be famines, pestilences, and earthquakes in various places. All these are the beginning of sorrows.

In the fifth chapter of Revelation, the apostle John was even more specific. At the beginning of the Tribulation, a scroll sealed with seven seals was in the right hand of Him who sits on the throne of heaven. A voice proclaimed, "Who is worthy to open the scroll and loose its seals?" John wept when no one in heaven or on the earth or under the earth was able to open the scroll.

But one of the elders comforted John: "Do not weep. Behold, the Lion of the tribe of Judah, the Root of David, has prevailed to open the scroll and to loose its seven seals" (Rev. 5:5).

While John watched, Jesus Christ came forth, looking like a Lamb that had been slain. While the elders and the Raptured Church watched, He, the perfect sacrificial Lamb, came forward before the host of believers, numbering "ten thousand times ten thousand and thousands of thousands" out of every tribe and tongue and people and nation. While the redeemed Church sang praises to Him, Jesus Christ stepped forward and opened the scroll. Several of the world's doomsday scenarios are about to move from the realm of possibility to stark reality.

MEET THE PRINCE WHO IS TO COME

At 6:55 A.M. the shrill ringing of the bedside alarm clock brings you awake, and you slap at it, then blink at the gray gloom filling your bedroom. Your heart is as heavy as the pile of blankets upon your chest; your emotions as confused as the so-called "experts" who have apparently taken over America's television programming. For weeks every network show and newscast has featured a panel of talking heads who have attempted to explain both the disappearance of millions of people and Russia's ignominious defeat on the northern slopes of Israel.

More out of habit than interest, your hand reaches for the television remote, and you punch the power on, hoping the sound of voices will help dispel the fog of sleep from your brain. You haven't been sleeping well. More than a dozen of your colleagues are among the missing, and your workload at the office seems to have doubled in the past few weeks.

The perky blonde on the morning news program is wearing a bright smile today, and the sight of it draws you out from under the covers. "Good morning, America," she exclaims, right on cue. "We've a welcome change of pace for you this morning. We have a wonderful guest today, and I'm absolutely delighted to be able to bring an exclusive interview to you."

She fairly twitters at the word *exclusive*, and as the camera draws back, you see the man seated across from her. His face is unfamiliar, but he's handsome and polished, with striking dark eyes, tousled thick hair, and an enigmatic smile that makes the Mona Lisa's look like a rueful grimace.

You lower your feet to the cold floor and send your toes on a quest for your slippers, never taking your eyes off the television screen.

"Our honored guest," the blonde is simpering now, flirting as if there's no tomorrow, "has taken time away from his busy schedule to be with us. Later today he will be addressing a joint session at the UN, then appearing at the White House, then hosting a meeting of ecumenical clergymen concerned with world peace."

She flutters her lashes and draws an exaggerated breath.

"Just thinking about such a schedule exhausts me! How do you do it all?"

The camera moves to the man's face, and his voice, vibrating with restrained power, fills your bedroom. "It's not difficult to maintain such a schedule when you're committed to important principles. I go where I am needed, and right now, the entire world seems to need me. I'm happy to do what I can."

The blonde shifts in her chair, then casts another look toward the camera—toward you. "We'll be back after this word from our sponsors," she says, her eyes sparkling in the lights. "And if you can't name our mystery guest, don't worry. His name will soon be as familiar as the sun and moon. This man, friends, is about to make a world of difference in a confused and trying time."

The blonde disappears, replaced by a singing coffee cup, and you swipe your hand through your hair, wondering if— and how—this man will affect your life.

THE FIRST SEAL—THE RIDER ON THE WHITE HORSE

After the breaking of the first seal, John saw a white horse. "He who sat on it had a bow; and a crown was given to him, and he went out conquering and to conquer" (Rev. 6:2).

The man on the horse was the Antichrist, a master imitator. Because prophecy tells us Jesus will return on a white horse at His Second Coming (Rev. 19:11), this man will ride a white horse, but he is no savior. He will be given a bow, a weapon of war, and a crown. He will go forth to conquer the world.

He will be successful.

The first and most noticeable sign of the Tribulation's advent is the rise of a global personality, a man whose name will be on everyone's lips. I don't know his name and wouldn't hazard a guess, but I believe he is alive at this moment and knows his satanic assignment.

Is the Antichrist a literal man? Listen to this quote from the *Dallas Morning News*:

> Many scholars argue that the Bible's authors never intended their work to be interpreted as literal prophecy. The Antichrist in Revelation, for example, alludes to the Roman emperor Nero, who represented evil to early Christians. The passage predicting Armageddon, scholars say, refers to the final victory of good over evil, not a literal battle. The Rapture, mentioned in 1 Thessalonians, is an expression of the apostle Paul's confidence that Christians will spend eternity with Jesus.[2]

My reaction to the above statement? Poppycock! First of all, any so-called "scholar" who talks about the Bible's "authors" doesn't understand how the Bible was written. You could talk about the Bible's "writers," "scribes," "amanuenses," or even "secretaries," but you don't dare talk about the Bible's "authors." An author is one who writes words he has pulled out of his mind or imagination. The Bible was *authored* by the Holy Spirit of God, not by man. Men recorded the words of God under the absolute control of the Holy Spirit so that the finished product was simply the Word of God!

Secondly, the men who wrote what the Holy Spirit dictated were not creating allegories or fables. John the Revelator wasn't trying to tactfully describe the Roman emperor Nero, nor was he being metaphorical when he described Armageddon with great and vivid detail. And if Paul merely wanted to reassure Christians that they would spend eternity with Jesus, why didn't he just say so? No, my friend. The Rapture is literal, Armageddon is an actual battle, and the Antichrist is a living, breathing person whom the Bible calls the son of perdition (2 Thess. 2:3).

John wasn't the only biblical writer to mention the Antichrist. Daniel was exposed to him not once, but three times. Let's look at the story beginning in Daniel's tenth chapter.

DANIEL'S FASTING AND PRAYER

In the third year of Cyrus, king of Persia, a message was revealed to Daniel, also called by his Babylonian name Belteshazzar. The year was about 534 B.C., about four years after Daniel received the vision of the seventy weeks. Daniel was very old, still respected, though probably retired from public service.

In the first few verses of the tenth chapter of his book, Daniel told us that he had been in mourning for three full weeks. "I ate no pleasant food, no meat or wine came into my mouth, nor did I anoint myself at all, till three whole weeks were fulfilled" (Dan. 10:3).

Something had shaken Daniel to his core, rocked him so severely that he didn't take a bath or comb his hair for three full weeks! We're not told why Daniel was in mourning, but we can hazard a guess. Since Daniel told us it was the third year of Cyrus's reign, and we know that in his *first* year

Cyrus proclaimed a decree that allowed any willing Hebrew to return to the land, Daniel may have been upset because so few of his people returned to Jerusalem. (This was still prior to the time when Nehemiah and his colaborers formed a committee to rebuild the walls.)

Daniel may have also been in mourning because he realized he would not return to his beloved Jerusalem, God's holy city. He was at least ninety, and perhaps he realized that he could be of more use to his people in his powerful palace position.

After deciding to seek the face of God, Daniel fasted, prayed, and sought the Lord for three full weeks. After twenty-one days, Daniel went outside to the banks of the Tigris River, and there he saw a vision unlike any he had ever seen. Some Bible scholars believe he saw the transfiguration of Jesus Christ.

> I lifted my eyes and looked, and behold, a certain man clothed in linen, whose waist was girded with gold of Uphaz! His body was like beryl, his face like the appearance of lightning, his eyes like torches of fire, his arms and feet like burnished bronze in color, and the sound of his words like the voice of a multitude. And I, Daniel, alone saw the vision, for the men who were with me did not see the vision; but a great terror fell upon them, so that they fled to hide themselves. Therefore I was left alone when I saw this great vision, and no strength remained in me, for my vigor was turned to frailty in me, and I retained no strength. Yet I heard the sound of his words; and while I heard the sound of his words I was in a deep sleep on my face, with my face to the ground. (Dan. 10:5–9)

Daniel's description of this heavenly visitor is strikingly similar to that of John, who saw Jesus and recorded his impression in Revelation. John saw:

> One like the Son of Man, clothed with a garment down to the feet and girded about the chest with a golden band. His head and His hair were white like wool, as white as snow, and His eyes like a flame of fire; His feet were like fine brass, as if refined in a furnace, and His voice as the sound of many waters. (Rev. 1:13–15)

Though others were with Daniel, they did not see the vision, but they were frightened enough to retreat and hide in the bushes along the river. The apostle Paul had a similar experience on the Damascus Road. He saw Jesus and heard His voice, while his frightened companions saw nothing. But on the Damascus Road and by the Tigris River, the supernatural power of God was clearly evident.

Overcome with the power and significance of what he had seen, Daniel, already weak from fasting, fainted dead away.

> Suddenly, a hand touched me, which made me tremble on my knees and on the palms of my hands . . . Then he said to me, "Do not fear, Daniel, for from the first day that you set your heart to understand, and to humble yourself before your God, your words were heard; and I have come because of your words. But the prince of the kingdom of Persia withstood me twenty-one days; and behold, Michael, one of the chief princes, came to help me, for I had been left alone there with the kings of Persia. Now I have come to make you understand what will happen to

your people in the latter days, for the vision refers to many days yet to come." (Dan. 10:10–14)

If the man Daniel saw at the first part of the vision was Jesus, the man speaking now definitely was not, for Jesus would not need help from the archangel Michael! This nameless angel—who most believe to be Gabriel, with whom Daniel had spoken before—explained that he was hindered by the prince of Persia, the satanic ruler over the kingdom of Persia for Satan, the god of this world. The holy angel was given his marching orders on the first day of Daniel's fasting and prayer but was blocked for twenty-one days by this demonic prince! We are not given a name for this being, but he was a high-ranking principality assigned by Satan to control the demonic activities in the kingdom of Persia where Daniel lived.

The devil, you see, has a host of fallen angels under his command, just as God has a host of angels. Both demons and angels are organized into hierarchies, and the mighty prince of Persia was able to hinder this messenger until Michael, the archangel, arrived to help clear the way. Demons are earth-bound creatures who walk the earth (Matt. 12:43) and crave the habitation of a body. When Jesus cast the demons out of the demoniac (Matt. 8:28–34), they begged to be permitted to enter the swine. Angels fly in the heavens and have bodies that are fully described in Scripture. Therefore, fallen angels are not demons. They are two different satanic battalions with the same commander-in-chief, Satan himself!

Why would Satan want to block an angel from appearing to Daniel? God wanted to give Daniel important prophetic information, and Satan didn't want Daniel to have it. In sharing this information about Satan's restraint and struggle via the Prince of Persia, the heavenly messenger lifted the curtain on the invisible warfare going on all around us. Paul wrote, "For we wrestle not against flesh and blood, but against principalities, against powers, against the rulers of the darkness of this world, against spiritual wickedness in high places" (Eph. 6:12, KJV). A *principality* in Satan's high command is a chief ruler of the highest rank (Eph. 1:21, Col. 2:10).

Interestingly enough, before he left, the angel told Daniel, "And now I must return to fight with the prince of Persia; and when I have gone forth, indeed the prince of Greece will come . . . (No one upholds me against these, except Michael your prince. Also in the first year of Darius the Mede, I, even I, stood up to confirm and strengthen him.)" (Dan. 10:20–11:1).

There's a wealth of assurance in the angel's parenthetical comment. "It was I," the angel confided in a daring whisper, "who strengthened King Darius after you were thrown into the lions' den. Do you remember how distraught he was? He spent a sleepless night worrying about you and beseeching God, so it was I who gave him the strength to trust that God would save your life."

The angel also mentioned that soon he would not only encounter the prince of Persia again, but also the prince of Greece. Why? Because the prophecy the angel related was concerning Greece.

The angel began his prophecy by explaining that it had to do with Daniel's people, in other words, the Jews. "Now I have come to make you understand what will happen to your people in the latter days, for the vision refers to many days yet to come" (Dan. 10:14).

Immediately after the Church is taken away in the

Rapture, God's prophetic time clock will begin to tick again, and the world will enter Daniel's seventieth week. The phrase "The vision is for many days" lets Daniel know that a long period of time was involved in the vision's fulfillment and before it would come to pass.

What followed was the most detailed account of history in all the Bible, yet it was prophetic when written. The angel's words covered events from approximately 529 B.C. to 164 B.C., and we will see how they were exactly fulfilled. It also covered just-as-certain events that will be fulfilled in the seven-year Tribulation that is just before us.

THE LAW OF DOUBLE REFERENCE

As we look at the next passage in Daniel, it's important to understand the prophetic *law of double reference.* This very important principle means simply this: Two events, widely separated by the time of their fulfillment, may be brought together into the scope of one prophecy. "This was done," said Dwight Pentecost, "because the prophet had a message for his own day as well as for a future time. By bringing two widely separated events into the scope of the prophecy both purposes could be fulfilled."[3]

R. B. Girdlestone explained it this way:

Yet another provision was made to confirm men's faith in utterances which had regard to the far future. It frequently happened that prophets who had to speak of such things were also commissioned to predict other things which would shortly come to pass; and the verification of these latter predictions in their own day and generation justified

167

men in believing the other utterances which pointed to a more distant time. The one was practically a 'sign' of the other, and if the one proved true the other might be trusted. Thus the birth of Isaac under the most unlikely circumstances would help Abraham to believe that in his seed all the families of the earth should be blessed.[4]

Daniel's vision in chapters 10–12 is a prophecy of double reference. It pertained to what would come in the near future, as well as what would come to pass in the latter days. Chapter 11 contains a remarkable example of prewritten history. The angel explained exactly what would happen in Greece, Egypt, and Syria during the years between the Old and New Testaments. When you read Daniel's prophecy and compare it to world history, you'll see why prophecy should never be confused with allegory or metaphor.

Many Bible scholars speak of the intertestamental period as a time of silence, but God was not at all silent about this time period. He predicted the course of human events, described the nations that would oppress the children of Israel for generations to come, and foretold the rise of a ruler, Antiochus Epiphanes, who would be a picture, or "type," of the prince who is spoken of in Daniel's vision of seventy weeks. Antiochus Epiphanes, however, was by far the lesser of two evils.

Because we are primarily concerned about events of the Tribulation, let me summarize the now-historical events included in this vision:

- Four additional Persian kings would rule after Cyrus, and the fourth would be the richest of them all! (Dan.

11:2). This actually happened, and Xerxes, the king who married Esther, was the wealthiest of the four.

- "A mighty king" would stand up (Dan. 11:3). This was Alexander the Great of Greece.

- This king would be uprooted, and his kingdom divided into four pieces and given to people not of his posterity (Dan. 11:4). Alexander died at age thirty-two, and his kingdom went to his four generals.

- "Also the king of the South shall become strong, as well as one of his princes" (Dan. 11:5). One of the generals, Ptolemy, began a dynasty in Egypt, while Seleucus did the same in Syria.

- "They shall join forces" (Dan. 11:6). Egypt and Syria made an alliance in 250 B.C., after both generals had died. Ptolemy II gave his daughter Bernice in marriage to the grandson of Seleucus, Antiochus II. Two years later, however, Ptolemy II died, and Antiochus II divorced Bernice and remarried his former wife, Laodice. Laodice then poisoned Antiochus and had Bernice killed. She appointed her son, Seleucus II, to the throne.

- "But from a branch of her roots one shall arise in his place" (Dan. 11:7). Back in Egypt, Bernice's brother, Ptolemy III now ruled. He invaded Syria and avenged his sister's death by executing Laodice. To save his own neck, Seleucus II ran away from the trouble.

- "And he shall also carry their gods captive to Egypt" (Dan. 11:8). Ptolemy III carried away tons of Syrian plunder, including 4,000 talents of gold, 40,000 talents of silver, and 2,500 golden idols.

- "Also the king of the North shall come" (Dan. 11:9). Seleucus II attempted to counterattack Egypt but was killed. He was succeeded by his son Antiochus III.

- "And the king of the South shall be moved with rage" (Dan. 11:10–17). The next few verses describe continuing warfare between Egypt and Syria. In 198 B.C. Antiochus III won control of Palestine at a battle outside Sidon. In 193 B.C. Antiochus gave his daughter Cleopatra (not the famous Cleopatra) in marriage to Ptolemy V. He hoped Cleopatra would foster Syrian interests in Egypt, but Cleopatra turned out to be a loyal wife . . . just as Daniel had predicted (Dan. 11:17).

- "After this he shall turn his face to the coastlands" (Dan. 11:18). Antiochus III joined with Hannibal and together they invaded Greece, but in 188 B.C. Roman warriors drove them out of their newly acquired territory.

- "There shall arise in his place one who imposes taxes" (Dan. 11:20). Seleucus IV ruled in his father's stead, but was soon murdered by his own prime minister.

ANTIOCHUS EPIPHANES: A PICTURE OF THE ANTICHRIST

Antiochus Epiphanes was the youngest son of Antiochus III, and the angel told Daniel that he was a "vile person." He would take the throne with an agenda of peace, the angel predicted, and would "seize the kingdom by intrigue" (Dan.

11:21). Let's look at the complete scriptural portrait of this historical character:

> And in his place shall arise a vile person, to whom they will not give the honor of royalty; but he shall come in peaceably, and seize the kingdom by intrigue. With the force of a flood they shall be swept away from before him and be broken, and also the prince of the covenant. And after the league is made with him he shall act deceitfully, for he shall come up and become strong with a small number of people. He shall enter peaceably, even into the richest places of the province; and he shall do what his fathers have not done, nor his forefathers: he shall disperse among them the plunder, spoil, and riches; and he shall devise his plans against the strongholds, but only for a time. (Dan. 11:21–24)

Harold Willmington has said that Antiochus Epiphanes was nicknamed "Epimanes," a word meaning *madman*, by those who knew him best. Apparently he pretended to be a second-century Robin Hood, stealing from one party and doling plunder out to others.[5]

> He shall stir up his power and his courage against the king of the South with a great army. And the king of the South shall be stirred up to battle with a very great and mighty army; but he shall not stand, for they shall devise plans against him. Yes, those who eat of the portion of his delicacies shall destroy him; his army shall be swept away, and many shall fall down slain. Both these kings' hearts shall be bent on evil, and they shall speak lies at the same table; but

FROM DANIEL TO DOOMSDAY

it shall not prosper, for the end will still be at the appointed time. (Dan. 11:25–27)

In 170 B.C., Antiochus Epiphanes defeated the Egyptian king Ptolemy Philometor at a battle east of the Nile delta. Ptolemy lost the battle because he was betrayed by counselors who sat at his own dinner table (Dan. 11:26).

"While returning to his land with great riches, his heart shall be moved against the holy covenant; so he shall do damage and return to his own land. At the appointed time he shall return and go toward the south; but it shall not be like the former or the latter. For ships from Cyprus shall come against him; therefore he shall be grieved, and return in rage against the holy covenant, and do damage. So he shall return and show regard for those who forsake the holy covenant. (Dan. 11:28–30)

Antiochus advanced in a second military campaign against Egypt but was stopped by Roman ships sailing from Cyprus. In his fury, he turned toward Palestine, breaking his peace treaty with the children of Israel. He wooed and flattered Jews who were willing to "forsake the holy covenant."

And forces shall be mustered by him, and they shall defile the sanctuary fortress; then they shall take away the daily sacrifices, and place there the abomination of desolation. (Dan. 11:31)

Armed with information from disloyal spies, Antiochus came against Jerusalem in 171 B.C. In a violent rage of frustration, he murdered over forty thousand Jews and sold an equal number into slavery. He took away the daily sacrifice from the temple (Zerubbabel's temple, which had been erected by the returned exiles), offered the blood of a pig upon the altar, and set up an image of Jupiter to be worshiped in the holy place.

THE ORIGIN OF HANUKKAH

Ever wonder where the Jewish holiday of Hanukkah originated? You'll find the answer in Daniel's prophetic time line.

Antiochus began his anti-Jewish campaign on September 6, 171 B.C. and continued until December 25, 165, when Judas Maccabeus restored true worship in the temple. This accounts for the 2,300 days of Daniel 8:14.[6] Chanukah, or Hanukkah, the eight-day festival that the children of Israel celebrate on the twenty-fifth day of the Hebrew month of Kislev, commemorates the victory of Judas Maccabeus and his followers over the forces of Antiochus Epiphanes. According to Talmudic legend, when the Hasmoneans recaptured and cleansed the temple, they were able to find only a single cruse of oil with the high priest's seal, sufficient for only one day's lighting of the menorah. But a miracle occurred, and the menorah burned for eight days.[7]

> Those who do wickedly against the covenant he shall corrupt with flattery; but the people who know their God shall be strong, and carry out great exploits. And those of the people who understand shall instruct many; yet for many days they shall fall by sword and flame, by captivity and plundering. Now when they fall, they shall be aided with a

little help; but many shall join with them by intrigue. And some of those of understanding shall fall, to refine them, purify them, and make them white, until the time of the end; because it is still for the appointed time. (Dan. 11:32–35)

In this portion of Daniel's prophecy, we can see that the years ahead were to be a time of great suffering. Gentile nations would continue to batter the nation of Israel—Syria from the north, Egypt from the South, Rome from the West. Many people would fall away from the faith and try to immerse themselves in the predominant culture. Others would remain faithful to the God of Abraham, Isaac, and Jacob. Those people, like the Maccabees, would be strong and "carry out great exploits." Some would fall and get up, being purged, refined, and strengthened as the end of time approached.

PROPHECY OF THE WILLFUL KING

Now the angel took Daniel over a prophetic gap of time. He moved from foretelling the future about Antiochus Epiphanes to speaking about a man who will be very much like that pagan Syrian. The angel began to speak of the Antichrist, and Daniel dutifully recorded the description:

Then the king shall do according to his own will: he shall exalt and magnify himself above every god, shall speak blasphemies against the God of gods, and shall prosper till the wrath has been accomplished; for what has been determined shall be done. He shall regard neither the God of his fathers nor the desire of women, nor regard any god; for he shall exalt himself above them all. But in their place he shall honor a god of fortresses; and a god which his fathers did not know he shall honor with gold and silver, with precious stones and pleasant things. Thus he shall act against the strongest fortresses with a foreign god, which he shall acknowledge, and advance its glory; and he shall cause them to rule over many, and divide the land for gain. (Dan. 11:36–39)

No doubt Daniel realized that he had heard about this willful prince before. He had seen the Antichrist in his vision of the four beasts (Dan. 7), heard the man speaking pompous words, and watched until the beast was slain, "its body destroyed, and given to the burning flame" (Dan. 7:11b).

Daniel had also learned about the Antichrist in his vision of the ram and goat. Here the angel told Daniel,

A king shall arise,
Having fierce features,
Who understands sinister schemes.
His power shall be mighty, but not by his own power;
He shall destroy fearfully,
And shall prosper and thrive;
He shall destroy the mighty, and also the holy people.

Through his cunning
He shall cause deceit to prosper under his hand;
And he shall exalt himself in his heart.
He shall destroy many in their prosperity.
He shall even rise against the Prince of princes;
But he shall be broken without human means.

And the vision of the evenings and mornings
Which was told is true;
Therefore seal up the vision,
For it refers to many days in the future. (Dan. 8:23–26)

THE FALSE MAN OF PEACE

Just like Antiochus Epiphanes, the Antichrist will make his debut upon the stage of world history with hypnotic charm and charisma. In Revelation 13:1, John described him: "Then I stood on the sand of the sea. And I saw a beast rising up out of the sea, having seven heads and ten horns, and on his horns ten crowns, and on his heads a blasphemous name."

Notice that the beast rose from the sea—the sea, in prophetic symbolism, represents the Gentile world. He will come from the European Union or a country or confederation that was once part of the Roman Empire, which stretched from Ireland to Egypt and included Turkey, Iran, and Iraq. In Daniel's vision of the four beasts, you'll recall that the fourth beast had ten horns, which represented ten kingdoms (Dan. 7:19–25). The "little horn" sprouted from among the other ten, which we believe are ten divisions of the old Roman Empire.

In his rise to power, the Antichrist will first weave his hypnotic spell over one nation in the ten-kingdom federation, then over all ten. He will conquer three of the ten nations, hence the seven heads and ten crowns of John's vision, then assume primacy over all of them. He may well be doing this during the time right before the Rapture or during the time of the Gog-Magog War. The Bible tells us that after his position is secure in the ten-nation federation, he will turn his ravenous eyes toward the Apple of God's eye—Israel.

While Israel is cleaning up after the terrible destruction of the war with Russia and her Arab allies, it is quite likely that this man will sense an opportunity to catapult himself onto the world stage. He will already have amalgamated his power in Europe, but controlling Israel is his chance to become a world peacemaker!

The Antichrist will be a man who has "paid his dues" in the military and the political sense, and many will willingly follow him. He will rule over those in his federation with absolute authority and will do as he pleases (Dan. 11:36).

We also know the Antichrist will enter the world stage with a reputation of being a powerful man of peace. Perhaps he will be a Nobel Peace Prize winner. He will defeat and merge three kingdoms. Daniel 8:25 says that by peace he "shall destroy many." He will step in and guarantee peace for Israel and the Middle East, which won't be difficult after Russia's pan-Islamic military juggernaut is destroyed. After all, those who have eyes to see will have just realized that God Himself defends Israel (Ps. 125:2)!

But you can dangle the truth right before some people, and they still won't believe it. Even after Israel's miraculous deliverance, millions of people will prefer to believe that mankind can solve its own problems. They'll credit Israel's deliverance to a fluke, a force of nature, or technology. And when this international peacemaker steps in to offer a seven-year treaty guaranteeing the peace of Israel, he will be applauded, lauded, and hailed as the Messiah, the world's new Caesar.

First John 2:18 boldly declares, "Little children, it is the last hour; and as you have heard that the Antichrist is coming, even now many antichrists have come, by which we know that it is the last hour." The Antichrist—capital *A*—is coming. Though many people through the years have been against Christ, there is coming a man who is the devil incarnate, the son of Satan, evil personified.

The Antichrist's three-point plan for world domination consists of a one-world economic system in which no one can buy or sell without a mark sanctioned by the Antichrist's administration, a one-world government, and a one-world religion that will eventually focus its worship on the Antichrist himself.

THE ONE WORLD ECONOMY

As America's economy shudders and sways above a crumbling foundation of global instability, the Antichrist will step in and end all of our problems. What could make more sense than a global currency? When Brazil devalues its currency, investors in America lose millions, so why not establish a currency that will bring parity to all nations? The European Union's Eurodollar may soon prove to be more stable and desirable than the American dollar. Why not extend the Euro, or something similar, to all nations?

The European Union is also considering a universal monetary system. *Time* magazine noted, "One month after the latest monetary crisis, Cabinet officers, legislators, and bankers on both sides of the Atlantic are intensely debating a lengthening list of ideas" for developing "a global financial system." Bank America has advertised the slogan, "The whole world welcomes world money."

The Antichrist's economy will be a cashless society in

which every financial transaction can be electronically monitored. John, inspired by the Holy Spirit to write the book of Revelation, described the situation:

> He causes all, both small and great, rich and poor, free and slave, to receive a mark on their right hand or on their foreheads, and that no one may buy or sell except one who has the mark or the name of the beast, or the number of his name. (Rev. 13:16–17)

The cashless society may ostensibly be presented to the world as a way to control drug lords, tax evaders, and the like. As I'm writing this, the Euro exists, but not in cash. If you are traveling in Europe, you could pay in Euros with your credit card, but not in coins or bills because they don't yet exist! The European Union is giving countries time to phase out their old currencies before minting and printing the new currency.

A cashless society may be presented as a foolproof way to end theft or as the ultimate shopping convenience. If you want to go to the grocery store, you can simply pass your hand—in which a microchip has been inserted beneath the skin—beneath a computer scanner. The amount of your purchase will instantly be deducted from your bank account.

This scenario doesn't sound nearly as far-fetched as it did in my father's day. My bank offers a debit card; today I don't need money to go to the grocery store. Everything is scanned these days, from library cards to thumbprints, and it doesn't require a great leap of imagination to see how this cashless, computerized system of buying and selling will be placed into operation. A day is coming when you will not even be able to buy a pack of gum without the proper approval, without having a chip in your hand or forehead.

The computer revolution has placed this phenomenal accomplishment well within our grasp. We have become accustomed to being managed by our "numbers." We cannot deduct our children on our income tax forms unless they have a Social Security number. We give our phone numbers to a representative from a catalog company, and sales clerks can find our address, sales history, and past purchases in an instant.

American politicians are now talking about implementing a national identity card, ostensibly to cut down on illegal aliens. Our government is putting on a full-court press that ultimately will give them the power to control cash transactions.

I believe the main reason the Antichrist will cause everyone to receive what is known as the "mark of the beast" is to control everyone and crush all who worship the God of Abraham, Isaac, and Jacob. If he cannot personally have the joy of controlling or killing them, he will have the satisfaction of knowing they will starve to death. Without his mark, no one will be able to buy a loaf of bread or a drop of milk. They may not be able to buy homes or make rent payments. They may not be able to hold jobs.

ONE-WORLD GOVERNMENT

Never in history has one government completely ruled the world, but the false man of peace will "devour the whole earth" (Dan. 7:23). He will rule over them by their own consent and with absolute and total authority (Dan. 11:36). His personality will be marked by great intelligence, persuasiveness, subtlety, and craft. His mouth will speak "pompous words" (Dan. 7:8), and he will be a "master of intrigue" (Dan. 8:23 NIV). He will be the world's most prominent, powerful, and popular personality.

The world—which no longer will have the true Church sprinkled throughout its nations—will not hesitate to give this man its full attention. The Antichrist will be free to set up his one-world government, but there's nothing new about his new world order! Satan has been scheming to institute one ever since Nimrod proposed to build a mighty tower on the plains of Shinar. The purpose of what we know as the Tower of Babel was to defy God's authority on earth—to cast God out and institute the government of man. While God commanded men to "Be fruitful and multiply, and fill the earth" (Gen. 9:1), the people of that day had a different idea:

> Now the whole earth had one language and one speech. And it came to pass, as they journeyed from the east, that they found a plain in the land of Shinar, and they dwelt there . . . And they said, "Come, let us build ourselves a city, and a tower whose top is in the heavens; let us make a name for ourselves, lest we be scattered abroad over the face of the whole earth." (Gen. 11:1–2, 4)

God endured the builders' brashness for a limited time, then He scattered them across the earth.

After World War I, "the war to end all wars," President Woodrow Wilson crafted the League of Nations to uphold peace through a one-world government. Adolf Hitler told the German people he would bring a "new order" to Europe. He did, dragging Europe into the bowels of a living hell and turning the streets crimson with rivers of human blood.

The communists of the former Soviet Union pledged to institute a new world order and erected an atheistic empire that collapsed like a house of cards. Now the United Nations wants to establish a new world order!

What does it mean? Brock Chisolm, director of the United Nations World Health Organization, said, "To achieve world government, it is necessary to remove from the minds of men their individualism, loyalty to their families, national patriotism, and religion."

Think about it: After the Rapture, after the Gog-Magog War of Ezekiel 38–39, after every nation has experienced terrible earthquakes, after nuclear war falls even upon nations not directly involved in the conflict, what hopes and ideals will remain to support mankind? True religion will be reduced to a dying ember—it will flame again, but not for a while. National patriotism will be trampled in the weariness of devastation. Loyalty to families may still exist, but even today it is waning. Our families are so fractured that family loyalty seems a thing of the past. And individualism? What's the point?

I believe simple apathy may be the prime force that draws men to the Antichrist. As men and nations struggle to pick up the pieces after the Rapture and the terrifying Gog-Magog War, they will look to one who promises peace, economic prosperity, and simple government. Why not hand him the reins of control?

THE ANTICHRIST'S ONE-WORLD RELIGION

What is the Antichrist's chief desire? He is a false christ. Satan knows the prophecy that one day every knee will bow before Jesus Christ, but so great is his hatred toward God that he's determined to lash out at God by keeping as many people from salvation as possible. Who knows; maybe Satan even thinks he can defeat the Lord God. During the Antichrist's limited time on earth, he will want to be worshiped. But he will proceed carefully, solidifying his positions in religion and politics, maintaining his false front as a global peacemaker.

Nowhere is he more careful and diplomatic than in Jerusalem. The Jewish temple will be rebuilt in the Holy City either shortly before or during the Antichrist's rise to power. During the first three and one-half years of the time of Tribulation, the Antichrist will allow the Jewish people to resume making daily sacrifices in the temple. They will rejoice, and many of them may believe him to be their messiah. In A.D. 1200, Moses Maimonides, a Jewish rabbi who wrote part of the Talmud, prophesied about the temple of the last days: "In the future, the Messianic king will arise and renew the Davidic dynasty, restoring it to its initial sovereignty. He will rebuild the Beis Ha Mikdash [the temple] and gather in the dispersed remnant of Israel."[8]

It could very well be that Maimonides was prophesying about Jesus and the Millennial Temple, but thousands of Jews may read this prophecy and link it with the Antichrist who has promised peace and allowed them to resume daily temple sacrifices.

The last time I was in Israel, I was amazed to discover that a Jewish temple society has already crafted all the implements necessary for temple worship to be reinstated exactly as in the days of Moses. Every detail in every instrument and every fabric has been replicated as they prepare to make sacrifices in the temple again. After the war of Gog-Magog, the hearts of the children of Israel will turn toward the God of Abraham, Isaac, and Jacob. In a surge of reawakening religious interest, they will rebuild the temple. In an ostentatious show of support, the Antichrist will praise these endeavors.

I wouldn't be surprised if, in a show of false humility, he visits the temple himself, accompanied by the Jewish leadership of Israel.

THE SECOND SEAL: THE RIDER OF THE RED HORSE

Shortly after the first seal was opened, John the Revelator saw Jesus break the second seal: "And another horse, fiery red, went out. And it was granted to the one who sat on it to take peace from the earth, and that people should kill one another; and there was given to him a great sword" (Rev. 6:3-4).

American essayist Robert Kaplan has said that the world has become an infinitely more dangerous place as distinctions weaken "between states and armies, armies and civilians, and armies and criminal gangs."[9] Under the red horseman, anarchy will reign as societies break down, the "haves" rioting against the "have nots."

The Antichrist's "peace" will be false and short-lived, for the second seal will propel the world toward increasing violence. I believe the rider on the red horse will instigate actual warfare between countries as well as violence between man and his neighbors. Remember the condition of the post-rapture earth—there are no Christians, and much of the world may be recovering from damage inflicted by nuclear fallout from the Gog-Magog War. As the rider of the red horse takes peace from the earth, people will kill one another on battlefields, in subways, on highways, in cities, in country fields. Such concepts as "common decency" and "human kindness" will fade to vague memories from another age. Nation will rise against nation, man will rise against his friend, children will rise against their parents. As cities turn into armed camps and nations hurl weapons at each other, the world will fall under a cloud of hopelessness and despair.

Remember the apocalyptic visions of a future world in movies like *Mad Max* and *Blade Runner*? Welcome to the world under the red horseman.

THE THIRD SEAL: THE RIDER
ON THE BLACK HORSE

John looked again and saw "a black horse, and its rider was holding a pair of scales in his hand. And a voice from among the four living beings said, 'A loaf of wheat bread or three loaves of barley for a day's pay. And don't waste the olive oil and wine'" (Rev. 6:5–6, NLT).

Fact: In 1995, for the third year in a row, the world produced less food than it ate, and its "carryover" stocks of emergency grain supplies sank to a record low. Lester Brown, president of the Worldwatch Institute, said we may now be witnessing a shift in the world's food economy "from a long-accustomed period of overall abundance to one of scarcity."[10]

Make no mistake; famine is on its way. The color of the black horse symbolizes the deep mourning that will fall upon the earth as the third seal is broken. As a result of war and God's mighty hand, the world will be stricken with a famine unlike anything in its past.

Listen how the prophet Jeremiah described death by famine:

Now their appearance is blacker than soot;
They go unrecognized in the streets;
Their skin clings to their bones,
It has become as dry as wood.
Those slain by the sword are better off
Than those who die of hunger;
For these pine away,
Stricken for lack of the fruits of the field. (Lam. 4:8–9)

While the Antichrist keeps himself aloof from the trouble, while violence and war wreak havoc in every nation, men, women, and children will begin to die of starvation. You'll notice that the rider of the black horse is told not to touch the wine and the olive oil. The wine and oil symbolize luxuries enjoyed by wealthy people. The rich will be able to obtain food and luxuries during this time, but the middle-class and the poor will not.

THE FOURTH SEAL: THE RIDER ON A PALE HORSE

As John the Revelator watched, Jesus broke open the fourth seal. A living creature beckoned John to "come and see."

"So I looked," John wrote,

> and behold, a pale horse. And the name of him who sat on it was Death, and Hades followed with him. And power was given to them over a fourth of the earth, to kill with sword, with hunger, with death [pestilence], and by the beasts of the earth" (Rev. 6:8).

Notice that Death and Hades rode together. J. Vernon McGee explained the pairing: "While Death takes the body, Hades is the place where the spirit of a lost man goes."[11]

Incredible! One-fourth of the earth's population will die as the rider on the pale horse goes forth. As anarchy, war, and famine continue, two new factors will be added to the scenario: pestilence and wild animal attacks. One agent almost certainly accounts for both—biological warfare. For the same reason a rabid raccoon will attack almost anything in its path, a biological or chemical attack could affect animals so that they lose their natural fear of man and attack without provocation.

Dr. Frank Holtman, head of the University of Tennessee's bacteriology department, said, "While the greater part of a city's population could be destroyed by an atomic bomb, the bacteria method might easily wipe out the *entire* population within a week" (emphasis added).[12]

The prophet Ezekiel foretold the path of the pale rider: "For thus says the Lord GOD: 'How much more it shall be when I send My four severe judgments on Jerusalem—the sword and famine and wild beasts and pestilence— to cut off man and beast from it?'" (Ezek. 14:21).

Notice that the order of the first four seals exactly follows Jesus' prediction about the beginning of the Tribulation: "For nation will rise against nation, and kingdom against kingdom [the red horse]. And there will be famines [the black horse], pestilences [the pale horse], and earthquakes in various places. All these are the beginning of sorrows" (Matt. 24:7–8).

THE FIFTH SEAL: PRAYERS OF THE MARTYRS

When Jesus opened the fifth seal, John saw under the altar,

> The souls of those who had been slain for the word of
> God and for the testimony which they held. And they
> cried with a loud voice, saying, "How long, O Lord, holy
> and true, until You judge and avenge our blood on those
> who dwell on the earth?" Then a white robe was given to
> each of them; and it was said to them that they should rest
> a little while longer, until both the number of their fellow
> servants and their brethren, who would be killed as they
> were, was completed. (Rev. 6:9–11)

The martyrs under the altar are those who will be
beheaded by the Antichrist in the first three and one-half years
of the Tribulation. They will be martyred in Daniel's seventieth week, between the Rapture and the fifth seal, for the same
reason John was on the isle of Patmos (see Rev. 1:9–10). Notice
that they are conscious and fully aware, not in "soul sleep."

THE SIXTH SEAL: NATURE REVOLTS

Jesus broke the sixth seal, and John recorded,

> Behold, there was a great earthquake; and the sun became
> black as sackcloth of hair, and the moon became like
> blood. And the stars of heaven fell to the earth, as a fig tree
> drops its late figs when it is shaken by a mighty wind. Then
> the sky receded as a scroll when it is rolled up, and every
> mountain and island was moved out of its place. And the
> kings of the earth, the great men, the rich men, the com-

manders, the mighty men, every slave and every free man, hid themselves in the caves and in the rocks of the mountains, and said to the mountains and rocks, "Fall on us and hide us from the face of Him who sits on the throne and from the wrath of the Lamb! For the great day of His wrath has come, and who is able to stand?" (Rev. 6:12–17)

John describes what seems remarkably like a meteor shower colliding with the earth. Scientists tell us that a collision with a huge meteor would result in an explosion much like that of a nuclear bomb, accompanied by enormous tidal waves, hurricanes moving at 600 miles per hour (the speed of sound), and months of darkness, caused by thick clouds of dust.[13] Astronomers predict that Earth's next close brush with a meteor will be in 2126 when the comet Swift-Tuttle comes near, but I believe God could bring a comet any time He chooses to accomplish His purposes.

THE SEVENTH SEAL: SILENCE IN HEAVEN

Just before the seventh seal was broken, John heard that 144,000 children of Israel, 12,000 from each tribe, were sealed. Terrible judgment was about to fall on the earth, and if these were not sealed, they would not escape.

These are the children of Israel who will spread the gospel throughout the entire world during the Tribulation. Notice that in Matthew 24, when Jesus was describing the Tribulation, he mentioned the martyrs (v. 9), false prophets (v. 11), and this great evangelistic team: "And this gospel of the kingdom will be preached in all the world as a witness to all the nations, and then the end will come" (v. 14).

Next John saw a great multitude of Gentiles who had come out of the Tribulation. They were clothed in white robes, and John was told that they had come "out of the great tribulation, and washed their robes and made them white in the blood of the Lamb" (Rev. 7:14).

That is a description of those who will be executed by the Antichrist during the Tribulation for "the word of their testimony, and they did not love their lives to the death" (Rev. 12:11). People will come to Christ during the Tribulation who did not hear the gospel during the Dispensation of Grace. They will hear the gospel preached by angels flying through the heavens saying, "Fear God and give glory to Him, for the hour of His judgment has come; and worship Him who made heaven and earth" (Rev. 14:7). They will refuse to take the mark of the Antichrist, and they will be killed.

Perhaps the Antichrist will charge them with treason. Perhaps he will condemn them for following what he calls "a dead religion for dead people." In any case, these martyrs will die for their faith, and their souls will wait in heaven until the Lord's purpose is complete.

Next in John's vision, Jesus, the Judge of the earth, stepped forward and broke the seventh seal. A solemn, tense hush fell over the assembly, and the silence lasted for "about half an hour" (Rev. 8:1).

This was not a hesitation or moment of indecision. This was the lull before the storm. The host of heaven saw what God was preparing to do, and they stood in absolute awe, total silence, of the coming divine annihilation of men on earth. The great Tribulation, when the full fury of the Lamb was unleashed, was coming next.

CHAPTER 7

11:56 P.M.
FOR THEN SHALL COME
GREAT TRIBULATION

*"I have read the Book of Revelation and, yes, I
believe the world is going to end—by an act
of God, I hope—but every day I think that
time is running out."*
—CASPAR WEINBERGER,
NEW YORK TIMES, AUGUST 23, 1982

M ama, what's this?" *Your four-year-old daughter, who
has been helping you clean out a box in the attic,
holds up a crumpled dollar bill.*

"That's what we used to use for money, sweetheart.
That's a dollar."

*She smoothes the bill with her fingers, easing out the
creases.* "Who's this man in the picture?"

"George Washington. Before the Leader came, we called
him the father of our country."

"What did you do with the dollars?"

"We took them to the stores. We'd give the storekeeper the dollar, and he'd give us something in exchange. A dollar would buy . . . well, a candy bar. Sometimes two."

She looks at you with a shadow of disbelief in her eyes. "You gave him this paper for candy? And he took it?"

You nod, not knowing quite how to explain it. "We didn't have the mark back then. And we only used scanners for things, not for people. All that was before the Leader came and made things simple."

"Oh." She holds the dollar beside her right hand, as if mentally comparing the tattooed lines of her mark with the fancy engraving and detailed art on the outmoded currency. "The dollar is prettier. But so old-fashioned."

"Yes, honey. A lot of things were prettier back then." You surrender to an overwhelming impulse to gather her into your arms, and she doesn't protest as you draw her close and breathe deeply of her hair, her skin. The Leader has changed many things, but the world itself has not changed. If anything, the darkness that fills men's souls has grown denser and more pronounced. Outside the burglar bars on your windows, what used to be a quiet, tree-lined street is deserted and patched, the houses silent and watchful.

"Tell me again, Mommy," your daughter says, still studying the dollar, "why Daddy wouldn't take the mark? Is it because he liked these dollars?"

A sludge of nausea moves in your stomach, and you close your eyes, steeling your heart against the memory of the execution, the guillotine, the somber, silent, approving crowd.

"Your daddy"—your voice breaks, but you push on— "believed that God was stronger than the Leader. So he *refused to get his mark, and he broke the law. It's that simple, honey."*

"Oh." Your daughter stares at the dollar bill for another moment, then, in the way of children, leaps from your arms and tosses it away, ready to dig for another treasure. But the crumpled bill falls to the dusty floor by your side, and you pick it up, fold it, and slip it into your pocket.

Your husband was a stubborn man, too rebellious for his own good. But there's no denying that he stood for a time when life seemed happier, when love blossomed frequently, when the bright prospect of hope lit the darkest places of the heart.

That world is gone now; it vanished like the dollars that were collected and burned shortly after the Leader's rise to power. But sometimes you think about the old world and grow nostalgic.

Will life ever be good again?

JOHN'S PORTRAIT OF THE GREAT TRIBULATION

In this chapter we will be taking a long look into Revelation, but John's book was not written in strict chronological order. Chapters 6 through 18 deal with the Tribulation period, but chapters 12 and 13 take time out for brief "biographical sketches" of several key characters with prominent roles in Daniel's seventieth week. And remember—while God's judgment is being poured out through the seven trumpets and vials, the Antichrist will continue to implement his program of world domination. To completely understand this period, you will have to see things from an earthly perspective *and* a heavenly one.

TRIBULATION CHARACTER SKETCH: THE WOMAN, THE CHILD, AND THE DRAGON

In Revelation 12:1 John wrote, "Now a great sign appeared in heaven." This is not a literal picture; by using the word *sign* John let us know the images are symbols. The woman described in Revelation 12:1–17 is Israel, from whom came the Child, Christ the Messiah. The dragon is Satan, who will persecute Israel throughout the Tribulation. The dragon's tail drew a third of the stars of heaven and threw them down to earth, symbolizing the angels who rebelled with Satan and were cast out of heaven before the creation of the world.

Make no mistake, friend. Though the Antichrist will appear to be controlling things during this last half of the Tribulation, he is inspired by the spirit of Satan himself.

THE ANTICHRIST WILL REVEAL HIS CHARACTER

Let's look back and see what Daniel had to say about these latter days and the evil man who will influence them:

> Then the king shall do according to his own will: he shall exalt and magnify himself above every god, shall speak blasphemies against the God of gods, and shall prosper till the wrath has been accomplished; for what has been determined shall be done. He shall regard neither the God of his fathers nor the desire of women, nor regard any god; for he shall exalt himself above them all. (Dan. 11:36)

The Antichrist will do "according to his own will," or as he pleases. If he has counselors, they are mere window dressing, for in the end he will do only what he wants to do. Compare his example to that of Jesus, the One he will imitate. Jesus said, "I can of Myself do nothing. As I hear, I judge; and My judgment is righteous, because I do not seek My own will but the will of the Father who sent Me" (John 5:30). In the garden of Gethsemane, Jesus prayed, "O My Father, if it is possible, let this cup pass from Me; nevertheless, not as I will, but as You will" (Matt. 26:39).

The Antichrist not only will be willful, but Daniel told us that he will not regard the "desire of women." This phrase could mean several things. First, and most obvious, it could mean that he will care nothing for the company of women— he will not possess normal desires for love, sex, and marriage. He may be a homosexual or, given that Daniel was writing in a pagan culture that exalted everything from gods of war to gods of childbirth, it may mean that the Antichrist will not honor the gods of men or those traditionally favored by women.

In examining the context of this verse, some prophecy scholars interpret this phrase to mean that the Antichrist will not regard the desire of Hebrew women to be the mother of the Messiah. The Messiah had not yet come at the time of Daniel's writing, and nearly every Hebrew woman yearned to be the mother of the One who would bring salvation to Israel. Daniel may have been saying, "He shall honor neither the true God, nor the coming Messiah, nor any god at all."

Though the Antichrist will come to the forefront of world events under a banner of peace and tolerance, he will quickly reveal his true colors. He will begin to persecute those who do not accept the mark that would allow them to buy and sell in the world markets, and he will portray those who refuse to swear allegiance to him as anarchists and dangerous subversives. His campaign of terror will escalate as he begins to criticize Bible-based worship in all its forms. He will promote a one-world religion and New Age concepts tolerant of all except Christians and Jews. The Antichrist will stop the daily sacrifice in the temple at Jerusalem, and he will demand that *he* be worshiped.

THE ANTICHRIST WILL CENTER HIS CULT IN JERUSALEM

Jerusalem! There is no city on the face of the earth like the Holy City. There are cities renowned for their massive size, their climate and beauty, or their industrial strength, but none can compare to the majestic city of Jerusalem. Why? Because Jerusalem is the city of God, the capital city of the nation God created by His spoken word (Gen. 12:1–3; 13:15), and with which He later made an eternally binding and unconditional blood covenant (Gen. 15:8–18).

This is the city God has chosen as His habitation: "Yet I have chosen Jerusalem . . . that My name may be there forever; and My eyes and My heart will be there perpetually . . . In this house and in Jerusalem, which I have chosen . . . I will put My name forever" (2 Chron. 6:6, 7:16, 33:7). King David, the man after God's own heart, the man who drove the Jebusites out of Jerusalem, wrote of the city of God with a holy passion, saying:

> Great is the Lord, and greatly to be praised
> In the city of our God . . .
> Beautiful in elevation,

The joy of the whole earth,
Is Mount Zion . . .
The city of the great King . . .
God will establish it forever. (Ps. 48:1–2, 8b)

The most passionate Scripture concerning Jerusalem was written by David: "If I forget you, O Jerusalem, / Let my right hand forget its skill! / If I do not remember you, / Let my tongue cling to the roof of my mouth— / If I do not exalt Jerusalem / Above my chief joy" (Ps. 137:5–6).

David was a musician and singer, so he was saying that as much as he loved music, if he forgot Jerusalem and God's purpose for that city, may his right hand no longer have the skill to play the harp, may he no longer be able to sing. A musician who cannot play and a singer who cannot sing have no purpose in life. Similarly, the man who forgets Jerusalem, the heart and soul of Israel, has no reason to live.

Jerusalem is a monument to the faithfulness of God. David wrote: "Those who trust in the LORD / Are like Mount Zion, / Which cannot be moved, but abides forever. / As the mountains surround Jerusalem, / So the LORD surrounds His people / From this time forth and forever" (Ps. 125:1–2).

Jerusalem is a living testimonial to all believers. We are sheltered in the arms of God just as Israel is cradled by the mountains and defended by God Himself.

Knowing all this, the Antichrist will decide to center his religious cult in Jerusalem, in the very heart of the temple itself. He will know full well that his actions are an affront to Holy God and His chosen people, the Jews.

Jesus confirmed that Satan's messiah would demand worldwide worship in Jerusalem. He said,

"Therefore when you see the 'abomination of desolation,' spoken of by Daniel the prophet, standing in the holy place" (whoever reads, let him understand), "then let those who are in Judea flee to the mountains." (Matt. 24:15)

THE ANTICHRIST'S COHORT: THE FALSE PROPHET

The Antichrist will not be alone in his diabolical deeds. He will have an assistant who is as thoroughly committed to evil as he is.

Remember this principle: Satan loves to mimic God's truth. He will continue doing so until the end of the age, and he will be particularly active during the last days.

The Antichrist will be part of a perverted satanic trinity that will function in much the same way as the Father, Son, and Holy Spirit. Satan, the "first person" of this triune partnership, will supply power to the Antichrist, who will be aided by the devilish "False Prophet."

> And he [the False Prophet] deceives those who dwell on the earth by those signs which he was granted to do in the sight of the beast, telling those who dwell on the earth to make an image to the beast who was wounded by the sword and lived. He was granted power to give breath to the image of the beast, that the image of the beast should both speak and cause as many as would not worship the image of the beast to be killed. (Rev. 13:14–15)

The image of the Antichrist is made to speak like a man. When it does, most people will bow and worship on the spot. Anyone who has ever been to Disney World and its "Hall of the Presidents" will tell you that the creation of a lifelike talking statue is no big deal. Either this statue possesses powers beyond what we're accustomed to, or the lesson here is the same lesson Daniel and his three friends learned back in Nebuchadnezzar's court. If you'll recall that story, Nebuchadnezzar had his craftsmen create a golden image of himself, ninety feet tall and nine feet wide, then he commanded everyone to fall down and worship it whenever they heard the musical cue (Dan. 3). Shadrach, Meshach, and Abed-Nego refused to bow and soon found themselves enjoying the roaring welcome of a fiery furnace. But God delivered them from the flames, sending His own Son to keep the young men company. Nebuchadnezzar was rightfully astonished and praised the Hebrews by saying, "Blessed be the God of Shadrach, Meshach, and Abed-Nego, who sent His Angel and delivered His servants who trusted in Him . . . [because they would] not serve nor worship any god except their own God!" (Dan. 3:28).

In the same way, the False Prophet will erect an image or statue of the Antichrist, and everyone will be commanded to worship it. And, just as He did generations ago, God will deliver those who refuse to bow.

In order to fully understand the Antichrist's agenda, it is important to grasp Satan's overall strategy. His goal is to "be like the Most High" (Isa. 14:14). He wants, in fact, to *dethrone* the Most High. Before the dawn of time, Satan convinced one-third of the angels to join him in his reckless attempt to overthrow God as the ruler of all. Though he was decisively defeated in a supernatural war, Satan has continued in open opposition to God, seeking every possible opportunity to lash out and attempt to destroy, deceive, or discredit that which is important to Him.

The very name *antichrist* hints at Satan's agenda. The Greek prefix *anti-* has two meanings. The first is the most obvious: *against*. The second is far more interesting, for *anti-* also means *in place of*. Both of these definitions apply here. Satan and his unholy conspirators are both against God and seeking to take His place.

Since Satan and his demons know what the Word of God says about their ultimate doom, why do they persist in this futile endeavor? Part of the answer undoubtedly lies in their evil, spiteful characters. Perhaps they truly believe they can alter their destiny and dethrone God Almighty. After all, Satan's defining sin is pride.

I believe one of Satan's purposes in the Tribulation is to imitate the worldwide rule of God in the Millennium. During the time of great Tribulation, Satan may feel he has the best shot he has ever had in usurping God's place. But though Satan seeks to impose a world government, the Antichrist will spend this half of the Tribulation fighting off one challenge after another. He will never fully succeed in claiming the world as his own.

Let's compare the two world rulers—Satan in the Tribulation, and Jesus in the Millennium:

- Jesus will rule a world of peace and prosperity, but the Antichrist will reign through seven years of war, violence, and chaos.

- While Jesus offers eternal salvation to those who trust Him, the Antichrist offers eternal damnation for those foolish enough to follow him.

- While the Holy Spirit testifies of Jesus and provides comfort, joy, and strength to those who trust the Savior, the False Prophet testifies of the Antichrist and enforces allegiance to him through threats, deception, and ruthless aggression.

- When Satan seeks to impose a world religion, a "great multitude no one can count" will reject him and recognize Jesus as the Messiah.

- While the Antichrist offers temporal salvation (the ability to buy and sell) to those who follow him, Jesus offers eternal salvation to those who trust Him.

TRIBULATION CHARACTER SKETCH:
THE BEASTS FROM THE SEA AND THE EARTH

The two beasts, one from the sea (Rev. 13:1–10) and one from the earth (13:11–18) are characters we have met before. The beast from the sea is the Antichrist, and the beast from the earth is the False Prophet, who institutes the apostate religious worship of the beast from the sea.

At some point in the great Tribulation, the Antichrist will be fatally wounded, perhaps by an assassination attempt, but he will not die. John says, "I saw one of his heads as if it had been mortally wounded, and his deadly wound was healed. And all the world marveled and followed the beast" (Rev. 13:3).

The Antichrist will emulate the death and resurrection of Jesus Christ. Just as he entered the stage of world prophecy riding a white horse to imitate Christ, he will also appear to die and miraculously rise again.

THE NUMBER OF A MAN

In Daniel, you will recall, the Antichrist was the "little horn" of chapter 7, the "king of fierce features" of chapter 8, the "prince who is to come" of chapter 9, and the "willful king" of chapter 11. John the Revelator gave us another way to identify him: "Here is wisdom. Let him who has understanding calculate the number of the beast, for it is the number of a man: His number is 666" (Rev. 13:18).

"The number of a man," according to Bible scholars, is *six*. Under Old Testament law, man's labor was limited to six days, for God commanded man to rest on the seventh day. The seventh day is God's day, and throughout Scripture seven is the number of divine completeness. Six falls short of seven, just as anything done by created beings falls short of the Creator's perfection.

The Antichrist's number, 666, could represent the satanic trinity: Satan, the Antichrist, and the False Prophet. For just as six falls short of seven, Satan falls short of being God the Father, the Antichrist falls short of being God the Son, and the False Prophet falls short of being God the Holy Spirit.

Another explanation for the Antichrist's number lies in the ancient Jewish practice of *Geometria*. As the apostle John wrote Revelation, he certainly knew that his readers were familiar with this practice, which involves substituting letters for numbers. The letters of the alphabet designated certain numbers in the same way that Roman numerals represent numbers. It would be a simple matter for members of the early church to convert a number into a name or a name into a number.

In Revelation 13:18, John made it possible for the world to identify the Antichrist by the number 666. This cryptic puzzle is not intended to point a finger at some unknown person. It is, however, intended to confirm someone already suspected as being the Antichrist.

This information is of no practical value to the Church, because we will be watching from the balconies of heaven by the time this lawless ruler is revealed. But for those of you reading this book after the Church has been taken away, you should be able to confirm which personality arising out of a European federation is the devil incarnate, the son of Satan.

During the late 1930s and early 1940s a flurry of pamphlets identified Adolf Hitler as the Antichrist. Others declared that Mussolini was the Antichrist because of his close relationship to Rome.

In his book *Is the Antichrist Alive and Well?* Ed Hindson listed several world leaders who have been suspected of being the Antichrist. The list includes Kaiser Wilhelm, Joseph Stalin, Nikita Krushchev, John F. Kennedy, Mikhail Gorbachev, Ronald Wilson Reagan (nominated because he had six letters in each of his three names), Saddam Hussein, and Bill Clinton, with Hillary as the False Prophet.[1] But no one who lives from the time of

Pentecost until the Rapture of the Church can possibly know who the Antichrist is because he will not make his appearance upon the world stage until the Church has been removed.

This so-called man of peace, this false messiah, is probably alive now and may even know his predestined demonic assignment. Although we do not know who he is, we certainly know what he will do.

THE ANTICHRIST WILL REVEAL HIS AGENDA

The Antichrist will care only about exalting himself. He will set up his image in the city of Jerusalem and demand that the nations of the world worship him—or face death by decapitation (Rev. 20:4). Daniel made it clear that the temple offerings will stop three and one-half years (1,290 days) before the end of the Tribulation. Why? Just like his forerunner, Antiochus Epiphanes, the Antichrist will introduce idolatrous worship inside the holy temple and set himself up as God:

> He will make a treaty with the people for a period of one set of seven [seven years], but after half this time, he will put an end to the sacrifices and offerings. Then as a climax to all his terrible deeds, he will set up a sacrilegious object that causes desecration, until the end that has been decreed is poured out on this defiler. (Dan. 9:27 NLT)

Paul also understood what would happen during the time of great Tribulation.

> He [the Antichrist] will exalt himself and defy every god
> there is and tear down every object of adoration and wor-
> ship. He will position himself in the temple of God, claim-
> ing that he himself is God . . . And you know what is
> holding him back, for he can be revealed only when his
> time is come. (2 Thess. 2:4, 6 NLT)

The Antichrist will speak so artfully, with such deception, that those who heard the gospel and rejected it before
the Rapture will be caught up in his lies. Paul told us,

> The coming of the lawless one is according to the work-
> ing of Satan, with all power, signs, and lying wonders,
> and with all unrighteous deception among those who
> perish, because they did not receive the love of the truth,
> that they might be saved. And for this reason God will
> send them strong delusion, that they should believe the
> lie, that they all may be condemned who did not believe
> the truth but had pleasure in unrighteousness. (2 Thess.
> 2:9–12)

Listen carefully, friend: The Rapture has not yet come, and
salvation of Jesus Christ is being extended to you. If you
reject it now, you will *not* be able to accept it later.

The son of Satan will be a counterfeit of the Son of God.
But we learn even more about the personality and plan of the
Antichrist by understanding how completely opposite he will
be from Jesus.

Christ came from heaven (John 6:38)	The Antichrist will come from hell (Rev. 11:7)
Christ came in His Father's name (John 5:43)	The Antichrist will come in his own name (John 5:43)
Christ humbled Himself (Phil. 2:8)	The Antichrist will exalt himself (2 Thess. 2:4)
Christ was despised and rejected (Isa. 53:3)	The Antichrist will be admired and lauded (Rev. 13:3–4)
Christ came to do His Father's will (John 6:38)	The Antichrist will come to do his own will (Dan. 11:36)
Christ came to save (Luke 19:10)	The Antichrist will come to destroy (Dan. 8:24)
Christ is the Good Shepherd (John 10)	The Antichrist will be the Evil Shepherd (Zech. 11:16–17)
Christ is the Truth (John 14:6)	The Antichrist will be "the lie" (2 Thess. 2:11)
Christ is the "mystery of godliness," God manifested in the flesh (1 Tim. 3:16)	The Antichrist will be the "mystery of lawlessness," Satan manifested in the flesh, the living son of Satan (2 Thess. 2:7)

TRIBULATION CHARACTER SKETCH:
THE TWO WITNESSES

The Antichrist will not be unimpeded, however. Along with a multitude of people who refuse to submit to his program, God will send two witnesses who will be a thorn in his side. Many Bible scholars believe the two witnesses who will appear on the earth during the Tribulation are Elijah and Enoch or Elijah and Moses (Rev. 11:1–15). I do not believe we can be dogmatic about who they are, for John didn't identify them, but there is a biblical basis for believing they could be Elijah and Moses.

In writing about the last days, the prophet Malachi wrote, "Behold, I will send you Elijah the prophet / Before the coming of the great and dreadful day of the LORD" (Mal. 4:5). Over the years, tradition has added the practice of "looking for Elijah" to the Jews' observance of the Passover feast. On the Seder table you will also find a special cup set for Elijah. Because the prophet is supposed to return as a forerunner of the Messiah, a cup is poured for him in the hope that he will appear, thus speeding the Messiah's appearance. Jesus Himself referred to this prophecy when He said, "Indeed Elijah is coming first and will restore all things" (Matt. 17:11).

Moses is a possible candidate for one of the two witnesses for several reasons. First, the miracles that the witnesses will perform are similar to those that Moses enacted during the Exodus. Second, some have suggested that Satan's effort to claim Moses' body (Jude 9) may have been motivated in part by his desire to prevent Moses' appearance at the Transfiguration and as one of these two witnesses. Moses has also been given the nod by some because he appeared with Elijah at the Transfiguration (Matt. 17:3).[2]

Whoever they are, these two witnesses will be filled with the Holy Spirit. They will preach the gospel and perform great miracles for three and one-half years. They will have the power to perform miracles, to call down fire from heaven, and to proclaim drought on the earth. They will be supernaturally protected until their mission is complete, then the Antichrist will kill them, leaving their bodies exposed for the world to see.

Scripture tells us that their dead bodies will literally lie in the streets of Jerusalem for three and a half days. The entire world, via television camera, will see their bodies and rejoice. No one will suggest that they be given a proper burial. Human decency and kindness will not be found in Satan's kingdom and certainly won't be found in the Antichrist's Jerusalem. The bodies of the two witnesses will lie in the gutter like dead animals while "those who dwell on the earth will rejoice over them, make merry, and send gifts to one another, because these two prophets tormented those who dwell on the earth" (Rev. 11:10).

It could be that the witnesses will die during Christmas, so the gift sending and receiving is part of those festivities. With no Christians to reinforce the *real* meaning of Christmas, the holiday will become totally pagan. I can just see a husband and wife toasting each other before a tinsel-draped fireplace, waiting for Santa and watching CNN's display of two dead bodies in the street. "Christmas came early for us this year," the newscaster says in a voice-over. "We finally got rid of those two cursed prophets! Glory to the Leader, and happy holidays to all!"

But, after three and one-half days, God will raise His prophets from the dead and take them to heaven. Before the unblinking eye of television cameras, they will stand to their feet, brush the dust and dried spittle from their rough garments, and lift their faces to heaven. The sky will thunder with a loud voice saying, "Come up here!" and up they'll go, courtesy of a heavenly cloud.

In that same hour there will be a great earthquake, and a tenth of Jerusalem will fall. Seven thousand men will be killed, but the trembling survivors will recognize the power of God.

THE VIEW FROM HEAVEN: THE SEVENTH SEAL LEADS TO SEVEN TRUMPETS

When He opened the seventh seal, there was silence in heaven for about half an hour. And I saw the seven angels who stand before God, and to them were given seven trumpets . . . So the seven angels who had the seven trumpets prepared themselves to sound. (Rev. 8:1–2, 6)

The seventh seal will inaugurate the seven trumpet judgments of Revelation 8:7–16, 21, which are reminders of the ten plagues God poured out on Egypt (Exod. 7–11). The first four judgments will affect the natural world; the last three will affect the unredeemed people of the earth. Everyone except the 144,000 Jewish evangelists will be subject to the plagues of the trumpet judgments. The horror announced by the first six trumpets will be beyond comprehension, but the seventh trumpet will announce the glory of the kingdom of Christ which is to come.

In the Old Testament we learn that God commanded that trumpets be used for calling the congregation together, either for the purpose of war or to sound an alarm. In Numbers 10:9 we read, "When you go to war in your land against the enemy who oppresses you, then you shall sound an alarm with the trumpets, and you will be remembered before the LORD your God, and you will be saved from your enemies."

J. Vernon McGee said, "As the trumpets of Israel were used at the battle of Jericho, so the walls of this world's opposition to God will crumble and fall during the Great Tribulation."[3] Amen!

THE TRUMPET JUDGMENTS

At the beginning of the great Tribulation, the angels of heaven will blow the trumpets against the earth ruled by the Antichrist. They will be sounding an alarm and a warning, for God will be about to pour out the full fury of His wrath.

> The first angel sounded: And hail and fire followed, min-
> gled with blood, and they were thrown to the earth. And
> a third of the trees were burned up, and all green grass was
> burned up. (Rev. 8:7)

This first judgment will be against the earth itself. Burning hail will strike the earth and destroy one-third of all plant life—trees, shrubs, grass, forests, gardens, parks. God used water, a flood, in His first judgment against the earth; now He will use fire. Plants were the first life forms to be created; now they will be the first to be destroyed.[4]

Then the second angel sounded: And something like a great mountain burning with fire was thrown into the sea, and a third of the sea became blood. And a third of the living creatures in the sea died, and a third of the ships were destroyed. (Rev. 8:8–9)

Another natural disaster will strike the earth as God moves His mighty hand. A massive meteor will strike the earth, causing tidal waves and vast pollution that will contaminate our oceans.

I don't know if you've seen a "red tide" before, but when it strikes beaches, hundreds of thousands of dead fish wash up on the shore, polluting the air for miles. This judgment will be far worse than a case of "red tide"; it will be a supernatural act of a wrathful God. One-third of all living creatures in the sea—dolphins and sharks, jellyfish and squid, microscopic plankton and great whales—will die, as well as any unfortunate seamen out on the ocean.

Then the third angel sounded: And a great star fell from heaven, burning like a torch, and it fell on a third of the rivers and on the springs of water. The name of the star is Wormwood. A third of the waters became wormwood, and many men died from the water, because it was made bitter. (Rev. 8:10–11)

The second trumpet will affect the salt water of the oceans. The third trumpet will affect *fresh* water, without which human life cannot exist. Chronic water shortages already affect 40 percent of the world's population, and when the angel poisons the waters, the situation will become dire. "Water wars" between countries over shared lakes and rivers could break out, with the Holy Land and northeast Africa being the most dramatically affected spots. According to Washington's World-Watch Institute, many of the skirmishes between Israeli settlers and Arabs have been exacerbated by the conflict over water rights.[5]

If water is such an urgent concern now, can you imagine how horrible the situation will be when Wormwood pollutes one-third of the world's fresh water?

Then the fourth angel sounded: And a third of the sun was struck, a third of the moon, and a third of the stars, so that a third of them were darkened. A third of the day did not shine, and likewise the night. (Rev. 8:12)

Like the heavy darkness that fell upon Egypt when Pharaoh made the lives of the Jewish people harsh with bitter bondage, darkness will cover the earth when the fourth angel sounds his trumpet. In Matthew 24:29, Jesus predicted that the heavens would declare the Tribulation: "Immediately after the tribulation of those days the sun will be darkened, and the moon will not give its light; the stars will fall from heaven, and the powers of the heavens will be shaken."

Whether from supernatural provision or as a result of the fire, the hail, and the meteor, God will allow a veil of thick fog to dim the light of sun, moon, and stars. He will not totally blot out sunshine and starlight, for in Genesis 8:22 He specifically promised that "While the earth remains, / Seedtime and harvest, / Cold and heat, / Winter and summer, / And day and night / Shall not cease."

God will keep His covenant with man. The earth will

still know day and night, but she will be darkened under a black cloud that will bring humanity deep depression and unspeakable emotional torment.

And I looked, and I heard an angel flying through the midst of heaven, saying with a loud voice, "Woe, woe, woe to the inhabitants of the earth, because of the remaining blasts of the trumpet of the three angels who are about to sound!" (Rev. 8:13)

The angel was warning that the judgments brought by the next three trumpets would be far worse than the others. The first four were judgments upon creation; the next three terrors will be judgments upon mankind.

THREE TRUMPETS OF TERROR

Then the fifth angel sounded: And I saw a star fallen from heaven to the earth. To him was given the key to the bottomless pit. And he opened the bottomless pit, and smoke arose out of the pit like the smoke of a great furnace. So the sun and the air were darkened because of the smoke of the pit. Then out of the smoke locusts came upon the earth. (Rev. 9:1–3)

These unnatural, demonic locusts will be released from the very pit of hell to torment men upon the earth. The "star fallen from heaven" will be Satan himself, and he will be given the authority to release these locusts upon the earth. Normal locusts eat plants, but these creatures do not. They will, however, sting men who are not sealed with the seal of

God. Their terribly painful sting will make men want to die, but they won't be able to. For five months these locusts, led by their demonic king Abaddon, will torment men upon the earth (Rev. 9:4–11).

John described these locusts as being the shape of a horse prepared for battle, their faces like the faces of men, their teeth like lion's teeth, and the sound of their wings like the sound of chariots with many horses running into battle (Rev. 7–10). This will be unspeakable and unstoppable terror! These are intelligent, spiritual beings, capable of commands and following the demonic leadership of Abaddon.

> Then the sixth angel sounded: And I heard a voice from the four horns of the golden altar which is before God, saying to the sixth angel who had the trumpet, "Release the four angels who are bound at the great river Euphrates." So the four angels, who had been prepared for the hour and day and month and year, were released to kill a third of mankind. (Rev. 9:13–15)

The four angels who were bound at the river Euphrates were evil angels, or they would not be bound. But now they will be loosed to kill a third of mankind, and they immediately will commence their evil assault. With one-quarter of humanity already dead from hunger, pestilence, sword, and wild beasts (Rev. 6:8), these angels will lead a demonic army 200 million strong. John said these hellish horsemen will have "breastplates of fiery red, hyacinth blue, and sulfur yellow; and the heads of the horses [will be] like the heads of lions; and out of their mouths [will come] fire, smoke, and brimstone" (Rev. 9:17).

I do not know if these are physical horses or symbols of a future weapon, but I do find the color combination intriguing. Just last week I picked up a *Newsweek* magazine and read an article on the European Union's new Eurodollar. In the picture, two men were dressed in colorful uniforms, and behind them a large circle, spangled with stars, displayed the emblem of the new currency.[6] The colors of their uniforms and the display? Hyacinth blue and yellow. Coincidence? I don't know. Perhaps the Antichrist will add his signature color, red, to the mix, and the horsemen of Revelation 9 will wear the official colors of his new world government.

Over one-half of the world's population will die in the Tribulation, yet the remainder will persist in idolatry, immorality, and rebellion against God (Rev. 9:20–21).

It is interesting to note that this great demonic army will issue from the vicinity of the Euphrates River. J. Vernon McGee pointed out that this area has great spiritual significance:

The Garden of Eden was somewhere in this section. The sin of man began here. The first murder was committed here. The first war was fought here. Here was where the Flood began and spread over the earth. Here is where the Tower of Babel was erected. To this area were brought the Israelites of the Babylonian captivity. Babylon was the fountainhead of idolatry. And here is the final surge of sin on the earth during the Great Tribulation.[7]

Harold Willmington said we should not marvel at the callousness of these people. The Bible provides several other examples of stubborn unbelief:

- the pre-Flood people, all but eight of whom were destroyed (1 Peter 3:20)
- Sodom, where not even ten were righteous (Gen. 18:32)
- the Exodus Israelites, all but two of whom died for their unbelief (Num. 14:29–30)
- the Canaanites, destroyed for their sin (Deut. 9:4)
- Israel, destroyed for disobedience (2 Kings 17:7–23; 2 Chron. 36:14–16)[8]

THE ANGEL AND THE LITTLE BOOK

An interlude falls between the sixth and seventh trumpet judgments. In Revelation 10:1-11, John prophesied the completion of the mystery of God concerning the nation of Israel. God's kingdom on earth would be established, but at a high cost to those who reject Him.

At this point in his vision, an angel gave John a "little book" and cried with a loud voice. He was answered by seven thunders, but John was not allowed to write the words he heard. This part of his revelation is the only part that remains sealed.

The angel planted one foot on the land and one on the sea—claiming God's dominion over both—and swore by God the Creator that the seventh trumpet was about to sound, and the "mystery of God" would be finished. Then John was commanded to take the book from the angel's hand and eat it. "It will make your stomach bitter," he was told, "but it will be as sweet as honey in your mouth."

So John ate. To that point he had seen the destruction of

Gentiles, but from that point on, he would see judgment upon his own people. At the beginning of Revelation 11, an angel told John to measure the temple of God, the altar, and the worshipers. He added that the outer court had been given to the Gentiles, who "will tread the holy city under foot for forty-two months" (Rev. 11:2).

These forty-two months correspond to the three and one-half years the Antichrist will control the temple (Dan. 12:11).

THE SEVENTH TRUMPET

At the blowing of the seventh trumpet, loud voices in heaven will cry out, "The kingdoms of this world have become the kingdoms of our Lord and of His Christ, and He shall reign forever and ever!" (Rev. 11:15–16). The end of the great Tribulation will be approaching. The world's suffering will be very nearly done, and Jesus Christ will be ready to claim His kingdom.

The twenty-four elders on their thrones will fall on their faces and worship God, saying,

We give You thanks, O Lord God Almighty,
The One who is and who was and who is to come,
Because You have taken Your great power and reigned.
The nations were angry, and Your wrath has come,
And the time of the dead, that they should be judged,
And that You should reward Your servants the prophets
    and the saints,
And those who fear Your name, small and great,

And should destroy those who destroy the earth. (Rev.
11:17–18)

TRIBULATION CHARACTER SKETCH:
THE THREE ANGELIC EVANGELISTS

The three angels (Rev. 14:5–13) are heavenly beings sent to
preach the message of God's righteous judgment on all the
nations of the earth. They will invite people to fear and glorify God before final judgment; they will announce the ultimate downfall of wicked Babylon, and they will warn
against worshiping the Antichrist.

"How tragic," wrote Harold Willmington, "that Christ,
at Calvary, drank this cup of wrath for the very sinners now
forced to drink it again."[9]

TRIBULATION CHARACTER SKETCH:
THE GREAT HARLOT

There is a vast difference between ignoring Scripture and
interpreting Scripture. To ignore the prophetic teaching of
Revelation 17 would be cowardly and irresponsible.
Anyone who interprets Revelation 17 runs the risk of being
labeled bigoted, extremist, and of course, politically incorrect.

In the New Testament, we find a clear presentation of an
apostate church that professes Christ without *possessing*
Him. In 1 Timothy 4:1, Paul wrote, "Now the Spirit
expressly says that in latter times some will depart from the
faith, giving heed to deceiving spirits and doctrines of
demons." And in 2 Peter 2:1–2, Peter told us,

But there were also false prophets among the people, even as there will be false teachers among you, who will secretly bring in destructive heresies, even denying the Lord who bought them, and bring on themselves swift destruction. And many will follow their destructive ways, because of whom the way of truth will be blasphemed.

After the Rapture of the true Church, or believers in Christ, a church will still exist on the earth, but she will be an *apostate* church. Revelation 17:1 labels the heretic church of the last days as "the great harlot who sits on many waters." A harlot is an individual who has been unfaithful in her wedding vows. Here John portrayed an apostate church that professed to be loyal to Christ but in fact cleaved to idols and a false religious system. This is spiritual adultery.

The apostate church will wield worldwide influence. God Himself told John the interpretation of the phrase "many waters" as "peoples, multitudes, nations, and tongues" (Rev. 17:15). This will be a worldwide false religious system.

In verse 2 we discover that this "great harlot" had seduced "the kings of the earth," not just the general population. The kings of the earth "were made drunk with the wine of her fornication." They were stupefied and mesmerized by this global religious system.

John further wrote, "So he carried me away in the Spirit into the wilderness. And I saw a woman [the great harlot] sitting on a scarlet beast which was full of names of blasphemy, having seven heads and ten horns" (Rev. 17:3). If you go back to Revelation 13:1, you will read, "Then I stood on the sand of the sea [the world]. And I saw a beast rising

FROM DANIEL TO DOOMSDAY

up out of the sea, having seven heads and ten horns." What we see in Revelation 17:3 and 13:1 is the same, so the beast that the great harlot sat upon was the revived Roman Empire under the control of the Antichrist. John described a world where the apostate church and the Antichrist have joined forces to rule the world.

The Harlot Is Beautiful but Deadly

In Revelation 17:4, John described the apparel of the great harlot: "The woman was arrayed in purple and scarlet, and adorned with gold and precious stones and pearls." She had the outward appearance of royalty; she was wearing gold and an array of jewels, meaning she had unlimited wealth. In her hand was "a golden cup full of abominations and the filthiness of her fornication." To the outward appearance the great harlot was beautiful, but the contents of her cup was poison to the nations of the world.

In Revelation 17:5, John identified the great harlot by saying, "And on her forehead a name was written: MYSTERY, BABYLON THE GREAT, THE MOTHER OF HARLOTS AND OF THE ABOMINATIONS OF THE EARTH."

The word *mystery* in the New Testament does not refer to something mysterious, but to some truth not previously made known by God to men. The mystery God was revealing was that in the last days there will be a worldwide apostate church that will reject Christ, dishonor God, and join forces with the Antichrist.

To identify Babylon, we must go to Genesis 10:8 and discover Nimrod, the arch-apostate of the postdiluvian world. Nimrod lived four generations after the Flood and was called "a mighty hunter before the LORD . . . And the beginning of his kingdom was Babel" (Rev. 17:9–10). The word *Bab-el* means the "gate of God."

It was Nimrod's generation that built the Tower of Babel for the purpose of casting God and His influence out of the earth. They proposed to build a great tower that would reach into heaven so they could have the benefits *of* God without submitting *to* God. In response to their presumptuous action, God confounded their language and scattered them over the earth.

This is the critical point—the first organized, idolatrous religious system in the history of the world was introduced at Babel. That's why John called Babylon "the mother of Harlots" (Rev. 17:5). Babylon was the birthplace of spiritual adultery. So the spiritual adultery of the end times is called by the name Babylon, the mother of harlots.

What is the end of this great harlot? Look carefully at Revelation 17:16–17:

And the ten horns which you saw on the beast [the European confederation which will produce the Antichrist], these will hate the harlot, make her desolate and naked, eat her flesh and burn her with fire. For God has put it into their hearts to fulfill His purpose, to be of one mind, and to give their kingdom to the beast, until the words of God are fulfilled.

John was saying that in the middle of the Tribulation, members of the European confederation that arises from the old Roman Empire will realize that they are mere puppets of the great harlot. The Antichrist, who will rule over the confederation, will be content for a time to share his power with her, then he will turn on her and destroy her with a vengeance. By eliminating the false church, the Antichrist will be clearing the way for his own cult and his own worship.

THE SEA OF GLASS AND THE SEVEN VIALS

The last set of judgments described in Revelation came with the seventh vial, or bowl, judgments (Rev. 16:1–21). A vial is a bowl, and these seven bowls of fierce judgment will be poured out in rapid succession at the end of the great Tribulation. As the seventh seal introduced the seven trumpet judgments, the seventh trumpet judgment introduces the seven bowl judgments, especially their final outcome. The bowl judgments are similar in kind to the trumpet judgments. But whereas the judgments of the trumpets are partial in their effects, the judgments poured on the earth from the bowls will be complete and final. The seventh and last bowl presages the great battle of Armageddon and foretells the final ruin of the Antichrist.

In Revelation 15:1–8, John the Revelator saw another seven angels preparing to pour out the seven last plagues. He described something "like a sea of glass mingled with fire," and told us that those who had been victorious over the beast were standing on the sea of glass, singing the song of Moses and the song of the Lamb. While John listened to their praise songs, the temple of the tabernacle in heaven was opened and out stepped the seven angels, clothed in pure white linen, having their chests girded with golden bands.

Without any delay, the angels were commanded to pour

out the bowls of God's wrath upon the earth. These terrible plagues followed one another in quick succession:

- The first angel poured out "foul and loathsome sore[s]" upon those who had the mark of the beast (Rev. 16:1–2).

- The second angel poured his bowl on the sea, and it became like the thick, coagulated blood of a dead man. Every living creature in the sea died (v. 3).

- The third angel poured his bowl on the rivers and springs of fresh water, and they, too, became as blood. The angel of the waters made a telling comment: "You are righteous, O Lord . . . / For they have shed the blood of the saints and prophets, / And You have given them blood to drink. / For it is their just due (vv. 5–6).

- The fourth angel poured his bowl on the sun, which began to burn hot enough to "scorch men with fire." Men cursed God, but they did not repent or give Him glory (vv. 8–9).

- The fifth angel poured his bowl on the throne of the beast, and his kingdom became full of darkness. His followers chewed their tongues in pain from the sores, the heat, and their thirst, but they did not repent (vv. 10–11).

- The sixth angel poured out his bowl on the great river Euphrates, and its waters dried up so the "kings from the east" could march across the dry riverbed and join God's other enemies for battle. At this time, three demons went forth to entice the kings of the world to gather at Armageddon. "You want a fight?" Satan was saying to God. "We're going to give You one" (vv. 12–16).

- The seventh angel poured his bowl into the air, and a voice from heaven proclaimed, "It is done!" (v. 17). A mighty earthquake unlike any other shook the earth.

Every city was destroyed; every mountain was laid low. Every island vanished into the sea as seventy-five-pound hailstones (each as heavy as the weight of one talent) fell from the sky. (Rev. 16:17–21)

Yet men still continued to curse and blaspheme God.

TRIBULATION CHARACTER SKETCH: THE REAPING ANGELS

The reaping angels (Rev. 14:14–20) are angels who will go forth at God's command to bring the wrath of God upon the unbelieving world. In this "sneak preview" of Armageddon, John saw that Christ would return to earth and, joined by these two reaping angels, would begin to harvest the earth with sharp sickles, resulting in a river of human blood two hundred miles long and as high as a horse's bridle.

The Old Testament prophets often spoke of the latter days in terms of harvest. Joel wrote, "Put in the sickle, for the harvest is ripe. / Come, go down; / For the winepress is full, / The vats overflow— / For their wickedness is great" (Joel 3:13).

Isaiah 63, the passage that inspired "The Battle Hymn of the Republic," the glorious old hymn sung throughout the

Civil War, shares Joel's vision of a vat of ripe grapes, ready to be trampled underfoot:

> Who is . . . This One who is glorious in His apparel,
> Traveling in the greatness of His strength? . . .
> Why is Your apparel red,
> And Your garments like one who treads in the winepress?
> "I have trodden the winepress alone,
> And from the peoples no one was with Me.
> For I have trodden them in My anger,
> And trampled them in My fury;
> Their blood is sprinkled upon My garments,
> And I have stained all My robes.
> For the day of vengeance is in My heart,
> And the year of My redeemed has come." (Isa. 63:1–4)

This is no weak-wristed, smiling Jesus who comes to pay the earth a condolence call. This is a furious Christ, ready to confront the gathered armies of the world on a plain called Armageddon.

The first time He came to earth, Jesus was the Lamb of God, led in silence to the slaughter. The next time He comes, He will be the Lion of the tribe of Judah who will trample His enemies until their blood stains His garments, and He shall rule with a rod of iron. Even so, come Lord Jesus!

CHAPTER 8

11:57 P.M.
INCHING TOWARD
ARMAGEDDON

*"I sometimes believe we're heading very fast for
Armageddon right now."*
—RONALD REAGAN, MAY 2, 1982[1]

The battle of Armageddon, the greatest blood bath in the
history of civilization, will be fought in Israel on the
plains of Megiddo. Though most Americans couldn't tell you
which battle the word *Armageddon* actually refers to, the
name carries connotations of catastrophe, as well it should.

Imagine, if you will, that you are one of the 144,000
children of Abraham sealed by God and living in the city of
Jerusalem at the time of the Tribulation. Unable to buy or
sell because you have not taken the identifying mark of the
Antichrist currently residing in Jerusalem, you are aware
that these terrible things that have come upon the world
could have come only from God . . .

You have wanted to read the Torah, but your house, your books, and all your belongings were confiscated years ago when the landlord reported you for not accepting the Universal Identification Chip. Now you and your loved ones live in a cavern-like chamber of rubble on the outskirts of the city with a few other vagrants. Sometimes the searchlights of the Global Police send you scrambling in the night . . . as they did the night you found a Bible in a trash heap.

You tucked it into your shirt and curled into the night shadows, then reached out to draw your little boy onto your lap. As you held your breath and prayed that the military police would grow bored and move on, some part of you wondered why your heart leapt at the sight of the Christian book. Before the time of trouble, you would have been reluctant to touch the book revered by those who had spent centuries torturing, murdering, and castigating your people, but now the book is a welcome sight, for it contains most of the Torah.

Now, as you crouch inside the remnant of an earthquake-ravaged building, you open the cracked leather binding. You begin to read, searching the writings of Old Testament prophets for a glimmer of hope, for strength to endure. And what you read in Zechariah makes your skin crawl.

> Behold, the day of the LORD is coming,
> And your spoil will be divided in your midst.
> For I will gather all the nations to battle against Jerusalem;
> The city shall be taken,
> The houses rifled,
> And the women ravished.

Half of the city shall go into captivity,
But the remnant of the people shall not be cut off from the
 city. (Zech. 14:1—2)

*The day of the Lord is coming. The day of the Lord was
mentioned by Isaiah, Ezekiel, Joel, Amos, Obadiah,
Zephaniah, Zechariah, and Malachi. It seems to be a period
of time in which many things happen, most of them unpleas-
ant. Zechariah was predicting another war against
Jerusalem, but this one would be different than Gog-Magog.
The Russians and their allies had been destroyed out on the
plains; but God says this time the enemy will enter
Jerusalem, storm into houses, and violate women. Half of
the city will be taken captive.*

Horrified, you read on.

Then the LORD will go forth
And fight against those nations,
He fights in the day of battle.
And in that day His feet will stand on the Mount of Olives,
Which faces Jerusalem on the east.
And the Mount of Olives shall be split in two,
From east to west,
Making a very large valley . . .
Then you shall flee through My mountain valley,
For the mountain valley shall reach to Azal.
Yes, you shall flee
As you fled from the earthquake
In the days of Uzziah king of Judah.
Thus the LORD my God will come,
And all the saints with You. (Zech. 14:3—5)

The Lord will go forth and fight. Though the sky is dark and oppressive overhead, your heart thrills with hope. This is a promise, strong and sure. You have already seen God's sheltering hand, for none in your family have been affected by the plague of boils sweeping the city. The stinging locusts have not touched you, nor has the sun burned your skin. And if these horrors come—no, when these horrors come—Israel's Messiah will come from heaven to defend His people and His holy city.

With an army of saints? One corner of your mouth quirks with a small smile. The believers. Not those imperious religious dictators who've been storming and ranting for the last seven years, but the quiet, confident "born agains" who vanished before all the trouble broke out.

You read further in the book of Zechariah:

And this shall be the plague with which the LORD will strike
    all the people who fought against Jerusalem:
Their flesh shall dissolve while they stand on their feet,
Their eyes shall dissolve in their sockets,
And their tongues shall dissolve in their mouths . . .
Such also shall be the plague
On the horse and the mule,
On the camel and the donkey,
And on all the cattle that will be in those camps.
So shall this plague be. (Zech. 14:12, 15)

Whatever's coming certainly won't be pretty. It could be nuclear war, biological weapons, or a chemical attack. You stand, wipe the grime out of your eyes, and peer out from the rubble to search for your wife and children. Time is short.

You and your family will have a better chance of surviving the holocaust out in the desert than here in Jerusalem.

STEP ONE: THE NATIONS WILL RISE AGAINST THE ANTICHRIST

Unlike Jesus Christ, whose throne will know no end, the Antichrist's days will be numbered. While God readies the armies of heaven, the nations of earth will rise against the Antichrist. Daniel tells us the Antichrist will constantly be at war with nations who rise against him, and this warfare will end at the fateful battle of Armageddon on the plain of Megiddo.

> At the time of the end the king of the South shall attack him; and the king of the North shall come against him like a whirlwind, with chariots, horsemen, and with many ships; and he shall enter the countries, overwhelm them, and pass through. He shall also enter the Glorious Land, and many countries shall be overthrown; but these shall escape from his hand: Edom, Moab, and the prominent people of Ammon. He shall stretch out his hand against the countries, and the land of Egypt shall not escape. He shall have power over the treasures of gold and silver, and over all the precious things of Egypt; also the Libyans and Ethiopians shall follow at his heels. (Dan. 11:40–43)

The Antichrist will do battle with Egypt, just as his precursor Antiochus Epiphanes did. He will defeat the Egyptians and take their treasures for his own use. He will also send his armies to the Holy Land, where he will have trouble with the Arabs. Libya and Ethiopia, however, will surrender to him, virtually guaranteeing his control over Africa. His domination of the world will not be complete, but it will be ruthless.

STEP TWO: THE ANTICHRIST WILL BLASPHEME GOD

Scripture tells us that "news from the east and the north shall trouble" the Antichrist (Dan. 11:44). His military intelligence will report that an army of 200 million Asians is marching down the dry bed of the Euphrates River to engage him in a titanic struggle for world supremacy. The Antichrist's one-world religious cult, headquartered in Jerusalem, will be the focus of the invading armies.

Revelation 13:6 tells that the Antichrist will open "his mouth in blasphemy against God, to blaspheme His name, His tabernacle, and those who dwell in heaven." As the Antichrist, indwelled by Satan, marshals his massive army for the battle of Armageddon, he will look into heaven at the angels who had the opportunity to follow him in his first rebellion against God. He will look at Christ, to whom Satan once offered the kingdoms of the world. He will look up at the raptured believers who stand with their Lord, and he will say, "Look, all of you! Look where you would be if you had followed me! You would be rulers of the earth! I *forbid* God to send His Son to earth to reign. I am God here! I rule and reign in this city! Jerusalem is *mine.*"

Why does the Antichrist covet Jerusalem? What inspires his hatred for the Jews? The answer is simple: God chose the nation of Israel so He would have a repository of divine

231

truth for generations to come. Through Israel God has given the world the Word of God, the patriarchs, the prophets, Jesus Christ, and the apostles. There would be no Christianity without Jewish contribution.

Satan's hatred for Israel and the Jewish people stems from God's love for Israel. Anti-Semitism is driven by a demon spirit because of the righteous contributions the Jewish people made to civilization.

Satan's purpose in this battle will be to exterminate every Jew on the face of the earth. The Lord Jesus Christ will return to earth to rule over the seed of Abraham, Isaac, and Jacob. If Satan, through the Antichrist, can destroy the Jews, there is no reason for Jesus to return, and Satan could continue as the world ruler. But the Antichrist cannot stop what God has already decreed.

STEP THREE: GOD WILL DRAW
THE NATIONS TO MEGIDDO

In Joel 3:2, God said, "I will also gather all nations, / And bring them down to the Valley of Jehoshaphat." Speaking through Zechariah, God said, "Behold, I will make Jerusalem a cup of drunkenness to all the surrounding peoples, when they lay siege against Judah and Jerusalem . . . I will gather all the nations to battle" (Zech. 12:2; 14:2).

The battle of Armageddon will begin on the plains of Megiddo to the north, continue down through the Valley of Jehoshaphat on the east, cover the land of Edom to the south and east, and revolve around Jerusalem. Fighting will begin almost immediately. The Antichrist's enemies will lay siege to Jerusalem, then overrun her defenses and city and wreak the havoc Zechariah so vividly described. They will take captives, murder, rape, and pillage until the streets run red with blood.

The Antichrist, who will be chasing the Jews who are fleeing Jerusalem for Petra, will hear of the trouble and direct his military juggernaut toward Armageddon to face the 200 million-man army advancing from China to capture the oil-rich Persian Gulf.

> But news from the east and the north shall trouble him; therefore he shall go out with great fury to destroy and annihilate many. And he shall plant the tents of his palace between the seas and the glorious holy mountain [Jerusalem]. (Dan. 11:44–45)

After hearing about the advancing eastern army and the attack on Jerusalem, the Antichrist will advance from the territory of the defeated king of the South to Armageddon, a natural battlefield, to face the armies from the North and East.

STEP FOUR: GOD WILL DISPATCH THE CAVALRY

Then God, who has patiently borne the blasphemies of the Antichrist, will say, "Son, take the armies of heaven—the angels and the Church—and return to earth as the King of kings and Lord of lords. Go—and make your enemies your footstool. Go and rule the earth with a rod of iron. Go and sit upon the throne of your forefather, King David."

Then will come the final invasion, not from the north, south, east, or west, but from heaven. It is the invasion described in Revelation 19, the attack led by Jesus Christ, the Lamb of God, the Lion of Judah, and the Lord of Glory!

Then the Lion of Judah shall mount His milk-white stallion, followed by His army wearing crowns and dazzling robes of white. I will be in that army, for it is composed of the loyal angels of God and those who were raptured with the Church! Enoch, the first prophet, prophesied about this day: "Behold, the Lord comes with ten thousands of His saints" (Jude 1:14).

Mounted upon a white horse, the King of kings will descend onto the battlefield at Armageddon. As He comes, His eyes will be like blazing fire, and the armies of heaven will follow Him. Out of the Messiah's mouth will come a sharp, two-edged sword, the Word of God with which He created the world out of chaos, raised Lazarus from the dead, and rebuked the unruly wind and waves on the Sea of Galilee. His spoken word will crush His enemies in milliseconds.

He is the Mighty Conqueror, and of His kingdom there shall be no end!

CHRIST'S BATTLE DRESS

In Revelation 19:12, John wrote that Jesus had a name "written on him that no one knew except Himself." As a Jew, John knew that God appeared to Abraham, Isaac, and Jacob by the name of God Almighty, *El Shaddai*. But God did not reveal Himself to them by the name of Jehovah (*Yahweh*). The patriarchs knew God as the Almighty One, but they had no concept of Him as an intimate friend and master, the One who delights to walk with His children "in the cool of the day" as God walked with Adam in the Garden of Eden.

Christ's robe, dipped in His innocent blood shed on the cross, is His prayer shawl. The *tzitzit* of His shawl spells

"Jehovah God is One" in Hebrew, meaning He is the King of kings and Lord of lords (Rev. 19:13,16).

When Jesus begins His descent, two opposing forces will be drawn up in battle array on the mountains of Israel—the armies of the Antichrist and the army of the kings of the East. Jesus told us, however, that before this battle begins there will be a sign in the heavens: "Then the sign of the Son of Man will appear in heaven, and then all the tribes of the earth will mourn, and they will see the Son of Man coming on the clouds of heaven with power and great glory" (Matt. 24:30).

We don't know what this sign will be, but it will be something so clear and obvious that it leaves no room for doubt— Jesus Christ, Messiah and Lord, is returning to earth!

At that point, the two armies will turn from each other and direct their weapons toward Christ Himself. John the Revelator said, "And I saw the beast, the kings of the earth, and their armies, gathered together to make war against Him who sat on the horse and against His army" (Rev. 19:19).

Jesus Christ, leading the armies of heaven, will dismount from His white horse and step out onto the Mount of Olives, cleaving the mountain in two. The terrified inhabitants of Jerusalem, who have been brutalized by the invading armies, will flee the city through the gap in the ancient mountain.

John the Revelator wrote that the mire of mingled blood and mud will form a lake that reaches to the bridle of a horse: "And the grapes were trodden in the winepress outside the city and blood flowed from the winepress in a stream about 180 miles long and as high as a horse's bridle" (Rev. 14:20, NLT). This blood will flow from the veins of men who came to destroy Israel but were themselves destroyed by God.

Daniel foretold the outcome of the Antichrist's encounter

with Jesus: "He [the Antichrist] shall even rise against the Prince of princes; / But he shall be broken without human means" (Dan. 8:25b).

Paul also gave us a word of prophecy: "And then the lawless one [the Antichrist] will be revealed, whom the Lord will consume with the breath of His mouth and destroy with the brightness of His coming" (2 Thess. 2:8).

Then the beast [Antichrist] was captured, and with him the false prophet who worked signs in his presence . . . These two were cast alive into the lake of fire burning with brimstone. And the rest were killed with the sword which proceeded from the mouth of Him who sat on the horse. And all the birds were filled with their flesh. (Rev. 19:20–21)

The Antichrist doesn't stand a chance! He who invaded Jerusalem, who murdered and killed righteous Jews who would not worship him, who conquered the world, will be cast alive and forever into the Lake of Fire with the False Prophet! And "that serpent of old, who is the devil and Satan" will be bound by an angel and cast "into the bottomless pit, and shut . . . up . . . so that he should deceive the nations no more till the thousand years were finished" (Rev. 20:2–3).

Returning to the earth with His bride, the Church, Jesus will clean house. Not only will the Antichrist and the False Prophet be thrown into hell, but Satan himself will be put away for a thousand years. Every hostile force that would challenge Christ's right to rule the earth will have been eradicated.

ARMAGEDDON'S AFTERMATH

Jesus Christ will win the battle at Armageddon for Jerusalem and Israel. In the aftermath of this battle, His people will finally understand who He really is and what He has come to offer them. The hearts of the Jewish people—warmed toward God because of His intervention—will fully turn to their true God. In that moment, Israel will look upon her Messiah with recognition.

> And I will pour on the house of David and on the inhabitants of Jerusalem the Spirit of grace and supplication; then they will look on Me whom they have pierced. Yes, they will mourn for Him as one mourns for his only son, and grieve for Him as one grieves for a firstborn. In that day there shall be a great mourning in Jerusalem . . . . And one will say to him, "What are these wounds between your arms?" Then he will answer, "Those with which I was wounded in the house of my friends." (Zech. 12:10–11, 13:6)

The "fullness of the Gentiles has come in," and "all Israel will be saved" as Paul predicted (Rom. 11:25–26).

Jesus Christ, the true Messiah, the Prince of Peace, the Blesser of Abraham, the Son of David, Shiloh, shall rule and reign forever from the city of Jerusalem, the city of God. Hallelujah to the Holy One of Israel! Of His kingdom there shall be no end!

CHAPTER 9

11:58 P.M.
THE MILLENNIUM DAWNS

"This war no longer bears the characteristics of
former inter-European conflicts.
It is one of those elemental conflicts which usher in
a new millennium
and which shake the world once in a
thousand years."
—ADOLF HITLER, APRIL 26, 1942

Hitler clearly had an overdeveloped sense of his own importance. World War II, as horrible as it was, was a mere skirmish compared to Armageddon, the war that will truly usher in the Millennium.

This interval of time, at two minutes till the ultimate doomsday, will be a time of great rejoicing for God's people. Jesus Christ, the Lord of Glory, will have come again and defeated the son of Satan, the Antichrist. Jesus will have regathered, regenerated, and restored faithful Israel. He will have called the remnant hiding in Petra and welcomed them back into His Holy City. Isaiah prophesied about this:

For the LORD will comfort Zion,
He will comfort all her waste places;
He will make her wilderness like Eden,
And her desert like the garden of the LORD;
Joy and gladness will be found in it,
Thanksgiving and the voice of melody . . .
For you shall go out with joy,
And be led out with peace;
The mountains and the hills
Shall break forth into singing before you,
And all the trees of the field shall clap their hands. (Isa.
    51:3, 55:12)

We who have returned in the armies of heaven will follow our King as He revisits His promised land. The barren, devastated lands around Jerusalem will miraculously burst forth with new life as the Messiah passes by, and we will breathe in the scents of sweet jasmine, the Rose of Sharon, and the Lily of the Valley. The faithful Jews who have anticipated His coming will follow, rejoicing in the arrival of their long-awaited Messiah. What a victory parade that will be!

Daniel 12:11–12 indicates there will be a period of seventy-five days between Christ's Second Coming and the institution of the millennial reign. Dr. S. Franklin Logsdon explained it this way:

We in the United States have a national analogy. The President is elected in the early part of November, but he is not inaugurated until January 20th. There is an interim of 70-plus days. During this time, he concerns himself with the appointment of Cabinet members, foreign envoys and others who will comprise his government. In the period of 75 days between the termination of the Great Tribulation and the Coronation, the King of glory likewise will attend to certain matters.[1]

Before Christ establishes His millennial kingdom, several events must occur.

THE JUDGMENT OF THE NATIONS

After the defeat of the Antichrist, Jesus will sit down on His throne and begin to execute judgment. This is not the Great White Throne Judgment, at which every unbeliever will be judged for his deeds, but a judgment to judge the Gentile nations of earth for the manner in which they treated the Jewish people and Israel (Gen. 12:1–3). Let's see how Jesus described it:

> When the Son of Man comes in His glory, and all the holy angels with Him, then He will sit on the throne of His glory. All the nations will be gathered before Him, and He will separate them one from another, as a shepherd divides his sheep from the goats. And He will set the sheep on His right hand, but the goats on the left. Then the King will say to those on His right hand, "Come, you blessed of My Father, inherit the kingdom prepared for you from the foundation of the world: for I was hungry and you gave Me food; I was thirsty and you gave Me drink; I was a stranger and you took Me in; I was naked and you clothed Me; I was sick and you visited Me; I was in prison and you came to Me."

Then the righteous will answer Him, saying, "Lord, when did we see You hungry and feed You, or thirsty and give You drink?" . . .

And the King will answer and say to them, "Assuredly, I say to you, inasmuch as you did it to one of the least of these My brethren, you did it to Me." Then He will also say to those on the left hand, "Depart from Me, you cursed, into the everlasting fire prepared for the devil and his angels: for I was hungry and you gave Me no food; I was thirsty and you gave Me no drink" . . .

Then they also will answer Him, saying, "Lord, when did we see You hungry or thirsty or a stranger or naked or sick or in prison, and did not minister to You?"

Then He will answer them, saying, "Assuredly, I say to you, inasmuch as you did not do it to one of the least of these, you did not do it to Me."

And these will go away into everlasting punishment, but the righteous into eternal life. (Matt. 25:31–46)

This judgment will be for Gentiles, who will be judged according to how they treated Jesus' "brethren," or the Jews, from the time of Genesis 12 to the judgment of the nations. God will judge Egypt and the Pharaoh that knew not Joseph for making the lives of the Jewish people bitter with harsh bondage. God will judge the Babylonians and the Persians. He will judge the Roman government that decreed the Jews were "sons of the devil," that they could not own land, that they could not vote or hold public office, that they could not practice their professions, that they must wear distinctive clothing marking them as Jews, that they could not live with Christians, and that it was good form to kill the "Christ-killers" during Holy Week.

During the Holy Inquisition of the Roman Catholic Church, the bones of dead Jews were dug up and put on trial in Spain. When the dead Jews could not prove they were not heretics, their fortunes were confiscated by the Roman Catholic Church.

The British Empire will be called to the judgment bar for their White Paper Policies during World War II and before. As Hitler was killing 25,000 people a day, multitudes of Jews tried to escape. Yet the British White Paper Policy allowed only 5,000 Jews a year to immigrate to Israel. Israel, under control of the British, returned helpless Jews to Hitler's death camps. The British captured Jews sneaking into Israel in leaky ships. The British closed the gates of mercy on Jews trying to escape. Almighty God will remember their actions on this judgment day.

The Gentiles who live during the Tribulation will answer for their treatment of the Jewish people and Israel. You will recall that during the Tribulation God will seal a believing remnant of Israel, 144,000 strong, to witness during the entire seven-year period. In Matthew 24:14, Jesus told us that this remnant will preach "this gospel of the kingdom . . . in all the world as a witness to all the nations, and then the end will come." These believing Jews will be successful in their endeavors, for in Revelation 7:9–17, we see that a great multitude has been redeemed during the dark Tribulation period.

Upon a casual reading of Matthew's passage, you might

think these Gentiles are being judged by their works—in other words, if they gave food and water to the ministering Jews, they will be allowed to obtain eternal life. This idea, however, contradicts the entire body of Scripture, for nowhere does God allow man to be saved through his own efforts. We are saved through faith in Jesus Christ, and our salvation *results* in good works. The works of kindness and compassion detailed in Jesus' words are not the criterion upon which these people will be judged, but *evidence* of the transformation of their hearts.

God will look at each individual who has come out of Tribulation terror and ask, "How did you treat the witness who came to visit you? Did you give him food and water and listen to his message? Or did you call the authorities and attempt to have him cast into prison?" I believe that society will be so dark, dismal, and paranoid that kindness and compassion will be found only in those whose hearts have been regenerated by the Spirit of God.

After this judgment, the "goats" will follow the Antichrist and the False Prophet into the lake of fire and brimstone. As they followed him in life, they will follow him in eternity. The "sheep" who know the Good Shepherd, Jesus, will follow Him to a glorious marriage feast.

THE FIRST RESURRECTION

The resurrection has three waves of ingathering. The first wave to be resurrected were those who came out of their graves at the Crucifixion. The second wave will be the Rapture of the Church, and the third wave will be those who are converted in the first three and one-half years of the

Tribulation. They will be taken into heaven in the middle of Daniel's seventieth week. Jesus Himself explained it to us:

"Do not marvel at this; for the hour is coming in which all who are in the graves will hear His [the Son of God's] voice and come forth—those who have done good, to the resurrection of life, and those who have done evil, to the resurrection of condemnation." (John 5:28–29)

Daniel told us, "And many of those who sleep in the dust of the earth shall awake, / Some to everlasting life, / Some to shame and everlasting contempt" (Dan. 12:2). Those who would wake to "contempt," however, will rise later, at the end of the millennial kingdom.

In Revelation 20:5–6 we learn that these two resurrections—of the good and evil—will be separated by the Millennium:

But the rest of the dead did not live again until the thousand years were finished. This is the first resurrection. Blessed and holy is he who has part in the first resurrection. Over such the second death has no power, but they shall be priests of God and of Christ, and shall reign with Him a thousand years.

As Daniel penned the last words of his book, the angel gave him a personal reassurance: "But you, go your way till the end; for you shall rest, and will arise to your inheritance at the end of the days" (Dan. 12:13). The angel was telling Daniel not to worry. He would die and take his rest but would rise with the Old Testament saints. When Jesus died at

Calvary, He descended into the bowels of the earth and took those who were in Paradise waiting for liberation by the Lamb of God. Daniel is now in heaven, waiting to be a part of the invasion of Planet Earth at the Battle of Armageddon.

THE MILLENNIAL KINGDOM WILL BE FOUNDED

What is the millennial kingdom of Christ? Though it is not often preached from Sunday pulpits, the Bible has much to say about the Millennium. It is known in Scripture as "the world to come" (Heb. 2:5), "the kingdom of heaven" (Matt. 5:10), "the kingdom of God" (Mark 1:14), "the last day" (John 6:40), and "the regeneration" (Matt. 19:28). Jesus told His disciples, "Assuredly I say to you, that in the regeneration, when the Son of Man sits on the throne of His glory, you who have followed Me will also sit on twelve thrones, judging the twelve tribes of Israel" (Matt. 19:28).

The Millennium was foreshadowed in the Old Testament by the Sabbath, a time of rest. A rest was to be observed after six work days, six work weeks, six work months, and six work years. In God's eternal plan, the earth will rest after six thousand years as well, as He ushers in the millennial kingdom of the Messiah.

The Millennium will be a time of rest for the people of God. Hebrews 4:8–9 tells us "for if [Jesus] had given them rest, then He would not afterward have spoken of another day. There remains therefore a rest for the people of God."

The prophet Isaiah echoed the thought: "And in that day there shall be a Root of Jesse, / Who shall stand as a banner to the people; / For the Gentiles shall seek Him, / And His resting place shall be glorious" (Isa. 11:10).

During the Millennium, the geography of Israel will be changed. Israel will be greatly enlarged, and the desert will become a fertile plain. For the first time Israel will possess all the land promised to Abraham in Genesis 15:18–21. A miraculous river will flow east to west from the Mount of Olives into both the Mediterranean and the Dead Sea. But it will be "dead" no longer!

Hear how Ezekiel described it:

> When I returned, there, along the bank of the river, were very many trees on one side and the other. Then he said to me: "This water flows toward the eastern region, goes down into the valley, and enters the [Dead] sea. When it reaches the sea, its waters are healed. And it shall be that every living thing that moves, wherever the rivers go, will live. There will be a very great multitude of fish, because these waters go there; for they will be healed, and everything will live wherever the river goes. It shall be that fishermen will stand by it from En Gedi to En Eglaim; they will be places for spreading their nets. Their fish will be of the same kinds as the fish of the Great Sea, exceedingly many. (Ezek. 47:7–10)

The prophet Ezekiel described fishermen catching all the fish at En Gedi (a city on the Dead Sea) that could be caught in the Mediterranean Sea. Indeed, the Dead Sea shall live, as will everything during the millennial kingdom when the Giver of Life sits upon the throne of His Father, King David.

Ezekiel stated that there will be trees on each side of this river, flowing out of the Temple Mount, and John the

Revelator further revealed that these trees will bear twelve kinds of fruit, one for each month of the year. The leaves of these trees will be for the healing of the nations (Rev. 22:2). Isaiah told us that we will enjoy unparalleled health: "In that day the deaf shall hear the words of the book, / And the eyes of the blind shall see out of obscurity and out of darkness" (Isa. 29:18).

Listen to how Zechariah described the land:

> And in that day it shall be
> That living waters shall flow from Jerusalem,
> Half of them toward the eastern sea
> And half of them toward the western sea;
> In both summer and winter it shall occur . . . .
> All the land shall be turned into a plain from Geba to
>   Rimmon south of Jerusalem. Jerusalem shall be raised
>   up and inhabited in her place from Benjamin's Gate to
>   the place of the First Gate and the Corner Gate, and
>   from the Tower of Hananel to the king's winepresses.
> The people shall dwell in it;
> And no longer shall there be utter destruction,
> But Jerusalem shall be safely inhabited . . .
>
> And it shall come to pass that everyone who is left of all
>   the nations which came against Jerusalem shall go up
>   from year to year to worship the King, the LORD of
>   hosts, and to keep the Feast of Tabernacles.
>   (Zech.14:8, 10–11, 16)

Jerusalem, the apple of God's eye, will become the joy of the world, for Jesus will reign there. The city will become the international worship center, and people from all over the world will make pilgrimages to worship in the holy temple. Kings, queens, princes, and presidents shall come to the Holy City so "that at the name of Jesus every knee should bow, of those in heaven and of those on earth . . . and that every tongue should confess that Jesus Christ is Lord, to the glory of God the Father" (Phil. 2:10–11).

The prophet Micah wrote of the millennial kingdom, and the poetry of his verse has inspired many a public building (including the United Nations headquarters) to be inscribed with a portion of his words. But Micah wasn't writing about the United Nations, London, or New York; the prophet was writing about God's millennial capital, Jerusalem:

> Now it shall come to pass in the latter days
> That the mountain of the LORD's house
> Shall be established on the top of the mountains,
> And shall be exalted above the hills;
> And peoples shall flow to it.
> Many nations shall come and say,
> "Come, and let us go up to the mountain of the LORD,
> To the house of the God of Jacob;
> He will teach us His ways,
> And we shall walk in His paths."
> For out of Zion the law shall go forth,
> And the word of the LORD from Jerusalem.
> He shall judge between many peoples,
> And rebuke strong nations afar off;
> They shall beat their swords into plowshares,
> And their spears into pruning hooks;

Nation shall not lift up sword against nation,
Neither shall they learn war any more. (Mic. 4:1–3)

The Holy City, now six miles in circumference, will occupy an elevated site and will be named *Jehovah-Shammah*, meaning "the Lord is there" (Ezek. 48:35) and *Jehovah Tsidkenu*, meaning "the Lord our righteousness" (Jer. 33:16).

Can you imagine a thousand years of perfect peace? The earth will cease from strife, and the lion shall lie down by the lamb without even showing his claws! Satan will be bound in the bottomless pit, and earthly problems will fade away.

BY WHAT RIGHT WILL JESUS CHRIST RULE THE EARTH?

God promised Abraham, "I will make you exceedingly fruitful; and I will make nations of you, and kings shall come from you" (Gen. 17:6). God was revealing how He planned to eventually rule over all the earth—through a king of His appointment.

In Genesis 49 Jacob the patriarch called his twelve sons around his bed to give them a final blessing and to speak a prophetic word over each of them. His word over Judah was especially provocative:

Judah, you are he whom your brothers shall praise;
Your hand shall be on the neck of your enemies;
Your father's children shall bow down before you . . .
The scepter shall not depart from Judah,
Nor a lawgiver from between his feet,
Until Shiloh comes. (Gen. 49:8, 10)

The word *Shiloh* may be rendered "He whose right it is to rule." Jacob thus prophesied that a man who had the right to be king would come out of Judah's lineage.

In 2 Samuel 7:16, God made this promise to King David: "And your house and your kingdom shall be established forever before you. Your throne shall be established forever." There are three important words in this verse: *house*, *kingdom*, and *throne*. "Your house" designates the descendants of David who would sit on his throne. "Your kingdom" represents the kingdom of Israel. "Your throne" is David's royal authority, the right to rule as God's representative. Twice in this one verse God assured David that his dynasty, kingdom, and throne would last *forever*.

The Gospel of Matthew opens with God breaking a silence of more than four hundred years. God proclaimed Jesus' royal lineage to Israel by saying, "The book of the genealogy of Jesus Christ, the Son of David, the Son of Abraham."

If Jesus Christ is the Son of Abraham, He is the Blesser promised to Abraham through whom all the families of the earth should be blessed (Gen. 12:3). If Jesus Christ is the Son of David, He is the one who has the right to rule. He is Shiloh!

The angel Gabriel appeared to the virgin Mary and said,

Do not be afraid, Mary, for you have found favor with God. And behold, you will conceive in your womb and bring forth a Son, and shall call His name JESUS. He will be great, and will be called the Son of the Highest; and the Lord God will give Him the throne of His father David. And He will reign over the house of Jacob forever, and of His kingdom there will be no end. (Luke 1:30–33)

Jesus Christ was born, lived as a Jewish rabbi, and was crucified by the Roman government on a Roman cross. When He ascended into heaven, God the Father said to Him, "Sit at My right hand, / Till I make Your enemies Your footstool" (Matt. 22:44).

Jesus Christ rules the Millennium because He alone is worthy. He rules by heritage, by holy decree, and by divine appointment. Blessing and honor and glory and power be to Him who will sit on the throne of His father, David!

THE KING AND HIS VICE-REGENT

Dr. Harold Willmington pointed out that though Jesus Christ will be supreme ruler during the Millennium, some prophetic passages strongly suggest He will be aided by a second-in-command: David, the man after God's own heart![2]

Let's look at the Scripture: "But they shall serve the LORD their God, / And David their king, / Whom I will raise up for them" (Jer. 30:9). Jeremiah wrote four hundred years after David's death, so he could not have been referring to David's earthly reign.

I will establish one shepherd over them, and he shall feed them—My servant David. He shall feed them and be their shepherd. And I, the LORD, will be their God, and My servant David a prince among them. (Ezek. 34:23–24, see also 37:24–25)

Afterward the children of Israel shall return, seek the LORD their God and David their king. They shall fear the LORD and His goodness in the latter days. (Hos. 3:5)

But King David won't be the only ruler. He will be aided by many:

- The Church (1 Cor. 6:3)
- The apostles (Matt. 19:28)
- Nobles (Jer. 30:21)
- Princes (Isa. 32:1, Ezek. 45:8–9)
- Judges (Zech. 3:7, Isa. 1:26)
- Lesser authorities (Zech. 3:7)[3]

If there is a lesson here for us, the waiting Church, it is that those who are faithful now will be given greater responsibility in heaven. "Well done, good and faithful servant," Christ told the man who multiplied the talents he had been given, "you have been faithful over a few things, I will make you ruler over many things. Enter into the joy of your lord" (Matt. 25:23).

THE PURPOSE OF THE MILLENNIUM

Why has God planned a Millennium? God has several reasons for instituting an earthly kingdom over which His Son will reign. First, He has promised to reward His children. Jesus said, "Then the King will say to those on His right hand, 'Come, you blessed of My Father, inherit the kingdom prepared for you from the foundation of the world'" (Matt. 25:34).

Second, God promised Abraham that Israel would become a mighty nation, which has already come to pass, and that his seed would someday own the Promised Land forever (Gen. 12:7; 13:14–17). Israel rightfully owns all the land God gave to Abraham by blood covenant: "from the river of Egypt to the great river, the River Euphrates," and "from the wilderness and Lebanon . . . even to the Western Sea" (Gen. 15:18, Deut. 11:24). Ezekiel 48:1 established the northern boundary of Israel as the city of Hamath; the southern boundary is established in Ezekiel 48:28 as the city of Kadesh. In modern terms, Israel rightfully owns all of present-day Israel, all of Lebanon, half of Syria, two-thirds of Jordan, all of Iraq, and the northern portion of Saudi Arabia. When Messiah comes, the seed of Abraham will be given that land down to the last square inch.

Third, God will establish the millennial kingdom to answer a million believers' prayers. When Jesus taught His disciples the model prayer, or "the Lord's prayer," He taught them to pray, "Your kingdom come" (Luke 11:1–4). The phrase "Your kingdom come" isn't just a little ditty meant to rhyme with "Your will be done"; it is a plea that God would soon establish His earthly kingdom!

Finally, God will establish a millennial kingdom to prove a point. In the Millennium, God will redeem creation, resulting in docile wild animals, plentiful crops, and pure water. The world will know one thousand years of peace, joy, holiness, glory, comfort, justice, health, protection, freedom, and prosperity. Satan will be bound and not able to wreak havoc on earth. King Jesus Himself will rule from Jerusalem, and immortal Christians with godly wisdom will rule other cities. But despite all these things, man's fallen nature will *still* pull him into sin and disobedience.

The Millennium will be a one-thousand-year lesson in

man's ultimate depravity. The humanistic idea that man can improve himself to the point of perfection will be proven false once and for all; the concept of utopia will vanish like the morning mist. For though Christians will live in their resurrected bodies, the Tribulation believers who go into the Millennium in their mortal bodies will bear children throughout the thousand years. The children, grandchildren, and great-grandchildren of the Millennium will still possess a sinful nature, and they will still have to choose whether or not to accept Christ as Savior.

The ages will witness one indisputable fact: without God, man has no hope. The Bible scholar Harold Willmington illustrated it this way:

- The age of innocence ended with willful disobedience (Gen. 3).
- The age of conscience ended with universal corruption (Gen. 6).
- The age of human government ended with devil-worshiping at the Tower of Babel (Gen. 11).
- The age of promise ended with God's people enslaved in Egypt (Ex. 1).
- The age of the law ended with the creatures killing their Creator (Matt. 27).
- The age of the Church will end with worldwide apostasy (1 Tim. 4).
- The age of the Millennium will end with an attempt to destroy God Himself (Rev. 20).[4]

THE MILLENNIUM IS WONDERFUL, BUT IT ISN'T HEAVENLY

Do you think our doomsday worries will end with the Tribulation? Think again. Millions of babies will be born during this thousand years, and they will be babies just like you and I once were, prone to sin and bent toward trouble. Though the Christian parents who enter the Millennium will teach their children right from wrong, some of these children will exercise their free will to choose wrong.

Some of them, Zechariah told us, will "not come up to Jerusalem to worship the King, the LORD of hosts" so on them "there will be no rain" (Zech. 14:17). Christ will have to rule with "a rod of iron" (Rev. 19:15).

Dr. Rene Pache explains the situation:

As beautiful as the Millennium is, it will not be heaven . . . Sin will still be possible during the thousand years. Certain families and nations will refuse to go up to Jerusalem to worship the Lord. Such deeds will be all the more inexcusable because the tempter will be absent and because the revelations of the Lord will be greater.[5]

Sin will still have a foothold in creation, and it must be eradicated. And at the end of the thousand-year reign of Christ, the final conflict between God and Satan will take place.

CHAPTER 10

11:59 P.M.
THE EARTH'S
FINAL CONFLICT

"Now this is not the end. It is not even the
beginning of the end.
But it is, perhaps, the end of the beginning."
—WINSTON CHURCHILL, NOVEMBER 10, 1942

Now when the thousand years have expired, Satan will be released from his prison and will go out to deceive the nations which are in the four corners of the earth, Gog and Magog, to gather them together to battle, whose number is as the sand of the sea. They went up on the breadth of the earth and surrounded the camp of the saints and the beloved city. And fire came down from God out of heaven and devoured them. (Rev. 20:7–9)

At the end of the Millennium, Satan will be loosed from his prison, and thousands of people from all the nations of the earth will believe his lies and follow him. They will gather around Jerusalem, Christ's capital city, and wage a great war.

What will make these people follow Satan? The prophet Jeremiah wrote, "The heart is deceitful above all things, / And desperately wicked; / Who can know it?" (Jer. 17:9).

Who can understand what drives men to sin? For those who are living in earthly bodies, even as we are now, the law of sin is like the law of gravity. No matter how much we want to rise above it, it draws us down. It is only through the power of Christ that we can rise above sin at all.

The Millennium will be a time similar to the Garden of Eden. In a perfect environment created by God, Adam and Eve chose to sin. Under ideal circumstances—an abundant earth, no sickness, no war—the human heart will prove that it remains unchanged unless regenerated by the power of Christ. When Satan is loosed on the earth, many will turn their backs on the God who has sustained them and will follow the evil one.

Notice that Revelation mentions Gog and Magog in this verse describing the final conflict, but this is not the same Gog-Magog War described in Ezekiel 38–39 J. Vernon McGee believed that "the rebellion of the godless forces from the north will have made such an impression on mankind that after one thousand years, the last rebellion of man bears the same label—Gog and Magog."[1] Just as we have called two conflicts World War I and World War II, the people may call this last battle *Gog-Magog II*.

These people will mount an army and advance against Jerusalem, where Jesus rules and reigns. There they will learn that rebellion always ends in destruction. To paraphrase Winston Churchill, this will truly be "the end of the beginning." Man will have rebelled against God for the last time.

To purge creation of the evil effects of sin finally and forever, God will destroy the earth with great heat and fire. Peter and John the Revelator told us,

> The heavens will pass away with a great noise, and the elements will melt with fervent heat; both the earth and the works that are in it will be burned up . . . Nevertheless we, according to His promise, look for new heavens and a new earth in which righteousness dwells. (2 Peter 3:10, 13)

> The devil, who deceived them, was cast into the lake of fire and brimstone where the beast and the false prophet are. And they will be tormented day and night forever and ever. (Rev. 20:10)

Our enemy—the one who has tormented, tempted, and tested Christians for generations—will be permanently put away. He will enter hell for the first time—during the Millennium he was chained in the abyss, and today he roams the earth, seeking those he may lead into deception.

But at the end of the Millennium, praise God, Satan the destroyer will receive God's permanent justice.

CHAPTER 11

MIDNIGHT:
DOOMSDAY AT THE GREAT
WHITE THRONE

You may juggle human laws, you may fool with
human courts,
but there is a judgment to come, and from it there
is no appeal.
—ORIN PHILIP GIFFORD[1]

The prophet Daniel peered through the periscope of prophecy and saw this terrible, final doomsday, the Great White Throne Judgment. Daniel 7:9–10 records his vision:

> I watched till thrones were put in place,
> And the Ancient of Days was seated;
> His garment was white as snow,
> And the hair of His head was like pure wool.
> His throne was a fiery flame,

Its wheels a burning fire;
A fiery stream issued
And came forth from before Him.
A thousand thousands ministered to Him;
Ten thousand times ten thousand stood before Him.
The court was seated,
And the books were opened.

The Great White Throne Judgment will take place after the millennial reign is completed. It will be held in an intermediate place, somewhere between heaven and earth. It cannot not occur on the earth because the earth will be gone (2 Peter 3:10–11). It will not occur in heaven, because sinners would never be permitted in the presence of a holy God.

Who will be the One sitting on the throne? Christ Himself! In John 5:27–29, Jesus Christ said that the Father

has given Him [the Son] authority to execute judgment also, because He is the Son of Man. Do not marvel at this; for the hour is coming in which all who are in the graves will hear His voice and come forth—those who have done good, to the resurrection of life, and those who have done evil, to the resurrection of condemnation.

We have already seen that there will be two resurrections: the resurrection of the just and that of the unjust (Acts 24:15). The Great White Throne Judgment will be the resurrection of the unjust, when every remaining soul is called to stand before the awe-inspiring throne of God. There will be no future judgments for believers. Christians will have been rewarded or reproved at the *bema* seat of Christ. The

Great White Throne Judgment will be for those who have rejected the Savior.

In Revelation 20:12–13, John continued to describe the Great White Throne Judgment, saying,

> And I saw the dead, small and great, standing before God, and books were opened. And another book was opened, which is the Book of Life. And the dead were judged according to their works, by the things which were written in the books. The sea gave up the dead who were in it, and Death and Hades delivered up the dead who were in them. And they were judged, each one according to his works.

Notice that God has two sets of books. The Book of Life contains the name of every person who accepted Jesus Christ while they were on the earth. When the wicked dead approach the Great White Throne, Jesus will first look for their names in the Book of Life. Obviously, they will not be recorded there. Then He will open the books that contain His written records of every word, thought, and deed of the wicked. The result? "And anyone not found written in the Book of Life was cast into the lake of fire" (Rev. 20:15).

HELL IS NOT THE LAKE OF FIRE

Hell, sometimes known as *Sheol* or *Hades*, is not to be confused with the lake of fire. In this life, the ungodly die and go to hell, where they wait until they are brought to the Great White Throne for the final judgment before God and sentenced to the lake of fire (Rev. 19:20, 20:10, 14–15).

Satan, fallen angels, demons, and all ungodly persons will be placed into the eternal lake of fire by the hand of God as judgment for rejecting Jesus Christ as the Son of God (Rev. 20:10–15; Jude 6–7).

In a secular society where there is no absolute right or wrong, many people scoff at the concept of a literal hell designed for those who violate the law of God. But Jesus believed in hell, and so did the prophets. Let's examine the Scriptures about hell, the abiding place of the lost before they face doomsday in front of the Great White Throne. We can learn many truths about hell from studying the parable Jesus told in Luke 16: 19–31.

- *Hell is a literal place.* Notice that Jesus began this story by saying, "There was . . ." This parable actually happened. The story is a literal tale of two beggars—Lazarus, who begged in this life, and the rich man, who begged throughout eternity.

- Christ's parable verifies the extreme difference in eternity for the righteous and the ungodly. This teaching is not a condemnation of wealth; it is a condemnation of any person who rejects Jesus Christ.

- This parable confirms that before Calvary, the saved were carried by angels into Paradise (Luke 16:22; 23:43). After Calvary, the righteous go to heaven (2 Cor. 5:8; Phil. 1:21–24; Rev. 6:9–11).

- *Hell is a place of eternal torment.* The unsaved go to hell when they die and are in a conscious state of eternal torment (Luke 16:23-28; Deut. 32:22; 2 Sam. 22:6; Isa. 14:9–11).

- *Hell is a place without mercy.* The rich man in hell cried out, saying, "Have mercy on me, and send Lazarus that he may dip the tip of his finger in water and cool my tongue; for I am tormented in this flame" (Luke 16:24).

- *Hell is a place without escape.* Jesus said, "Between us and you there is a great gulf fixed, so that those who want to pass from here to you cannot, nor can those from there pass to us" (Luke 16:26). When you arrive in hell, the prayers of ten thousand saints cannot save you.

- *People in hell are aware of people on earth.* The rich man begged for someone to warn his family, "for I have five brothers, that he [Lazarus] may testify to them, lest they also come to this place of torment" (Luke 16:28).

- *Souls are immortal in hell and heaven* (Luke 16:22–32; 1 Peter 3:4, Luke 20:38; 2 Cor. 5:8).

- *Hell is located in "the lower parts of the earth"* (Ps. 63:9; Eph. 4:8–10; Matt. 12:40).

John the Revelator concluded his description of the Great White Throne Judgment by saying, "Then Death and Hades were cast into the lake of fire . . . And anyone not found written in the Book of Life was cast into the lake of fire" (Rev. 20:14–15).

Paul wrote,

For as in Adam all die, even so in Christ all shall be made alive . . . Then comes the end, when He delivers the king-

263

dom to God the Father, when He puts an end to all rule and all authority and power. For He must reign till He has put all enemies under His feet. The last enemy that will be destroyed is death . . . O Death, where is your sting? O Hades, where is your victory? (1 Cor. 15:22, 24–26, 55).

After the Great White Throne Judgment, death and hell will be finished, and eternity will loom. The best is yet to come. Glory!

CHAPTER 12

ETERNITY:
HEAVEN AND
EARTH REBORN!

"For behold, I create new heavens and a new earth;
And the former shall not be remembered or come to
mind.
But be glad and rejoice forever in what I create;
For behold, I create Jerusalem as a rejoicing,
And her people a joy.
I will rejoice in Jerusalem,
And joy in My people;
The voice of weeping shall no longer be heard in her,
Nor the voice of crying." (Isa. 65:17–18)

After the Great White Throne Judgment, God will present us with a new heaven and a new earth, to which a New Jerusalem will descend from heaven. John the Revelator wrote,

Now I saw a new heaven and a new earth, for the first heaven and the first earth had passed away. Also there was no more sea. Then I, John, saw the holy city, New Jerusalem, coming down out of heaven from God, prepared as a bride adorned for her husband. And I heard a loud voice from heaven saying, "Behold, the tabernacle of God is with men, and He will dwell with them, and they shall be His people. God Himself will be with them and be their God. (Rev. 21:1–3)

Speaking of Jesus Christ, the apostle John told us, "And the Word became flesh and dwelt [tabernacled] among us, and we beheld His glory, the glory as of the only begotten of the Father, full of grace and truth" (John 1:14).

Writing to a primarily Jewish audience, John used the Greek word *sk'enos* (meaning "shelter or covering") and the metaphor of a tabernacle to describe Christ's incarnation. The same word appeared in Revelation 21:3, when the New Jerusalem came down from heaven and God said, "Behold, the tabernacle of God is with men." We will be able to talk with God in the cool of the day as Adam did. The sinlessness of Eden will be recreated on earth, and in immortal bodies we will fellowship with God forever.

THE NEW JERUSALEM: GOD'S GOLDEN, GLORIOUS CITY

In Revelation chapters 21 and 22, John offered a panoramic view of the new Jerusalem:

Then one of the seven angels who had the seven bowls filled with the seven last plagues came to me and talked with me, saying, "Come, I will show you the bride, the

Lamb's wife." And he carried me away in the Spirit to a great and high mountain, and showed me the great city, the holy Jerusalem, descending out of heaven from God, having the glory of God. Her light was like a most precious stone, like a jasper stone, clear as crystal. Also she had a great and high wall with twelve gates, and twelve angels at the gates, and names written on them, which are the names of the twelve tribes of the children of Israel: three gates on the east, three gates on the north, three gates on the south, and three gates on the west. Now the wall of the city had twelve foundations, and on them were the names of the twelve apostles of the Lamb. And he who talked with me had a gold reed to measure the city, its gates, and its wall. The city is laid out as a square; its length is as great as its breadth. And he measured the city with the reed: twelve thousand furlongs [about 1400 miles]. Its length, breadth, and height are equal. Then he measured its wall: one hundred and forty-four cubits [about 200 feet], according to the measure of a man, that is, of an angel.

The construction of its wall was of jasper; and the city was pure gold, like clear glass. The foundations of the wall of the city were adorned with all kinds of precious stones: the first foundation was jasper, the second sapphire, the third chalcedony, the fourth emerald, the fifth sardonyx, the sixth sardius, the seventh chrysolite, the eighth beryl, the ninth topaz, the tenth chrysoprase, the eleventh jacinth, and the twelfth amethyst. The twelve gates were twelve pearls: each individual gate was of one pearl. And the street of the city was pure gold, like transparent glass.

But I saw no temple in it, for the Lord God Almighty and the Lamb are its temple. The city had no need of the sun or of the moon to shine in it, for the glory of God illuminated it. The Lamb is its light. And the nations of those who are saved shall walk in its light, and the kings of the earth bring their glory and honor into it. Its gates shall not be shut at all by day (there shall be no night there). And they shall bring the glory and the honor of the nations into it. But there shall by no means enter it anything that defiles, or causes an abomination or a lie, but only those who are written in the Lamb's Book of Life.

And he showed me a pure river of water of life, clear as crystal, proceeding from the throne of God and of the Lamb. In the middle of its street, and on either side of the river, was the tree of life, which bore twelve fruits, each tree yielding its fruit every month. The leaves of the tree were for the healing of the nations. And there shall be no more curse, but the throne of God and of the Lamb shall be in it, and His servants shall serve Him. They shall see His face, and His name shall be on their foreheads. There shall be no night there: They need no lamp nor light of the sun, for the Lord God gives them light. And they shall reign forever and ever. (Rev. 21: 9–27; 22:1–5)

John described the New Jerusalem as a city that is four-square and 1500 hundred miles up, down, and across (Rev. 21:15–18). If you put it on a map of the U.S.A., it would extend from the northernmost point of Maine to the southern tip of Florida, and from the Atlantic Ocean on the east to the western Rocky Mountains. It would be as large as all of Western Europe and half of Russia. Each street is one-half the length of the diameter of the earth. The levels rise one mile above the others, equaling eight million miles of beautiful golden avenues. The twelve gates of pearl are built upon twelve jeweled foundations, and they will open to believers from every kindred, tribe, and nation (Rev. 21:14).

The citizens of Jerusalem, that ancient city that has seen so much suffering, will exchange streets that have flowed with blood for streets of pure gold! The desert sun will yield to the light of the Lamb, and the hatred of warring nations to the peace of God! The protective walls of Jerusalem, which were built and rebuilt with much toil and struggle, will be replaced by walls designed solely for beauty and glory. The tree of life, not seen or enjoyed since Eden, will grow in the center of the city. Nations will no longer look upon Jerusalem with jealousy or resentment but will look to it for the light of God's glory.

The apostle Paul was permitted to see heaven, and words failed him when he tried to describe its beauty. He summed it up by quoting the prophet Isaiah: "Eye has not seen, nor ear heard, / Nor have entered into the heart of man / The things which God has prepared for those who love Him" (1 Cor. 2:9).

A CENSUS OF HEAVEN

Who will live in this holy city? The holy angels, Gentiles who have placed their faith and trust in Christ, and redeemed Israel. Although the New Jerusalem is a wedding present from the Bridegroom to His bride, Israel will be invited to dwell within these beautiful walls.[1]

In Hebrews 11, the "roll call of faith," the author testifies of Jewish saints who placed their faith in God and obeyed His commands. They will be invited to dwell in His heavenly city: "But now they desire a better, that is, a heavenly country. Therefore God is not ashamed to be called their God, for He has prepared a city for them" (Heb. 11:16).

How many people will be dwelling on the new earth, in the new heaven, and in the heavenly city? Harold Willmington has devised a formula by which we can take an informal "census" of heaven's future residents. He estimated that approximately 40 billion people have lived on our planet since Adam's creation. With that figure, we can extrapolate a rough formula:

Several anthropologists and sociologists have calculated that as many as 70 percent of all humans born never live to celebrate their eighth birthday; they are killed by disease, war, starvation, etc. What happens to the souls of all these little ones? Various verses make it clear that they go to be with Jesus. (See 2 Sam. 12:23, Matt. 18:1–6, 10; 19:14; Luke 18:15–17.) Now, add to this figure the millions of babies murdered by abortion each year, 40 million world-wide . . . Abortion is now the number one cause of death in the U.S. These victims of abortion, like those children dying outside the womb, also go to be with Christ. Finally, let us suggest that 10 percent of those 40 billion human beings born on the earth accept Christ as Savior sometime after reaching the age of accountability. Put this figure with the rest and total it up.[2]

The column would read:

28,000,000,000 (70% who died before age 8)
1,040,000,000 (those killed by abortion since 1973)
<u>1,200,000,000</u> (those who accept Christ as Savior)

30,240,000,000 Grand Total

If you were disenchanted by the low figure of only 10 percent who accept Christ, notice that the total figure indicates that nearly three-fourths of all human beings will enjoy heaven and the new earth!

BUT WHAT WILL WE *DO* IN ETERNITY?

We're not going to sit around heaven and pluck on harps all day. No, indeed. Scripture tells us that heaven will be a very busy place for active people.

- *Heaven will be a place of praise.* We will sing praise to God for all He has done (Isa. 44:23; Rev. 14:3; Rev. 15:3).

- *Heaven will be a place of fellowship.* We will not only know each other, but we will be able to talk to the Old Testament saints, the prophets, Adam and Eve, the apostles, and the Lord Jesus Himself!

- *Heaven will be a place of serving* (Rev. 22:3; 7:15).

- *Heaven will be a place of learning* (1 Cor. 13:9–10). If you enjoy learning new things, exploring new worlds, visiting new places, then heaven will be the perfect place for you. Imagine being able to fly to new planets where no man has gone before or exploring a new continent on the new earth. Best of all, we will learn about God, about our Savior, and His plan for us. The Holy Scriptures will come together in our minds, and all mysteries will be revealed.

- *Heaven will be a place of joy and perfection.* "But when that which is perfect has come," Paul wrote, "then that which is in part will be done away" (1 Cor. 13:10). There will be no sorrow, no pain, no trouble there.

- *Heaven is a place of unbelievable real estate.* Jesus taught, "In My Father's house are many mansions; if it were not so, I would have told you" (John 14:2).

HEAVEN IS A REAL PLACE

There are some who say heaven is "a state of mind, a fancy, a dream, an abstraction," but Jesus Himself called heaven a real place. He came from heaven to earth and then returned to heaven where He awaits the day when His church shall join Him in the mansions He has prepared for His own. Jesus called heaven "a house, a dwelling place." Heaven is not an illusion. It's just as real as the home in which you live right now.

In Acts 1:11, the angel told the disciples, "Men of Galilee, why do you stand gazing up into heaven? This same Jesus, who was taken up from you into heaven, will so come in like manner as you saw Him go into heaven."

Did Jesus go up into a state of mind? Did He enter an abstraction? No! Jesus went to a real place, an eternal home, a place of perfection God has prepared as a place of reward for those who love Him.

Jesus prayed, "Our Father who art in heaven . . ." He did not say, "Our Father who art in a state of mind" or "an eternal illusion." His Father and ours was in heaven, a real place.

Our citizenship lies in heaven. Paul wrote, "For our citizenship is in heaven, from which we also eagerly wait for the Savior, the Lord Jesus Christ" (Phil. 3:20).

Our names are written in heaven: Luke said, "Nevertheless do not rejoice in this, that the spirits are subject to you, but rather rejoice because your names are written in heaven" (Luke 10:20).

Our treasures are stored in heaven: "Do not lay up for yourselves treasure on earth . . . but lay up for yourselves treasures in heaven, where neither moth nor rust destroys and where thieves do not break in and steal" (Matt. 6:19–20).

These words, friend, are faithful and true. They are our guiding light through dark days and troubled times. Though the world shudders around us in doomsday perils real and imagined, we have placed our trust in Jesus Christ and His Revelation. Doomsday is coming, but not for those who believe!

FACE THE FUTURE WITHOUT FEAR

Upbraiding his frantic disciples in the midst of a storm, Jesus told them to "fear not." From Genesis to Revelation, from Abraham to John the Revelator on the Isle of Patmos, God has told us over and over again: "Fear not!"

That command was given to Abraham, Israel, Moses, David, Daniel, the disciples, and to Mary the mother of Jesus. Jesus called those words to Peter when he was sinking in a stormy sea. He whispered those words to Paul as a rolling wave capsized the ship in which he was sailing. "Fear not!" He still speaks those words to us today.

You can fear the unknown. You can fear the past. You can fear many things!

Face this fact, friend: Either you will conquer fear, or fear will conquer you. We know what the future holds; that's why God gave us a wealth of prophecy in the Scripture. God wanted Daniel to look into the future and be assured. When it came time for that mighty prophet to die, I'm sure he lay down on his Babylonian couch, wrapped his cloak about him, and closed his eyes as if yielding to pleasant dreams. He knew he'd be resurrected in the first resurrection. He knew he would see His Lord and Savior, the One in whom He had placed His trust.

Fear is a product of the Prince of Darkness. If you live in fear of a technological, economic, or military doomsday, the spirit of fear will break your spirit. Regardless of your profession of faith, if you live with the spirit of fear in these areas, you are living like an atheist. "For God has not given us a spirit of fear," wrote Paul, "but of power and of love and of a sound mind" (2 Tim. 1:7).

Fear entered the world with sin, when Adam and Eve ate the forbidden fruit. Before that event, God had walked with Adam in the garden, talked to him, shared his thoughts and hopes. But when Adam sinned, he heard the voice of God and was afraid. Fear comes in by sin, is sustained by sin, and, like a virus, invades the soul.

But faith, that mighty weapon, can conquer fear. We are more than conquerors through Christ, and prophecy proves we have nothing to fear! If you are a child of God living before the Rapture, you do not have to fear the Tribulation, the Antichrist, or the judgment at the Great White Throne! Fear would have you cowering before the nightly news, worrying about the stock market, fretting about your retirement fund. Don't be foolish; do be prepared, but do not fear!

Fear is contagious. Like a disease, it spreads panic among the population. Spreading on the wings of doubt, fear destroys peace like the plague. But faith is the victory that overcomes the world. Faith believes God will take care of His people.

Faith compelled Abraham to look for a city whose builder and architect was God. He will one day live in that city, the New Jerusalem.

Faith drove Moses into Pharaoh's court and gave him the courage to demand, "Let my people go!" Faith parted the waters of the Red Sea and crumbled the walls of Jericho.

Faith urged David to face Goliath while forty thousand cowards watched from the hillside. "You come at me with a sword and a spear," David shouted, his faith like a rock of determination inside him. "I come to you in the name of the Lord!"

Faith enabled Paul and Silas to sing in prison at the dark midnight hour.

Faith can turn the desert into springs of living water. Faith can calm the troubled sea. Faith is the victory that overcomes the world.

Fear can rob you of your spiritual inheritance. Moses sent twelve spies into the Promised Land, and ten came back shaking their heads with disappointment. Only Joshua and Caleb said, "We can take the land!" and consequently, only Joshua and Caleb lived to enter the land flowing with milk and honey.

Some of you reading this book are afraid of what people will think if you surrender your life to Christ. You will allow fear to rob you of eternal salvation and happiness even as you make your own personal date with doomsday.

Some of you Christians reading this book are afraid of what people will think if you actually talk about Christ in the workplace or at secular social gatherings. You are allowing fear to rob your friends and family of heaven. By remaining silent, you are denying them an opportunity to trust Christ before the Rapture.

Fear not!

Fear not, because the Father is with you. Jesus the Son is with you, and so is the Holy Spirit. Remember Daniel's prayers in Babylon? Angels were dispatched from heaven the moment he began to pray, and, child of God, angels are watching over you right now.

Fear not, because God will strengthen you to do the work He has called you to do. God gave Samson the strength to kill a thousand enemies with the jawbone of an ass. He gave David strength enough to kill a lion with his bare hands. He gave a donkey the ability and courage to rebuke Balaam. If God can use a donkey, He can certainly use you!

God is looking for men and women who are not afraid to fulfill His purposes on the earth. When God formed the world, He created the man Adam and made him guardian of the Garden of Eden. When God wanted to form a new nation, He found the man Abraham, and Israel was born.

When God chose to destroy the world by flood, He found a man, Noah, to build an ark for the salvation of his family and the human race. When Pharaoh ordered that all baby boys be killed, God found a woman, Moses' mother, who had faith enough to send her son forth on the Nile. When the people of Jericho were about to close in on the Hebrew spies, God found a woman, Rahab, with courage enough to risk her life and send them to safety over the wall. When the Philistines terrorized Israel, God found a man, Samson, to break the yoke of tyranny over the chosen people. When the virgin Mary was found to be with child, God found a man, Joseph, whose faith was greater than the skepticism of society, and the Son of God was born. When Jesus Christ left this earth, He found a man, Paul, to establish the New Testament Church.

On and on I could continue, listing the names of Deborah, the judge of Israel; Gideon, the timid warrior; Daniel, the captive prophet; Hannah, the sacrificial mother. My point is this: God is still looking for a few good men and women to accomplish His purposes. He needs men who will be loving fathers and devoted husbands, ending the social chaos of the collapsing American home. He needs women who will not be afraid to stand up against the tide of immorality drowning our nation. He needs people who are not afraid to share the gospel with a world on a certain path to doomsday.

Where do you stand, friend?

Every person reading this book is either saved or lost, wheat or tares, sheep or goats, walking the narrow way that leads to heaven or the broad way that leads to hell. You are either looking for Jesus Christ or the Antichrist. You are either a friend of God or His enemy. James wrote, "Do you not know that friendship with the world is enmity with God? Whoever therefore wants to be a friend of the world makes himself an enemy of God" (James 4:4).

Where do you stand?

Jesus said, "He that is not for me is against me." Have you become a carnal, compromising, lukewarm Christian whom the Revelation describes as "neither cold nor hot, [so Christ] will vomit you out of [His] mouth" (Rev. 3:16)? Are you cursed with a casual Christianity that has a form of godliness but denies the power thereof? You can have ritual without righteousness. You can profess Christ without possessing Christ.

Christ could come today. Doomsday could begin tomorrow. Are you prepared?

NOTES

INTRODUCTION

1. http://www.geocities.com/SoHo/1147/Future.htm
2. Deborah Solomon, "1899: The Names Have Changed, but the Worries Remain," *Newsweek,* 11 January 1999, 10.
3. David Nicholson-Lord, "What's Going to Get You First?" *Independent on Sunday,* 5 January 1997, 4–5, 7.

CHAPTER 1

1. "Year 2000 Cultists Arrive Home, Hide," A Knight Ridder Newspapers report, *Tampa Tribune,* 10 January 1999, 2A.
2. Jack Katzenell, "Israeli Police Fear Christian Suicides on Temple Mount," AP Online, 23 November 1998.
3. Judy Siegel-Itzkovich, "Preparing for the False Prophet," *Jerusalem Post,* 4 January 1999, 17.
4. J. Vernon McGee, *Daniel* (Nashville: Thomas Nelson, 1991), ix.
5. Henry H. Halley, *Halley's Bible Handbook* (Grand Rapids, Mich.: Zondervan, 1965), 336.
6. William Kelly, *Notes on Daniel* (New York: Loizeaux Brothers, 1952), 50.

CHAPTER 2

1. McGee, *Daniel,* 153.
2. Harold L. Willmington, *Willmington's Bible Handbook* (Wheaton, Ill.: Tyndale, 1997), 438.
3. J. Dwight Pentecost, *Things to Come* (Grand Rapids, Mich.: Zondervan, 1964), 245–46.
4. McGee, *Daniel,* 157.
5. Ibid., 155–56.

CHAPTER 3

1. Harold Willmington, *Basic Stages in the Book of Ages* (Lynchburg, Va.: Thomas Road Bible Institute, 1975), 375.

2. Adapted from Internet material on Net Fax, published by Leadership Network, 31 August 1998, http://www.leadnet.org.

3. *The New York Public Library Book of Twentieth-Century American Quotations* (New York: Warner Books, 1992), 367, 378.

4. Ibid., 376.

5. Arieh O'Sullivan, "Virtual Terror: Threat of a New World Disorder," *Jerusalem Post*, 27 March 1998, 15.

6. Ibid.

7. Ibid.

8. Ibid.

9. Ibid.

10. "Concord Coalition: The National Debt Continues to Increase Despite Today's Budget 'Surplus' Celebration," US Newswire, 30 September 1998.

11. Ibid.

12. Eric Black, "A Glimmer Behind the Deficit Glaze," Minneapolis *Star Tribune*, 8 February 1998, 21A.

13. James C. Lawson, "The U.S. Debt Debacle," *The World & I* (1 January 1996), 96.

14. Ibid.

15. Ron Blue, *Master Your Money* (Nashville: Thomas Nelson, 1986), 15.

16. William F. Lauber, "America's Failed War on Poverty," *The World & I*, 10 (1 September 1995), 28.

17. Ibid.

18. Ibid.

19. Pat Robertson, *The New World Order* (Nashville: Word, 1991), 119–20.

20. John Hanchette, "Fed's Alan Greenspan: Messiah or Megalomaniac?" Gannett News Service, 15 February 1995.

21. Ibid.

22. Bill Deener, "What a Year! As Market Recuperates from a Wild '98, Most Analysts Expect a Strong '99," *The Dallas Morning News*, 2 January 1999, 1F.

23. Robert J. Samuelson, "The Crash of '99?" *Newsweek*, 12 October 1998, 28.

24. Dan Walz, Professor at Trinity University, Department of Business Administration, notes, 14 October 1998.

25. Samuelson, "Crash of '99?" 28.

26. Allan Sloan and Rich Thomas, "Riding for a Fall," *Newsweek*, 5 October 1998, 56.

27. Ibid.

28. David Hendricks, "Experts Say Economy Not Quite in the Clear," *San Antonio Express News*, 7 November 1998, 1E.

29. Samuelson, "Crash of '99?" 28.

30. "Germ Warfare," *Primetime Live*, 29 July 1998, transcript.

31. Gustav Andersson, "Warfare, Chemical and Biological," 28 February 1996, *Colliers Encyclopedia CD ROM*, Vol. 23.

32. Ibid.

33. Ibid.

34. Ibid.

35. Ibid.

36. "Germ Warfare."

37. Ibid.

38. Sue Goetinck, "Plague Protection," *Dallas Morning News*, 12 October 1998.

39. "Germ Warfare."

40. Andersson, "Warfare, Chemical and Biological."

41. "Germ Warfare."

42. John Hanchette, "Pentagon Trying to Develop Anti-Biological Warfare Vaccine," Gannett News Service, 7 April 1997.

43. U.S. Senator Richard Shelby (R-AL) Chairman holds hearing on the threat of biological weapons, Washington Transcript Service, 4 March 1998.

44. Hanchette, "Anti-Biological Warfare Vaccine."

45. "Germ Warfare."

46. Ibid.

47. Ibid.

48. Stephen Joseph and Gordon Soper, "Bio-Terrorism: The Hometown Scenario," *The Washington Times*, 28 December 1998.

49. Ibid.

50. "Germ Warfare."

51. Ibid.

52. Ibid.

53. Ibid.
54. "Holds News Briefing on Anthrax," Washington Transcript Service, 14 August 1998.
55. Ibid.
56. "Germ Warfare."
57. "Pentagon to Help Cities Combat Weapons of Mass Terror; Defense: L.A. Is Among 120 Municipalities to Get Training in Chemical, Biological, Nuclear Threats," *Los Angeles Times*, 17 April 1997, 16.
58. John Omicinski, "U.S. Fears Rogue Nations Experimenting with Bio-Chem Agents," Gannett News Service, 4 April 1998, ARC.
59. Fred Bayles, "Anti-Terrorism Plans Falling Short," *USA Today*, 13 October 1998, 15A.
60. Ibid.
61. Michael Kelly, "Another Clinton Administration Crisis," *Arkansas Democrat-Gazette*, 5 November 1998, B12.
62. Ibid.
63. Gary L. Bauer, Washington Update, 28 August 1998.
64. Kelly, "Clinton Administration Crisis."
65. George Will, "Threat of Kindness Riles ACLU," *San Antonio Express-News*, 7 December 1998, 13A.
66. Ibid.
67. Ibid.

CHAPTER 4
1. Rodney Andrews, "End of the World in Sight?" *Anglican Journal*, April 1998.
2. Grant Jeffrey, *Final Warning* (Toronto, Ontario: Frontier Research Publications, Inc., 1995), 306.
3. For examples of Scriptural references, see 1 Cor. 8:6, Eph. 4:6, Matt. 28:19, John 14:26, John 15:26, 2 Cor. 13:14, and 1 Peter 1:2.
4. Jeffrey, *Final Warning*, 314–15.
5. J. Vernon McGee, *Revelation, Chapters 14–22* (Nashville: Thomas Nelson, 1991), 128.
6. Pentecost, *Things to Come*, 223.
7. Ibid.

CHAPTER 5
1. John Wesley White, *Thinking the Unthinkable* (Lake Mary, Fla.: Creation House, 1992), 150.

2. J. Vernon McGee, *Ezekiel* (Nashville: Thomas Nelson, 1991), 187.

3. "Commonwealth of Independent States," *The Encarta '99 Desk Encyclopedia*. Copyright 1998 Microsoft Corporation. All rights reserved.

4. Moris Farhi, *The Last of Days* (New York: Kensington Publishing Corp., 1983), 201.

5. Press Bulletin from the Israel Government Press Office, 2 December 1998.

6. Ibid.

7. Ibrahim Sarbal, leader of the Islamic Jihad Movement in Palestine—al Aqsa Brigades. Quote is provided by the Anti-Defamation League of B'nai B'rith.

8. Quote provided by the Anti-Defamation League of B'nai B'rith.

9. Douglas J. Feith, "Wye and the Road to War," *Commentary*, 107, the American Jewish Committee, 1 January 1999, 43.

10. Martin Regg Cohn, "Decades-Old Palestinian Charter Thorn in Mideast Peace Process," *The Toronto Star*, 23 November 1998.

11. Arafat's quotes from Press Bulletin issued from the Israel Government Press Office, 2 December 1998.

12. Nadav Shragai, "Refusal to Recognize Israel Widespread on Palestinian TV," *Ha'aretz News*, 3 September 1998.

13. Uri Dan and Dennis Eisenberg, "Kremlin's Lust for Oil," *Jerusalem Post*, 19 September 1996, 6.

14. Ibid.

15. Stephen Blank, "Russia's Return to the Middle East," *The World & I*, 11 (1 November 1996).

16. Ibid.

17. Ibid.

18. Scott Peterson, "Israel Uses 'Deliberate Ambiguity' in Nuclear Policy," *The Washington Times*, 12 August 1998, A13.

19. Stan Goodenough, "A Narrowing of Choices," *Jerusalem Post*, 12 April 1995.

20. Ibid.

21. "Researcher Says Russians Have Nuclear Doomsday Device," *All Things Considered*, National Public Radio, 8 October 1993, transcript.

22. Tim Zimmermann, "Just When You Thought You Were Safe . . ." *U.S. News & World Report*, 10 November 1997, 38–40.

23. White, *Thinking the Unthinkable*, 145.

24. Tim LaHaye, *The Beginning of the End* (Wheaton, Ill.: Tyndale, 1988), 65.

25. D. M. Panton, "The Jew God's Dial," *Dawn*, 15 August 1924, 197–201.

26. Peter C. Craigie, *Ezekiel* (Philadelphia, Penn.: Westminster Press, 1983), 273.

CHAPTER 6

1. Deborah Kovach Caldwell, "Apocalypse Soon? As New Millennium Rapidly Approaches, Interest in End of World Is at All-Time High," *The Dallas Morning News*, 24 October 1998, 1A.

2. Ibid.

3. Pentecost, *Things to Come*, 46.

4. Ibid., 47.

5. Willmington, *Basic Stages*, 373.

6. Willmington, *Bible Handbook*, 437.

7. Peter S. Knobel, ed., *Gates of the Seasons* (New York: Central Conference of American Rabbis, 1983), 90.

8. Jeffrey L. Sheler, and Mike Tharp, "Dark Prophecies," *U.S. News & World Report*, 15 December 1997, 62.

9. Nicholson-Lord, "What's Going to Get You First?" 4–7.

10. Ibid.

11. J. Vernon McGee, *Revelation, Chapters 6–13* (Nashville: Thomas Nelson, 1991), 45.

12. Ibid.

13. Nicholson-Lord, "What's Going to Get You First?" 4–7.

CHAPTER 7

1. Ed Hindson, *Is the Antichrist Alive and Well?* (Eugene, Oreg.: Harvest House, 1998), 19–21.

2. Harold Willmington, *Bible Handbook*, p. 801.

3. McGee, *Revelation, Chapters 6–13*, 86.

4. Ibid.

5. Nicholson-Lord, "What's Going to Get You First?", 4–5, 7.

6. For photo, see "The Euro: No Worries in Washington," *Newsweek*, 19 January 1999, 41.

7. McGee, *Revelation, Chapters 6–13*, 106.

8. Harold Willmington, *Willmington's Guide to the Bible* (Wheaton, Ill.: Tyndale, 1997), 800.

9. Ibid.

CHAPTER 8

1. James L. Franklin, "The Religious Right and the New Apocalypse," *Boston Globe*, 2 May 1982.

CHAPTER 9

1. S. Franklin Logdson, *Profiles of Prophecy* (Grand Rapids, Mich.: Zondervan, 1964), 81.
2. Harold Willmington, *The King Is Coming* (Wheaton, Ill.: Tyndale, 1988), 250.
3. Adapted from Willmington, *The King Is Coming*, 250.
4. Ibid., 241–42.
5. Rene Pache, *The Return of Jesus Christ* (Chicago, Ill: Moody Press, 1955), 428.

CHAPTER 10

1. McGee, *Revelation, Chapters 14–22*, 152.

CHAPTER 11

1. Frank S. Mead, ed., *The Encyclopedia of Religious Quotations* (Old Tappan, N.J.: Revell, 1965), 259.

CHAPTER 12

1. Willmington, *The King Is Coming*, 300.
2. Ibid., 304. Numbers in the tally have been adjusted to reflect 1999 figures.

ABOUT THE AUTHOR

Dr. John C. Hagee is the founder and senior pastor of Cornerstone Church, a nondenominational evangelical church in San Antonio, Texas, with more than 17,000 active members. Dr. Hagee is the author of nine books, three of which are bestsellers: *Beginning of the End, Day of Deception,* and *Final Dawn Over Jerusalem.*

Dr. Hagee is the president of Global Evangelism Television, which broadcasts Pastor Hagee's daily and weekly programs on television and radio throughout the United States and around the world.

Dr. Hagee is married to Diana Castro Hagee, and they are blessed with five children: Tish, Christopher, Christina, Matthew, and Sandy.

Dr. Hagee has been to Israel numerous times and has met with every prime minister since Menachem Begin. John Hagee Ministries has given $1.2 million to bring Soviet Jews from the former Soviet Union to Israel and has given thousands of dollars to Hadassah Hospital and other Jewish organizations. Dr. Hagee is known around the world for his strong stand against anti-Semitism and his support of the nation of Israel.

OTHER TITLES
BY JOHN HAGEE

Beginning of the End
A *New York Times* Bestseller
The world was stunned and saddened
in 1995 when Israli prime minister
Yitzhak Rabin was cruelly struck
down by an assassin's bullet. Dr.
Hagee takes a close look at Rabin's
assassination and explains how it fits
into events prophesied centuries ago in
the Bible.

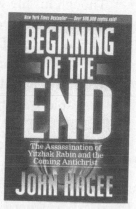

ISBN 0-7852-7370-0 • Trade Paperback • 208 pages
Also available in audio: ISBN 0-7852-7115-5

Day of Deception
In this powerful exposé, Dr. Hagee
reveals deception at work in our government, our schools, our media, our
culture, and even our religious institutions. This book shows readers how to
discern truth from falsehood and how
to appropriate the power of God to
emerge victorious.

ISBN 0-7852-7573-8 • Trade Paperback • 240 pages
Also available in audio: ISBN 0-7852-7116-3

Final Dawn Over Jerusalem
Pastor John Hagee never dreamed that his life would change the night he took a bold stand against terrorism and anti-Semitism in his hometown. Though his life was threatened, his property destroyed, and his peace of mind rocked, Dr. Hagee uncovers secret treasures of spiritual insights for all believers, as well as a blueprint for the rapidly approaching end times.

ISBN 0-7852-7571-1 • Trade Paperback • 228 pages
Also available in audio: ISBN 0-7852-7082-5

His Glory Revealed
This seven-week devotional explores the feasts of Israel: The Feast of Passover, The Feast of Unleavened Bread, The Feast of Firstfruits, The Feast of Pentecost, The Feast of Trumpets (Rosh Hashanah), The Feast of Atonement (Yom Kippur), and the Feast of Tabernacles. *His Glory Revealed* helps readers understand not only the meaning of each of these feasts but also the prophetic significance of each festival.
ISBN 0-7852-6965-7 • Hardcover • 192 pages